"For those considering network storage consolidation, *Straight to the Core* walks the reader through both the how and why of IP and Ethernet's flexibility."

Larry Boucher, CEO, Alacritech

"Orenstein communicates complex storage architecture concepts effortlessly. Unlike traditional storage networking analysis, *Straight to the Core* goes beyond technical descriptions to the business reasons and justifications for implementing a storage architecture."

Doug Ingraham, Senior Manager, Cisco Storage Technology Group

"As today's enterprise continues to become more data-intensive, customers demand the best storage solutions to fit their unique computing environment, cost and total solution purchase criteria. This, oftentimes, means having a single storage platform that has NAS, SAN and iSCSI solutions," said Steve Kleiman, senior vice president and chief technology officer at Network Appliance. "*Straight to the Core* provides a fresh perspective on storage networking, highlighting open, standards-based approaches to solve customer needs."

Steve Kleiman, CTO of Network Appliance

"*Straight to the Core* delivers the details to get IT professionals up to speed and provides an overview that gives executives a big picture perspective."

Bob Herbold, Executive Vice President and Chief Operating Officer (Retired), Microsoft Corporation

"Widespread customer familiarity with IP and Ethernet networks gives iSCSI a head-start to a receptive audience. *Straight to the Core* effectively highlights the broad range of user options and ease of use in deploying IP storage solutions."

Clod Barrera, Director of Storage Strategy, IBM Systems Group

"A must for customers investigating network storage assessment and deployment."

Tricia Bregman, Glasshouse Technologies

"IP Storage promises to revolutionize the network storage landscape by making it easy to deploy storage networking. *Straight to the Core* provides a good foundation for understanding this change."

Jamie Gruener, Senior Analyst, The Yankee Group

"IP SANs make redundant, resilient data accessible to midsized enterprises and departments by optimizing their storage assets with lower cost and complexity. IP SANs also compliment and extend Fibre Channel SANs in ways that IT managers and CIOs are only just beginning to realize. *Straight to the Core* clearly conveys this range of deployment strategies and technology."

Bill Huber, VP Engineering and CTO ,
StoneFly Networks

"An insightful look into technology shifts and new solutions which hold the potential to shift network storage industry dynamics."

Charles Beeler, General Partner,
El Dorado Ventures

"iSCSI invites the broader population of well-trained LAN administrators to manage storage area networks. The door is now wide open for their collective IP and Ethernet expertise to work its way into creative and robust storage solutions made possibly by this exciting technology."

Bryce Mackin, chair of the IP Storage Forum
of the Storage Networking Industry Association
(SNIA) and product line manager for Adaptec

"Gary Orenstein's experience and insight give him a unique position to cover the future of IP networks in storage and system network applications. *Straight to the Core* introduces key considerations for both the technology and financial ramifications to the storage industry."

Robert Montague, Managing Director,
RBC Capital Markets

"Enter the brave new world where mission-critical computing meets economies-of-scale. These pages capture the Core Concept: leverage current IT architectures alongside future technologies without forklift upgrades—winning strategies for IT managers, CFOs, and technology investors."

Joaquin Ruiz, Vice President, Product Management
and Marketing, Sistina Software

"*Straight to the Core* effectively portrays the capabilities of IP Storage and iSCSI to solve both storage networking challenges and business-wide solutions."

Ahmad Zamer, iSCSI Chair, SNIA IP Storage
Forum and Senior Product Line Marketing
Engineer, Intel Corporation

IP Storage Networking

Straight to the Core

Gary Orenstein

✦▾Addison-Wesley

Boston • San Francisco • New York • Toronto • Montreal
London • Munich • Paris • Madrid • Capetown
Sydney • Tokyo • Singapore • Mexico City

The publisher offers discounts on this book when ordered in quantity for special sales. For more information, please contact:

Pearson Education Corporate Sales Division
201 W. 103rd Street
Indianapolis, IN 46290
(800) 428-5331
corpsales@pearsontechgroup.com

Visit AW on the Web: www.awprofessional.com

Library of Congress Cataloging-in-Publication Data

A CIP data record for this book can be obtained from the Library of Congress.

ISBN 0-321-15960-8
Text printed on recycled paper
First printing, June, 2003

Contents

Appendix A   IT Service Recovery Strategy: Best Opportunity for Success   307

Appendix B   The Broadview Storage Perspective   333

Foreword

STORAGE WAS ONCE a peripheral. To mainframe systems managers it was DASD—a direct-access storage device inextricably tied to big iron processors in the data center. While those days are gone, they are by no means forgotten. The majority of the world's data still resides on storage devices that remain hardwired to a single server.

Yet, there is now a near universal understanding among IT systems managers that data should not always be hidden behind, or bottled up inside, a single server. It should be positioned so that it can be made quickly but securely available to other applications and departments within the enterprise and with entities external to the enterprise as well. In short, data and the information it represents should be made fluid.

Why? Data—translated into information—has grown in value to the point that for many enterprises, it is the most valuable corporate asset. Used effectively, data is a competitive differentiator. And with the advent of e-commerce, it has risen in importance to become mission-critical to the very enterprise as viewed from the outside through the Web portal. The data storage domain is now the single most important IT resource for assuring that enterprise data will always be accessible, will always be "on"—just like electricity. Lost access to data can be severely damaging and possibly fatal to the enterprise. In a health-care setting, for example, continuous access to data could make the difference between life and death.

The concept of the fluidity of data plays an essential role in understanding how to make data persistently available. Consider the legacy mainframe storage environment once again. When data centers had only one mainframe system with direct-attached storage, deciding where to put data was easy—it had to reside on one of the volumes that the mainframe controlled.

Similarly in the open systems world, customers running environments in which storage is directly attached to servers had only one place to allocate data—on the direct-attached storage. Data security was more or less assured so long as the operating system managing the data was trusted to perform this critical function. However, data availability was severely compromised. To get to data held captive behind a server—mainframe or otherwise—an application had to first negotiate its way through bandwidth and operating system interoperability issues, adding an intolerable degree of latency. If the server in question was out of service, so to was its captive data.

With the advent of Network-Attached Storage (NAS) and storage area networks (SANs), IT administrators can now build environments with many different servers running their own operating systems connected to many different storage platforms. They can choose where to put the data for a particular application or set of applications—on high speed arrays or slower arrays, SAN, NAS, or whatever may be appropriate. As a result, data rarely remains where it was originally created.

While data fluidity becomes more prevalent within enterprises, so too does the commoditization of the enterprise storage domain. Large, heavy, resource-hungry disk subsystems, for example, have given way to RAID arrays built up of small, modular, and inexpensive disk drives introduced to the mass market by the proliferation of PCs. The drives themselves are of questionable reliability when considered for use in mission-critical business applications. But the industry has found ways to bypass those shortcomings. Now, big iron disk is gone, replaced by disks that originated in the commodity PC world. The further commoditization of storage is inevitable and in fact even desirable.

Internet Protocol, as both a networking standard and a ubiquitous data transport utility, stands at the crossroads of these two storage megatrends—data fluidity and the commoditization of the storage domain. IP is an obvious enabler of data fluidity. Its use in data communications is so commonplace that it is taken for granted. Its ubiquity in turn breeds commoditization and mass-market distribution of IP-related hardware and software. Its widespread adoption has led to standardization as well within all industries and all computing environments

Therefore, the marriage of IP and data storage is inevitable as well. The advantages that IP storage proponents claim over other alternatives, such as Fibre Channel, are numerous. IP is switchable and therefore capable of supporting high-speed, shared-resource applications. IP is mature (e.g., free of interoperability issues that were settled years ago), is well understood by the

IT community at large, and has a huge mass of management software and service offerings available to users

On the surface, it's a compelling argument. IP is a known quantity with a mature infrastructure complete with management facilities. But just below the surface of IP storage, things get complex rather quickly. First, IP alone does not guarantee delivery of packets from source to target. Yet SCSI, the standard storage I/O protocol, requires that data packets not only arrive at a target destination, but also arrive in the exact order they were sent from the source. Therefore, if you want to send SCSI storage packets over an IP network, some method has to be devised that satisfies the guaranteed delivery requirements of the SCSI protocol and is done in such a way that packets are presented at the target destination in the same order they were sent.

Second, satisfying the requirements of the SCSI protocol and delivering acceptable performance for a broad range of applications and workloads will require that much of the necessary code be implemented in specialized chipset hardware. This will not be a trivial task, even for the most expert of IP networking vendors. Additionally, like Fibre Channel, a standard method for coding and decoding IP storage transmissions must be established. No vendor will make a serious commitment to low-cost, high-volume production of the required chipsets until standards have been established. The good news is that IP storage standards are now established that satisfy the requirements of the SCSI protocol and are currently in the process of productization.

Regardless of the current limitations, whatever they may be, with regard to the application of IP to storage, there is a belief that somehow those limitations will be overcome. Remember that RAID storage evolved from just a pile of inexpensive PC drives to disk arrays capable of supporting today's most critical business applications without interruption or data loss. The economic advantages of RAID drove creative and resourceful vendors to meet enterprise-user objections to the new technology. Then, pioneering IT administrators found RAID arrays to be worthy additions to production data centers. RAID implementations are now as commonplace as IP in enterprise computing.

Enterprise computing is now dominated by technologies created for the mass market. We have only to witness the rise of behemoths like Intel and Microsoft to understand the powerful influence commoditization wields. IP is firmly embedded in the world of commodity computing as well. It is the heart of the Internet. A seemingly infinite number of IP tentacles now reach into millions of households and businesses.

Storage networking stands squarely in the path of commoditization. In fact, no computing technology can hide from the onslaught commoditization. IP's march into the storage domain—as both an enabler of data fluidity and a byproduct of commoditization—is inevitable and inexorable.

John Webster
Data Mobility Group

Preface

You cannot simply replace data. You can easily reinstall a computer application, but you cannot go to the store and buy another copy of your data warehouse. The computer storage industry thrives on this fundamental fact, creating sophisticated and elaborate mechanisms to ensure that whatever happens, a second copy of the data is available if needed. Sometimes there is also a third copy, and a fourth, and so on.

A couple of years ago, I noticed that everything taking place in the storage networking industry became almost singularly focused on data protection. This was probably due to increasing commercial reliance on data to run businesses and the stark realization that even when we think everything is safe, it may not be.

Looking a bit closer, I found that many of the early campaigns for storage networking were being left out or left behind. The initial impetus for storage networks was derived largely by a need to manage data more effectively. In the midst of an all-out recovery focus, many of the industry's driving forces were stunted, while business continuity planning stole the show.

Meanwhile, important new storage networking technology developments were taking place. For the first time, IP networks were proven to be a reliable, high-performance means to transmit block-level data. Long the domain of parallel SCSI buses and Fibre Channel networks, the storage transport had a new friend in IP networks—and that friendship would begin to rewrite the storage networking guidelines.

Watching the industry transform, I felt that a protection-only view of the world was serving neither the customers nor the industry. Only by adopting plans to return to the roots of storage networking—a means to handle and manage almost unstoppable data growth—would everyone benefit. Fortunately, the proactive strategies for storage networking fit hand in hand with strategies for data protection, yet only in concert do the greatest returns materialize.

Recognizing the need to bring storage networking back into the forward-thinking planning process, I focused my efforts in this book on IP storage networking—one of the most important storage networking steps since the initial SCSI command set serialization into Fibre Channel. IP storage networks promise to unite the once-restricted storage functions with the rest of the enterprise, allowing coordinated information technology planning across compute and storage functions with a common platform.

IP Storage Networking: Straight to the Core is targeted to both a technical and business audience. The aim is to include information about new storage networking technology but also to keep a reality check on the business aspects of storage networking implementation. Understanding and evaluating both the technical and business implications of new technology helps all of our organizations. As such, many parties in the storage industry, such as storage networking planners and implementers, business-focused managers, senior financial planners, industry press and analysts, and technology investors, are likely to benefit from the material.

Chapters 1 through 3 provide the background necessary for almost anyone in this group to get up to speed on the storage networking industry. With the industry changing so quickly, even those with detailed knowledge are sure to find some new information.

Chapters 4 and 5 lay the foundation for building effective storage network roadmaps. Chapter 4 presents a history of data storage architectures and how the intelligence piece of the equation has evolved across server platforms, disk subsystems, and now within networking fabrics. Chapter 5 outlines both defensive, protection-oriented strategies and offensive strategies for storage deployment using new technologies enabled by IP storage networking.

The primary business continuance applications are covered in Chapter 6 in a clear, incremental framework from basic recovery mechanisms to sophisticated real-time availability. Chapter 7 examines means to increase efficiency and productivity, and to create a flexible data storage infrastructure to serve the organization through dramatic and unpredictable information growth.

The tactical roadmap begins in Chapter 8 and extends through 9 and 10. From an exploration of the infrastructure design shifts to crafting an effective migration, Chapter 8 assists in this decision making. Chapter 9 serves as a comprehensive review of networking options, and rounding out the tactical storage roadmap, Chapter 10 reviews specific applications across wide area networks.

With the appropriate storage infrastructure in place, business and IT managers still have the task of maintaining and managing storage policies. Chapter 11 presents options for creating overall enterprise storage policies, and Chapter 12 concludes by tying the material together and presenting some forward-looking options.

There is plenty ahead for IP storage networking. Read on and enjoy!

Acknowledgments

As with any large project, there is a cast far beyond those featured who contribute to the overall success. I would like to recognize these individuals for their contributions, participation, and assistance in helping me create *IP Storage Networking: Straight to the Core.*

Tom Clark deserves credit for his input and support though the genesis of the book through to completion. With his insight, understanding, and spirited sense of humor, I had a trusted guide and colleague that made overall endeavor a true pleasure.

John Webster, senior analyst and founder of the Data Mobility Group, continues to provide thought leadership in the storage networking industry and has long understood the larger implications of IP storage networking. In addition to contributing the introduction, John and Data Mobility Group co-founder Perry Harris provided extensive material to Chapter Eleven (Managing the Storage Domain.) John and Perry's plan of attack provides a unique view to designing the organizational structure behind storage management.

Randy Fardal contributed an endless amount of networking expertise to Chapters Nine (Assessing Network Connectivity) and Ten (Applications Across Wide Area Networks). The technical detail in Chapter Ten has long eluded the novice and expert storage administrator alike. Through a series of detailed steps, Randy's analysis helps us navigate through potentially complicated remote storage scenarios made simple through his innovative approach.

In what will likely become a useful template for assessing high-availability requirements, Rajiev Rajavasireddy of VERITAS helped outline the entire spectrum of protection mechanisms from simple backup to wide area failover configuration in Chapter Six (Business Continuity for Mission Critical Applications.) Rajiev's exceptional capability to boil down the range of solutions to a clear, easy-to-follow framework makes this chapter an enjoyable read for even the most knowledgeable on backup and recovery procedures.

Christian Tate drew on his experience at Storage Networks for Chapter Seven (Options for Operational Agility) which focuses primarily on the storage service provider model. Christian's intimacy with this sector, and additional background at Sun Microsystems storage division and Cable and Wireless enabled him to provide a comprehensive overview of past and present trends in outsourced storage services.

Glenn Haar kindly contributed his detailed report on IT Service Recovery for Appendix A. Glenn has twenty four years of experience in the information technology field encompassing development, support, and operations. As a project leader, he implemented a revenue processing system used by the State of Idaho for 20 years. As an early adopter of technology, he was awarded a Hewlett-Packard Technology Award for Technology Integration and been listed in the International Who's Who of Information Technology.

In one of the most insightful industry reports available, Jason Yip delivers a logical, comprehensive structure to understand the storage landscape from software through systems to semiconductors. Jason's in depth expertise as an analyst at Broadview, a leading technology-focused global M&A advisor and private equity investor, helps clarify the dizzying array of new market entrants and where they fit within the larger storage environment.

Ben Nelson and Bala Parthasarathy of Snapfish graciously donated their time and experience to an educational case study on network storage in Chapter Eight (Initiating Deployment.) Ben's business foresight combined with Bala's technical acuity has produced an innovative storage growth story.

Following an inventive presentation on managing storage at Storage Networking World Fall 2002, Geoffrey Moore graciously contributed his framework on Core versus Context to Chapter Eleven. This fresh approach to looking at storage management tasks will make even the most experienced managers reevaluate their time and resource commitments.

Drawing upon his routing expertise and intimate knowledge of distributed systems, Roy D'Cruz assisted in the overall framework for Chapter Four (Storage Systems Control Points.) Roy's parallels between networking and storage distributed systems provide uncanny insight towards future storage deployments.

Aamer Latif provided his network control points model in Chapter Four. This model was used extensively in the early days of the IP storage industry to convey the market forces shaping storage network evolution.

With extensive experience on the investment and operation sides of the storage industry, Eric Bohren shared his views and perspective in parts of Chapter Four and Eight. His intimacy with the email storage sector provided the email centric case study.

Craig LeGrande of Mainstay Partners kindly contributed material to Chapters Eight and Twelve (Perfecting the Storage Engine) related to IT portfolio management. Craig's in-depth understanding of managing large IT initiatives shows visibly in his strategic approach.

I would also like to thank Bill Lozoff of NeoScale Systems, Ken Steinhardt of EMC, Sara Radicati of the Radicati Group, Inc., and Steve Duplessie of the Enterprise Storage Group for their contributions, and Josh Tseng and Charles Monia for their many educational hallway conversations.

Of course, none of this would have happened without the support of the editorial, production, and marketing teams at Addison Wesley and Prentice Hall to whom I am most thankful. I also appreciate the insightful comments of numerous editors who made this book a better read for all.

Finally, I owe true gratitude to Ching-Yee and my family for their patience during the busier times of this challenging and rewarding project.

1   Storage in a Wired World

As we race through the digital age, the natural byproduct of our high-speed journey accumulates at increasing rates that we have only begun to imagine. This byproduct, information, comes in all shapes and sizes—from databases to emails, Web pages to imaging archives. It grows continuously with our push to electronic commerce, 24/7 availability, and our requirement, real or perceived, to record every last transaction in our business exchanges. In our direct interaction with computers over the last 20 years, we witnessed the information explosion as our data storage went from a single floppy disk drive at 1.44 Megabytes (MB) to hard disk drives with capacities at 100 Gigabytes (GB)—a staggering 70-million fold increase. Applying growth of that magnitude to the business world virtually guarantees chaotic planning and mandates a radical restructuring to deal with an apparently uncontrollable byproduct.

The shift from a seemingly controllable to uncontrollable byproduct occurred as we began to network our computers. In the pre-Internet era, a significant amount of information exchanged in the business environment passed through human gatekeepers. Orders, inventory, customer support, and corporate correspondence, to name a few, typically flowed through an organization only as fast as a person could send or receive it. Today, the human gatekeepers no longer place artificial bottlenecks on the flow of information, and computers within and across organizations now generate communication and data at astronomical rates. Supply-chain management, real-time inventory tracking, automated monitoring systems of all types perpetually send data that must be tracked and ultimately stored.

Coupled with the sheer amount of information they generate, corporations face increasing pressure to accommodate, maintain, and protect it. Whether for customer relationship management software, electronic commerce Web sites, or corporate communications email infrastructure, today's business expectations place the utmost priority on data accessibility anytime, anywhere. Customers, partners, and employees demand that the information required for them to operate be there when they need it. The consequences of unavailable data quickly skyrocket to lost customers, disgruntled partners, and unproductive employees.

Behind the scenes of every corporation's mission-critical information technology (IT) operations, lies the foundation layer of data storage. Typically in the form of large disk subsystems and tape libraries, the media upon which the bits and bytes are stored empower the information flow. Couple this core with an effective software layer, the appropriate network interconnect, and precise administration, and you have the makings of a complete data storage system to drive organizational success.

1.1 Storage Takes Center Stage

In the early days of large-scale, enterprise computing, the data storage infrastructure simply came as part of the overall system. If you had an IBM mainframe, you were certain to find IBM storage attached as part of the deal. Few questioned this model, and in centralized data centers having a single point of contact for both mainframes and storage made sense. At that time, computing equipment purchases focused on the application platform first and the rest followed. This model continued through the migration to more open systems, including mid-range to high-end servers from a variety of vendors. Over time, storage capacity for applications grew as separate dedicated pools, with each application's capacity requirements managed independently within the organization.

As we moved to networked business environments, with more transactions, interactions, and information to capture, storage pools dramatically increased in size. Our push through the digital age caused thousandfold and millionfold increases in required storage capacity. Many companies were locked in to buying additional storage from their original mainframe or server vendor, often at inflated prices. Without options for any other kind of storage or the ability to share storage pools, you can imagine the margins that existed, and the vendors' enthusiasm to exploit them.

In the early 1990s, one storage vendor took note of this phenomenon and dove headfirst into the fray. EMC Corporation set out to attack IBM's market for captive storage, specifically in the mainframe market. Within several years, EMC was selling more storage for IBM mainframes than IBM was. The dam had broken, the vendor lock for homogenous configuration of mainframes and storage disappeared, and the storage market emerged.

Today, a cabal of companies controls the high-end enterprise market and fights daily for treasured data center territory. The bunch includes EMC, IBM, Sun Microsystems, Hewlett-Packard, Dell, and Hitachi Data Systems. The wars within this group for the crown of best "Terabyte Tower" perhaps are best expressed by the vigor of the product names. IBM called its latest salvo into the enterprise storage market Shark. Hitachi Data Systems calls its product line Freedom Data Storage, as if in some way to indicate that it offers choice to the downtrodden.

Now, more than ever, customers face a myriad of choices for their storage infrastructure. That may not be such a bad thing, especially considering that the storage component of IT deployments comprises as much as 70 percent of the total equipment cost. Management attention will always focus on the critical piece of the system and likely find areas that are bottlenecks, costly, complex, or competitive differentiators. Critical IT expenditures in storage indicate the central role it plays in corporate technology direction.

In the wired world, best-practice storage deployments require three focal points. The first is utilization and efficiency. Often the largest share of new IT expenditures, storage must be utilized to full capacity. A poor utilization rate is nothing short of leaving money on the table. To maintain an optimal storage infrastructure, executives and IT managers alike must maximize storage utilization rates. With storage networked together, the ability to exchange data and available space across the entire infrastructure becomes another routine corporate function.

In a wired world, with access to local, metropolitan, wide, and wireless networks 24 hours a day, 7 days a week, data must be everywhere, all the time. The second piece of best-practice deployment is availability. Even the most temporary outage of access to data, such as an unavailable Web page, can have a meaningful impact on customer goodwill. While all companies agree that business continuity must be maintained, few have spent the time and effort to see a thorough plan through completion.

In a wired world, power and intelligence reside in the network. There is no better example of this than what we have witnessed with the Internet. Its reach, impact, capabilities, and ongoing transformation speak volumes about what can happen when a bunch of computers are linked together, as if engaged in a never-ending dialogue. Storage on a network is no different. Though the development of storage networks is relatively new (5 years, perhaps) compared to the Internet (25 years), the potential can be equal or

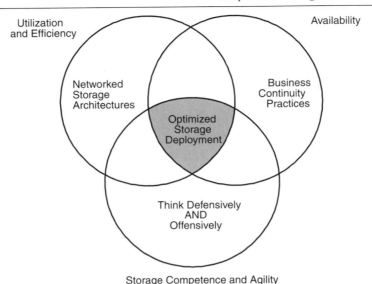

Figure 1–1 Components of optimized storage deployment.

greater. Harnessing this power in the form of optimized, agile data storage infrastructure will set a class of companies above the rest and provide a platform for competitive differentiation. This third pillar of effective deployment is the overall agility and competence of the system.

1.2 The Need for Business Continuance

Data storage lies at the epicenter of corporate mission-critical applications. Given this essential organizational function, there is no time for gaps in storage availability. The data storage infrastructure acts as an information source for customers, partners, and employees, and they all expect access anywhere, anytime.

Downtime, as it is typically referred to when IT systems become unavailable for whatever reason, was once accepted as a necessary evil in dealing with computers. Today *availability* has taken over, with a range of modifiers from "high," to "24/7," to that additional stretch of "24/7/365." Perhaps our next sustained availability window will broach a decade! But downtime has real consequences, both in terms of business or revenue lost and the goodwill of any human contact in the disrupted exchange. An interrupt of a back-office database replication might delay the launch of a new service, but the replication software doesn't mind trying again . . . immediately. Yet, a corrupted On-Line Tranaction Processing (OLTP) exchange with a Web visitor could result in a lost transaction and a lost customer.

In either case, as measured in short term or long, faulty data storage translates to lost business and productivity. Expectations on business continuity go beyond simple customer expectations to a measure of corporate competence. Combating this potential black mark, companies have moved to implement business continuity plans, ranging from system-level redundancy and backups within the data center to sophisticated off-site protection schemes that replicate mission-critical data instantly.

Business continuity comes packed with dozens of questions about its defined meaning. Do we need 24/7 availability? How long can we afford to be down? Are we protected from system failure, site failure, and natural disasters? What data are we trying to protect, and why? Who is involved? Where should our second site be located? These questions underscore the complexity of a well-executed business continuity plan. The first step to executing such a plan is having the appropriate tools. When it comes to data storage, a networked storage environment provides the easiest way to get on track to a highly available storage environment.

1.3 Driving Towards Operational Agility

The rise in current and anticipated storage spending is evidenced by increasing customer requirements as well as the clamoring among storage vendors for market share. Much of the spending increase can be linked to customer requirements to maintain a highly available storage infrastructure that meets today's business continuance requirements. Few CEOs are willing to consider the possibility of a sustained data storage service outage within their company, and they sign checks to protect against these risks.

But too often, the infrastructure investment in storage focuses primarily on protection and business continuity. While a worthy objective for existing or new data storage deployments, this singular focus on risk prevention accomplishes only part of the long-term goals—to establish an effective and nimble data storage infrastructure. IT executives and implementers need to recognize that the storage spending on risk-prevention mechanisms must be coupled with operational agility mechanisms. Only through this combined defensive and offensive approach will a company be able to navigate the chaotic growth and change of data storage infrastructures.

Cost savings and return on investment can be difficult to measure for risk-prevention approaches. The impact of sustained service outages is frequently defined in lost dollars per hour or a similar metric. But can anyone really anticipate the costs of a full-scale disaster that wipes out a data center? On the offensive side, however, more easily measured metrics help justify the spending on upgraded and new data storage deployments.

Planning for a more agile enterprise, IT executives have a variety of parameters at their disposal to measure and justify expenditures. Application efficiency, capacity efficiency, simplified training, management, and maintenance, deployment time for new applications, and new storage capacity—these productivity considerations link to real cost savings within the IT budget. By including an offensive approach to a storage strategy, IT executives can couple risk prevention with operational agility to build a more robust, flexible data storage system.

1.4 Charting a Storage Networking Roadmap

Behind every successful corporation lies a set of core competencies that provide a competitive edge—FedEx has logistics; Wal-Mart, inventory management; Dell, supplier management. Today, with information as a key corporate asset, data storage management is as vital to business success as other operational functions. The starting point for developing data storage management as a core competence is an effective roadmap.

Certain companies are known to "get" technology. They are frequently the ones that have integrated business planning with IT development. By fostering a corporate culture that supports exchanges between business units and technology development, positive reactions develop that lead to defending, supporting, and expanding existing business. Additionally, the interaction can drive new business and lead to broader technology capabilities of a more effective organization.

As the lifeblood information assets of corporations, data storage requires development of independent plans and strategies that integrate with business objectives and related technology investments. Specifically from the storage perspective, three areas form the basis of an effective roadmap. The first is utilization and efficiency—ensuring adequate, yet not overprovisioned storage resources to serve the organization. A well-designed infrastructure using networked storage makes this feasible. Business continuity is the second component of the roadmap, guaranteeing data availability to all participants anytime, anywhere. Finally, storage competency, or storage agility, completes the roadmap. Those organizations that develop the best infrastructure, policies, and procedures to deal with explosive storage growth stand to lead the

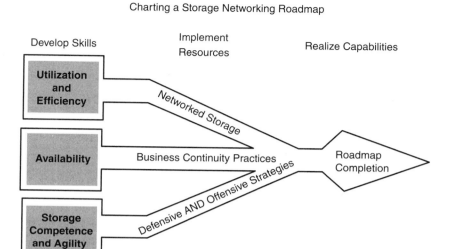

Figure 1–2 Charting an effective storage networking roadmap.

pack. Storage competency translates to business-savvy operational agility for maneuvering ahead of the competition.

The following chapters outline a complete storage networking roadmap, as shown in Figure 1–2, for organizations starting from the ground up or looking to improve upon longstanding installed infrastructure. From architectural basics, to control points, to strategies for continuity and agility, the book serves as both practical guide and navigational companion to understand the world of storage networking.

1.5 Audience and Text Overview

1.5.1 Target Audience

IP Storage Networking—Straight to the Core was written to serve IT and business managers. As these two groups need to understand each other's objectives to develop coherent action plans, it makes sense to cover considerations for both sides. On the business side, the book covers strategies for storage network deployment, options for outsourcing, and insight into storage vendor control points. On the technical side, the book presents comprehensive infrastructure explanations along with new and emerging developments in storage networking, specifically the recent integration of storage with mainstream IP networking. This area, which brings networking and storage professionals together for a common cause, presents the greatest opportunities for organizations to deploy innovative and valuable infrastructure.

Beyond senior IT and business management, the book addresses a wider range of constituents involved, directly or indirectly, with the deployment of enterprise storage. CIOs, CEOs, and CFOs will benefit from understanding the mix between technical and financial opportunities, particularly in the case of multimillion dollar deployments with disaster recovery plans that may require board approval. Research and development teams will benefit by seeing new architectural designs for application deployment. Technology investors, industry press, and analysts will benefit from a deeper understanding of the market forces behind the technology innovation.

All of these groups have a stake in the enterprise storage industry, and as such, can be considered "straight to the core" ambassadors, as shown in Figure 1–3.

1.5.2 Text Overview

Chapters 2 and 3 cover the background of storage hardware and software respectively. Storage professionals will likely grasp these details easily. However, Chapter 2, "The Storage Architectural Landscape," pays special attention to the differences between network-attached storage, operating at the file layer, and storage area networks, operating at the block layer. As these two useful storage technologies merge to a common communications medium of IP networking, a review of each should prove helpful. Chapter 3, "The Software Spectrum," presents a detailed overview of the software spectrum around data storage management. Moving more quickly than other areas of the infrastructure, the software components can make a storage

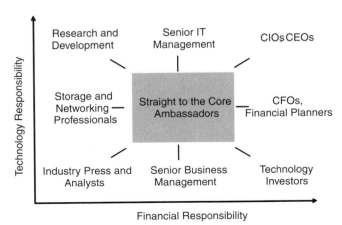

Figure 1–3 Target audience for IP Storage Networking—Straight to the Core.

administrator's life easier and provide business value for the corporation. New market segments, specifically virtualization, are particularly interesting given the rapid development underway. While current virtualization software may not be appropriate for all organizations presently, these powerful capabilities will enhance storage administration, and any organization looking toward new investments must keep this component in the design plan.

Chapter 4, "Storage System Control Points," and Chapter 5, "Reaping Value from Storage Networks," lay the foundation for building effective storage network roadmaps. Chapter 4 presents a history of data storage architectures and how the intelligence piece of the equation has evolved across server platforms, disk subsystems, and now within networking fabrics. This dynamic shift, if managed appropriately, can be used toward customer advantage in balancing multivendor configurations. Building these kinds of strategies into a storage networking roadmap can provide significant cost savings at future junctures. Similarly, Chapter 5 outlines the defensive strategies for data storage most often associated with disaster recovery and business continuity. *IP Storage Networking—Straight to the Core* goes one step beyond the typical analysis by providing offensive strategies for storage deployment, fostering operational agility, and anticipating future changes to the overall architecture. Finally, the chapter concludes with techniques to measure returns on defensive and offensive tacks, allowing business and IT managers to justify expenditures and be recognized for cost efficiency and profit contribution.

The primary business continuance applications are covered in Chapter 6, "Business Continuity for Mission-Critical Applications." Most organizations have some or all of these applications running at present. The chapter begins by outlining the business continuity objectives for each application, for example, designing "classes" of storage. It also breaks down the differences between server availability and storage availability, and the required interaction. Storage-specific requirements of these applications are reviewed, particularly, mechanisms to optimize performance while maintaining business continuity. Conclusions about enabling uptime allow business and IT managers to draft the appropriate business continuity plans to meet their objectives.

Chapter 7, "Options for Operational Agility," examines means to increase efficiency and productivity, and create a flexible data storage infrastructure to serve the organization through dramatic and unpredictable information growth. By applying business models of ownership, financing, inventory management, and forecasting, business and IT mangers can create solid roadmaps for an agile enterprise. Specific topics covered include the emergence of outsourced storage models, recommendations for managing service level agreements, accelerating application deployment, and incorporating data storage into proven models for corporate asset management.

The tactical roadmap begins in Chapter 8, "Initiating Deployment," and extends through Chapters 9 and 10. From an exploration of the infrastructure design shifts to crafting an effective migration, Chapter 8 assists in this decision making. It also includes guidelines for calculating the total cost of ownership and identifying the true cost components of an enterprise data storage deployment.

Chapter 9, "Assessing Network Connectivity," serves as a comprehensive review of networking options. In cases of both business continuity and operational agility, the networking component plays a critical role. The ability to network storage devices within and across organizations presents opportunities for innovating architectures. Recently, with the introduction of new IP storage technologies such as iSCSI, choosing the right networking option is more important than ever. Topics such as network technologies, topologies, and carriers are covered thoroughly in this chapter, including security for storage across networks.

Rounding out the tactical storage roadmap, Chapter 10, "Long-Distance Storage Networking Applications," reviews specific applications across wide area networks. Historically, storage applications have been designed for the data center, with little consideration for the associated latency of running these applications across long distance. Today, sophisticated techniques exist that mitigate the effects of distance and enable storage applications to run between virtually any locations. These techniques are outlined in the chapter.

With the appropriate storage infrastructure in place, business and IT managers still have the task of maintaining and managing storage policies. Chapter 11, "Managing the Storage Domain," presents options for creating overall enterprise storage policies with a focus on data protection and disaster recovery scenarios. As these functions are inextricably linked with the need to administer overall growth, aspects of managing storage expansion are included in this section.

1.6 Chapter Summary

Storage in a Wired World

- Data storage growth is continuing astronomically.

- Information grows automatically, regardless of human influence.

- Anytime, anywhere availability is required.

1.1 Storage Takes Center Stage

- Storage was traditionally an afterthought to the server or mainframe purchase.

- The storage infrastructure is now paramount to the server and communications infrastructure.

- Elements of best-practice storage deployment are

    - Utilization and efficiency

    - Availability

    - Storage competence/storage agility

1.2 The Need for Business Continuance

- Downtime is no longer an option. Availability is everything.

- Demands for business continuity go beyond routine expectations to a measure of corporate competence.

- Business continuity as a practice comes loaded with questions that must be identified, outlined, and addressed.

1.3 Driving Towards Operational Agility

- Storage investments must extend beyond protection schemes to offensive mechanisms to improve operational agility

- While risk-prevention projects may be difficult to justify quantitatively, more agile enterprise storage deployments often have easily measured cost savings.

1.4 Charting a Storage Networking Roadmap

- Develop data storage management as a core competence.

- Extend corporate culture among business units and technology development.

- Deploy storage with appropriate focal points:

    - **Utilization and efficiency**—Create networked storage architectures

    - **Availability**—Make use of business continuity practices

    - **Storage competence/storage agility**—Think defensively and offensively

2

The Storage Architectural Landscape

IP Storage Networking: Straight to the Core provides readers with an understanding of storage networking technologies as well as a roadmap to optimized deployment. In order to accomplish this mission, we need to closely examine the architectural landscape of data storage, specifically the hardware that makes up these ever-increasing capital investments. Through this understanding, we can effectively integrate the hardware decision-making process into overall objectives for utilization and efficiency, availability, and storage agility.

The information data storage repositories, from disk drives to multimillion-dollar dedicated "storage computers," reside at the edge of the overall infrastructure. These devices have grown in sophistication and complexity to the point that many new enterprise storage deployment budgets allocate more money for storage than for servers. Their importance cannot be underestimated as storage is freed from single-server restrictions.

Moving from the end storage devices, network connectivity comes into play, both in the form of Network-Attached Storage (NAS) and storage area networks (SANs). These complementary technologies, once physically restricted to two separate network domains, now converge with the introduction of IP storage networks (IP SANs). Appropriately managing the balance between NAS and SAN, from performance, to usability, to vendor-or-technology lock-in, requires an updated look at the origins and evolution of these architectures.

IP SANs entered the market in 2002 and represent the newest turbo boost into the overall storage equation. By merging still high-margin storage markets with dynamic networking markets (operating by different technology conventions), innovation, investment, and new product development flourish. Today's market offerings, from new storage networking hardware to new storage management software, provide more opportunities for rewriting the rules of data storage management than ever before.

This chapter outlines the architectural and technological basics to effectively approach SANs as a fundamental component of optimized storage deployment.

2.1 Storage Building Blocks

The basic elements of a computing storage system haven't changed in the last 30 or so years. The equipment and areas that control the primary interaction may have moved around, but at the end of the day, an operating system still initiates a request to a file system, which in turns talks to a volume management layer, and ultimately the storage devices themselves, as shown in Figure 2–1.

The earliest server implementations of this architecture took place internal to the system but have since expanded outside the box into specialized equipment and software platforms. Intelligent disk arrays, switching infrastructure, and network transports have shattered the traditional blueprint for storage designs. This newfound geographic freedom for a wide variety of storage functions presents IT professionals with previously unavailable architectural options. In today's global computing environments, these options help save time and money.

The SNIA shared storage model serves as an excellent reference for outlining storage architectures. Specifically, the model provides a navigable map for the variety of functions that make up a complete storage system.

2.1.1 STORAGE GUIDANCE: File Systems, Volumes, and Blocks

The model in Figure 2–2 provides an abstraction of how applications address storage, allowing IT administrators to effectively plan complete architectures. It carries the simplified model in Figure 2–1 further by calling out spe-

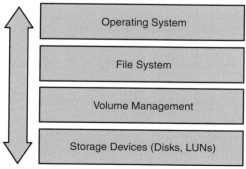

Figure 2–1 Basic storage building blocks.

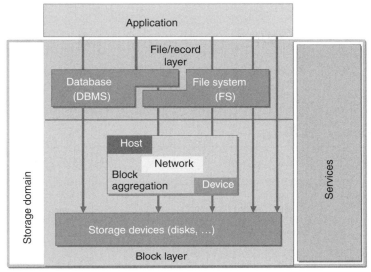

© Storage Networking Industry Association

Figure 2–2 The SNIA shared storage model.

cific mechanisms that file systems and volume management use to access storage devices. In the case of the SNIA model, one can roughly equate volume management with block aggregation.

Applications are the common starting point for the model. From there, all other mechanisms fall into the storage domain—database management systems (DBMS), file systems (FS), and all of the ways to connect to disks. The connection to the physical disk drive may be direct from the server or host, through a storage network, or through a device such as a NAS head or NAS server. Each of these areas—host, network, and device—may perform the block aggregation functions required to deliver blocks to the upper-layer file or record layer.

One benefit of the SNIA shared storage model is the ability to map a variety of storage architectures onto a single framework. In the case of large corporations with storage deployments spanning direct-attached storage (DAS), NAS, and SAN-attached storage, viewing these seemingly separate hardware infrastructure across common dimensions can help rationalize purchases and resources across the storage organization. Further, this optimized view helps IT managers plan and architect corporatewide solutions serving multiple departments, enabling greater efficiency.

Figure 2–3 highlights the versatility of the model in depicting multiple architectures within one framework. Item one, DAS, connects directly from a host, or server, with its own logical volume management (LVM) to a set of disks. In this case, the host provides software redundant array of independent disks (RAID) functionality to the unintelligent disks, often referred to as just a bunch of disks (JBOD). File system and volume management functions reside on the host. Note that the host box covers the entire space of the file/record layer, and covers *host block aggregation* in the block layer of the diagram. Item two is similar, but now the host connects to a disk array across a SAN. It still has some host block aggregation (i.e., volume management), but now some of the aggregation, such as the RAID functions, are shared by the device, which overlaps with *device block aggregation* in the block layer of the diagram.

Items three and four change the storage access mechanisms to file-based, as opposed to block-based. Note that a local area network (LAN) resides between the host and the NAS head and NAS server, and that each NAS unit overlaps into the file/record layer. The communication requests from the hosts to the NAS units are file-based, used for corporate file sharing, for example, compared to block-based hosts (items one and two), which use a SCSI-based access mechanism (SCSI, Fibre Channel, iSCSI) to communicate with the disks.

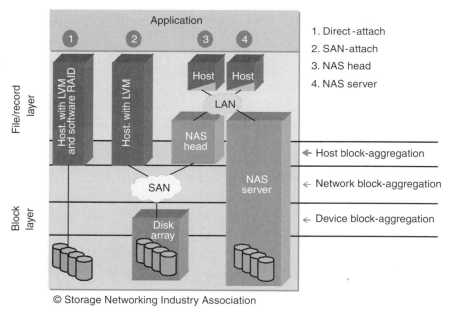

© Storage Networking Industry Association

Figure 2–3 The SNIA shared storage model depicting direct-attached, SAN-attached, and network-attached storage.

2.2 Internal Storage/Server-based storage

In early computing designs, storage devices were located within the computing system itself, such as a server. In this case, all storage components (file system, volume management, and storage devices) are internal. This simple implementation is easy for administrators to deploy, with each server having specific storage allocations met by internal disk drives.

Disk drive interfaces vary between SCSI (Small Computer System Interface), IDE (Integrated Device Electronics), and ATA (Advanced Technology Attachment), with each providing a cost/performance optimization suited to varying market segments. Inside an enclosure, the disk drive interface has little effect on the overall enterprise computing system design. But placing individual storage devices within each server leads to scalability issues. In an internal-only storage environment, each application is largely constrained by the amount of storage that can fit inside the box. Beyond that, the only options left are moving outside the server.

2.3 External Storage (JBOD, RAID, Tape, Optical, Other)

External to the server, storage devices have the flexibility to evolve to highly specific task-oriented machines, from JBODs at the low end of the disk-based media spectrum to high-end RAID systems. Similarly, tape, optical, solid-state, and other forms of storage come in all shapes and sizes to suit specific needs. This section covers the basics of external storage devices leading up to transition from direct-attached to networked storage.

An understanding of these basic storage components provides significant value as IT professionals begin to chart their storage networking roadmaps. Since external storage devices vary in size, cost, and complexity, effective use of these basic building blocks helps offset potential pitfalls as the entire storage infrastructure scales.

2.3.1 Just a Bunch of Disks (JBOD)

While some may place JBODs at the low end of the storage food chain, a careful look at the overall storage networking picture reveals more sophisticated uses for these devices. With a relatively low cost per megabyte for disk-based storage, JBODs provide excellent value where redundancy and intelligence can be added elsewhere in the overall architecture, for example within a host or network.

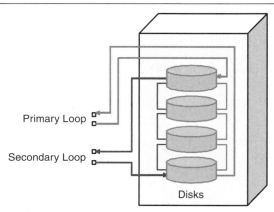

Figure 2–4 Basic JBOD design.

The basic JBOD is an enclosure for 3.5-inch hard disk drives that provides a daisy-chain mechanism to link the devices together. In SCSI terms, the disk drives are independent devices on a parallel SCSI bus. In Fibre Channel terms, the disk drives are independent devices on a Fibre Channel loop. A typical JBOD architecture based on Fibre Channel loop is outlined in Figure 2–4.

2.3.2 Redundant Array of Independent/Inexpensive Disks (RAID)

RAID can be implemented directly in storage hardware devices or in storage controllers, such as host bus adapters (HBAs), or in software. While these options offer choice in terms of cost and performance, the basic principles of RAID remain the same. RAID architectures protect disk drive-based data with several redundancy mechanisms to protect against disk failure. Implemented properly, storage systems using RAID will be unaffected by disk drive loss and can go uninterrupted through the cycle of disk failure and repair.

RAID grew considerably with the introduction of inexpensive 5.25-inch and 3.5-inch drives. Manufacturers valued the opportunity to use less expensive components with a cost curve similar to the PC industry, but also had to contend with the potential failure of such low-end components. The specific terminology used to describe the life of a disk drive is mean time between failure (MTBF). By removing individual disk drive failure from the overall system MTBF, RAID systems could guarantee higher availability and continuous uptime for users.

Today, high-end RAID systems offer a variety of redundancy measures and storage management features that contend directly with similar offerings in the rest of the enterprise. A mirror, or exact copy of the data on an additional set of disk drives, can operate directly within a RAID system for optimized performance. Similar functions can also be accomplished directly with host-based software or within a storage network.

The primary RAID functions include striping, mirroring, and parity. IT professionals should be familiar with these functions and terminology, as outlined next in Section 2.3.3.

2.3.3 STORAGE GUIDANCE: RAID Levels

Basic RAID features break down into a series of defined RAID levels as originally documented by David A. Patterson, Garth A. Gibson, and Randy H. Katz of the University of California at Berkeley in 1988. Six basic levels were defined—RAID 0 through 5 (see Figure 2–5). Each represents a unique mechanism to achieve higher performance and availability with common disk drive components. The numbers do not directly correlate with degrees of performance or availability and should be viewed categorically. In practice, RAID 0, 1, and 5 are the most commonly implemented RAID mechanisms. RAID 2 required special disk features. Given the economics of volume production, the cost of such features favored simply using other RAID levels. RAID 3 and 4 also are not frequently implemented due to the performance impact of dedicated parity disks.

RAID levels, outlined in Figure 2–5, can be combined to create even higher levels of availability. For example, a RAID 0 array may also be mirrored. Known as RAID 0+1, this provides the performance of RAID 0 striping with the redundancy of RAID 1 mirroring. Another configuration, RAID 10, stripes data across two independent mirrored disk volumes. Similar combinations exist with RAID 0 and RAID 5.

2.3.4 Tape Drives and Tape Libraries

Purchasing decisions for storage devices measure performance, features, capacity, and cost. At the high end of the performance, feature, and cost equation are large RAID arrays. While it would be convenient for enterprises to standardize on a single set of media devices, economics come into play and create opportunities for other device types.

Tape drives and tape libraries offer high-capacity, low-cost storage when compared to disk arrays. Tape density for single tape drives and cartridge density for automated tape libraries far outweigh the equivalent capacity of a disk-based unit with a similar footprint. Further, the ability to swap tape cartridges provides flexibility to add capacity and the ability to remotely locate tapes for disaster recovery purposes.

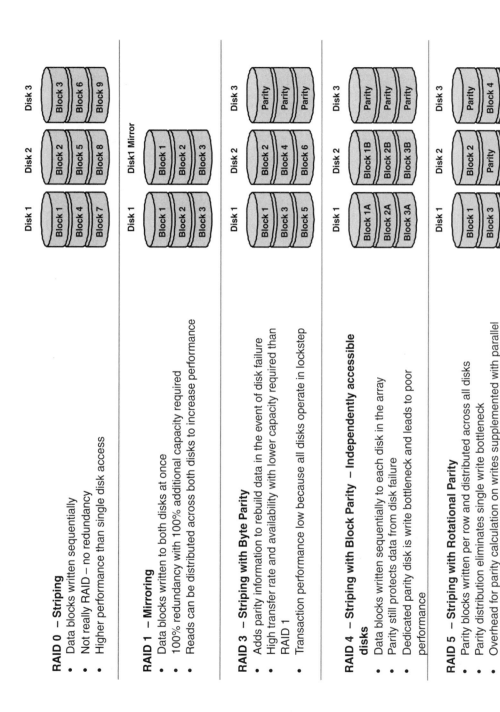

RAID 0 – Striping
- Data blocks written sequentially
- Not really RAID – no redundancy
- Higher performance than single disk access

RAID 1 – Mirroring
- Data blocks written to both disks at once
- 100% redundancy with 100% additional capacity required
- Reads can be distributed across both disks to increase performance

RAID 3 – Striping with Byte Parity
- Adds parity information to rebuild data in the event of disk failure
- High transfer rate and availability with lower capacity required than RAID 1
- Transaction performance low because all disks operate in lockstep

RAID 4 – Striping with Block Parity – Independently accessible disks
- Data blocks written sequentially to each disk in the array
- Parity still protects data from disk failure
- Dedicated parity disk is write bottleneck and leads to poor performance

RAID 5 – Striping with Rotational Parity
- Parity blocks written per row and distributed across all disks
- Parity distribution eliminates single write bottleneck
- Overhead for parity calculation on writes supplemented with parallel microprocessors or caching

Figure 2–5 RAID levels.

Today, SANs allow consolidated sharing of tape libraries across a number of servers. Whereas previously, each server required its own tape drive, or servers had to share traffic on the LAN for access to a central backup server, SANs allow direct connections between servers and tape libraries for simplified backup, offloading a potentially overburdened LAN. Coupled with the appropriate backup software package, this provides an economical, easily managed backup system.

Tape media comes in a variety of forms, such as digital linear tape (DLT), linear tape-open (LTO), and advanced intelligent tape (AIT), each offering its own capacity, performance, and cost equation that will manifest itself in the overall system specifications. Choice of a tape library should focus more on system features within the context of the enterprise storage architecture rather than choice of a specific media type. However, purchasers should be advised that media types do have a life of their own. Yearly checks to assure both media type and subsystem availability should be part of data center operating procedures. To protect against outdated media types and potential data loss due to tape degradation or magnetic interference, IT managers often re-record data to fresh tapes every year. This guarantees recovery mechanisms but also adds the cost of tape replenishment.

2.3.5 Other Storage (Optical, Solid State)

Other media technologies include optical, which is often compared to tape, but since it uses electromagnetic recording mechanisms, the shelf life of the discs far exceeds that of tape. Electromagnetic mechanisms for optical recording operate at much higher temperatures than traditional magnetic disk and tape recording. This prevents interference from nearby magnetic material or environmental impacts due to low or high temperatures. In fact, if kept in a properly controlled environment, optical media suffers virtually no degradation over time.

Optical media comes in recordable CD/DVD form, 5.25-inch WORM (write once, read many), and 12-inch optical disks. These magnetic-optic (MO) drives operate independently or can be assembled in to a library (often called a jukebox) to provide high-capacity optical storage similar to tape libraries. In an automated jukebox, mechanics allow for recording on both sides of the optical disk.

Solid-state storage media sits highest on both the performance measure and cost measure. It is often used for performance-critical applications that operate from a small data set. As the name implies, solid-state storage relies upon memory chips to provide capacity. This implementation provides extremely high throughput and I/O operations per second. However, due to cost and capacity limitations, solid-state storage is used in limited market segments.

2.4 Direct-Attached Storage

DAS expands server storage capacity. It provides easily configurable storage that looks local, or internal, to a server, yet has scalable capacity benefits of being outside the server itself. External storage can extend server life by providing not only additional capacity but a range of storage features, such as redundancy, that help protect data.

With DAS, servers access blocks of data. The file system and volume management layers are host-based. Other data storage functions implemented independent of the server, such as RAID, provide greater performance and leave the server free to focus on its priority tasks, such as application processing. Most external storage devices attach to servers via high speed parallel SCSI or Fibre Channel cabling. Traditionally, the speed difference between SCSI and Fibre Channel compared to LANs has been significant, although today's high-speed networking interconnects, such as Gigabit Ethernet, level the playing field. See Section 2.6.3, "SAN GUIDANCE: Comparing Ethernet/IP and Fibre Channel Fabrics," for a more complete overview of storage and networking interconnects.

However, even DAS has its limits. Adding additional storage usually requires incremental servers, and one server does not have direct access to another server's storage. This captive storage model makes resource sharing difficult and leaves servers susceptible to single points of failure. The basic DAS model is shown in Figure 2–6.

Reaching the limits of the captive storage model, solutions with additional scalability arose that networked storage together. This development took shape in the mid-1980s, well before the introduction of high-speed serial storage technologies such as Fibre Channel and iSCSI. Therefore, without a means to serialize the high-speed parallel SCSI interconnects between servers and DAS devices, the only other available network was the Ethernet and IP-based LAN. This led to the introduction of NAS.

2.5 Network-Attached Storage

NAS devices overcame several barriers when introduced to the storage market. First, NAS broke the DAS captive model. Second, it provided a mecha-

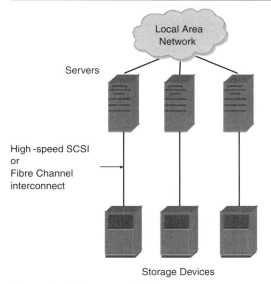

Figure 2–6 Direct-attached storage.

nism to link storage across Ethernet and IP networks, a completely new foot-print for storage administrators. Most importantly, and in part to support the architectural change, NAS moved the file system and volume manage-ment functions from the server to a NAS device, often called a filer. Keep in mind that the "filing" function remains no matter what the storage model. The location of this function has traditionally separated the distinction of NAS and SAN. See the following section for a more complete outline of the differences between NAS and SAN.

2.5.1 STORAGE GUIDANCE: SAN and NAS

A discussion about accessing storage via IP and Ethernet, such as with IP storage adapters, invariably begs the question about the difference between SAN and NAS. The SNIA shared storage model outlines file-level and block-level distinctions, which are further clarified in Figure 2–7.

SANs provide scalable performance with direct access to storage devices. Since the storage system resides on the distributed hosts, this architecture works well for databases and online transaction processing.

NAS provides crossplatform scalability, but not the performance scala-bility due to its use of a high level of file abstraction between applications and storage. While a NAS filer offloads some server workload required to

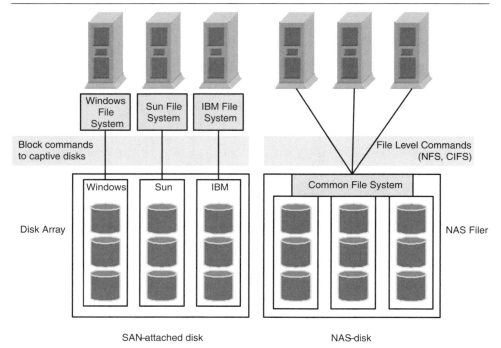

Figure 2–7 Comparing SAN and NAS.

map files into physical storage, it adds significant workload to the filer itself. NAS delivers a central storage system (file system) that is ideal for file sharing, Web serving, and similar applications.

A NAS device is essentially a highly optimized file-delivery server. Depending on the specific implementation, NAS devices may have internal storage (similar to a traditional server), or they may be directly connected to a RAID device for additional capacity or to a tape library for backup functions. Additionally, some NAS devices can connect directly to a block-based storage network.

Traditional servers access NAS devices through the Ethernet and IP network by means of a file request. Since the file system resides on the NAS device, servers with different operating systems can all easily access the same data. This crossplatform access gives NAS a considerable advantage in terms of simplicity. It also allows the NAS device to provide lock functions for particular files. Since the device knows if one server is accessing a file, the second server will not be able to write or modify that file.

NAS has made tremendous inroads to certain market segments where the architecture suits the applications. Web-related functions, such as serving

HTTP requests, are ideal applications. The relatively small file size combined with the crossplatform access across Ethernet and IP networks makes NAS a winner.

Similarly, corporate file sharing is easily addressed by NAS. To add more storage capacity to such a configuration, a storage administrator would simply need to plug another NAS device into the IP network. Of course, if for the new NAS device to be completely integrated with other NAS devices in a network—for example, where the NAS devices could pool storage capacity—purchasing the unit from the same vendor becomes a requirement.

Figure 2–8 outlines a basic NAS architecture. As shown, application servers access NAS filers over the IP network, providing greater scalability and crossplatform access than DAS provides. However, NAS doesn't alleviate LAN congestion, and the expansion of block-oriented storage remains disruptive. Additionally, each filer owns the storage that it maintains (except in some homogeneous, pooled NAS environments), and in general, NAS has a unique OS that must be maintained across all filers for ease of management. Finally, the high level of file abstraction inherent to NAS design doesn't suit certain application requirements accustomed to block-level storage.

The gap between high-performance DAS and flexible NAS became the sweet spot for SANs. Traditionally, block-oriented SANs solved a combination of problems between DAS and NAS with Fibre Channel networks. More

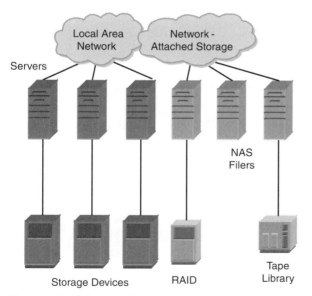

Pros:
- Uses standard Ethernet and IP
- Optimized file handling performance
- Improved scalability over DAS

Cons:
- Doesn't alleviate LAN congestion
- Disruptive "block" storage expansion/maintenance
- Filer "owns" storage resource
- Unique OS

Figure 2–8 Network-attached storage.

recently, SANs have been able to fill this gap with block-oriented IP SANs, using IP storage protocols such as iSCSI. The following sections cover the details of both Fibre Channel and IP SAN infrastructure.

2.6 Storage Area Networks

Entire books have been written about SANs. Two notable volumes are *Designing Storage Area Networks* and *IP SANs*, both by Tom Clark. For those interested in the next level of technical detail, they both serve as excellent references.

Achieving the roadmap objectives of *IP Storage Networking—Straight to the Core* requires a thorough understanding of SANs and the underlying infrastructure of both Fibre Channel and IP SANs. This section covers such material with the intent to quickly move on to the software spectrum that maximizes the impact of a flexible, well-architected infrastructure.

2.6.1 SAN History and Background

In the mid-1990s, IT professionals recognized the gap between DAS and NAS, and momentum grew for a mechanism that combined the performance and direct access of DAS with the network flexibility of NAS. The solution that emerged was Fibre Channel.

Fibre Channel is actually a SCSI-based implementation, only in a serial format. SCSI commands are at the root of all storage exchanges between imitators and targets. Commands such as write, read, and acknowledge provide the rules of engagement between two devices. This SCSI command set has proved invaluable as the lingua franca for storage.

Originally, the SCSI command set could operate only on top of a SCSI parallel bus. This cabling mechanism involved the use of large, high-density cabling with as many as 68 wires per cable. SCSI cabling cannot extend beyond 25 meters and can effectively support only a handful of devices.

Fibre Channel solved SCSI limitations of device count and distance with the Fibre Channel Protocol (FCP) and Fibre Channel networks (see Figure 2–9). It is important to remember that these two components do not necessarily need to operate together, especially when considering implementations of IP storage. With the ability to layer the SCSI command set on to FCP, and then transmit the information across a serial high-speed network built with Fibre Channel, IT professionals could now build networked storage infrastructures where servers have direct access to storage devices, new storage devices could easily be added to the network, and storage capacity could be

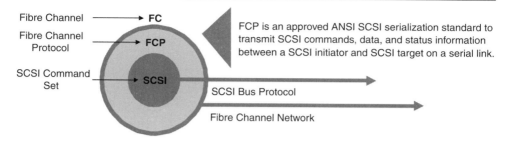

SCSI	Core command set for hosts and device communication
FCP Layer	Routable packaging (SCSI serialization) for network connectivity

Figure 2–9 Basics of Fibre Channel Protocol (FCP).

shared among multiple servers. These SAN benefits, including the ability for storage professionals to manage the ever-increasing amount of data, led to the adoption of this architecture by virtually all large corporations.

With the routable packaging in place via FCP shown in Figure 2–9, the network build-out for storage could take place with Fibre Channel SANs, shown in Figure 2–10.

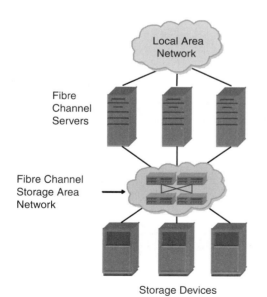

Pros:
- Gigabit speed performance
- Distance storage connectivity ~10KM
- Scales to thousands of storage nodes
- Enables storage resource sharing

- **Cons:**
- Unresolved Fibre Channel interoperability issues
- Lack of customer Fibre Channel trained staff
- Introduces second network technology
- Requires separate management system

Figure 2–10 Fibre Channel storage area networks.

Fibre Channel SANs proved invaluable for storage professionals looking to expand direct access storage capacity and utilization. However, Fibre Channel SANs came with their own set of issues that left the end-to-end solution incomplete. This includes unresolved interoperability issues between multiple vendors' products. While compatibility between Fibre Channel adapters in servers and Fibre Channel storage devices is mature, the interoperability required to build Fibre Channel fabrics with switches and directors from multiple vendors remains a difficult and complex process.

Fibre Channel SANs, through the inherent nature of introducing a new network technology different from IP and Ethernet, requires new staff training, new equipment, and new management systems. These factors add considerably to the overall total cost of the storage infrastructure.

Finally, Fibre Channel networking was designed as a data center technology, not intended to travel long distances across WANs. With today's requirements for high-availability across geographic areas, Fibre Channel networks cannot compete independently, even with the help of extenders or Dense Wave Division Multiplexing (DWDM) products. At a maximum, these solutions can extend Fibre Channel traffic to around 100 kilometers.

2.6.2 Pure IP Storage Networks

Starting in 2000, the concept of a pure IP SAN took hold. The basic concept of this implementation was to create a method of connecting servers and storage devices, with the direct access block methods applications expected, via an Ethernet and IP network. This would provide IT professionals the ability to utilize existing, well-understood, mature networking technology in conjunction with block-addressable storage devices. The underlying technology enabling this architecture is known as Internet Small Computer Systems Interface, or iSCSI (see Figure 2–11).

iSCSI, in its simplest form, represents a mechanism to take block-oriented SCSI commands and map them to an IP network. This protocol can be implemented directly on servers or storage devices to allow native connectivity to IP and Ethernet networks or fabrics. Once accomplished, storage applications requiring direct access to storage devices can extend that connection across an IP and Ethernet network, which has a nearly ubiquitous footprint across corporate and carrier infrastructures. The basics of the iSCSI protocol are outlined in Figure 2–11, while an implementation example is shown in Figure 2–12.

This wholehearted embrace of underlying IP and Ethernet technologies—mature network technology, installed base, software integration,

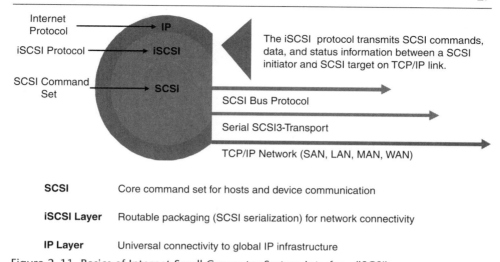

SCSI | Core command set for hosts and device communication

iSCSI Layer | Routable packaging (SCSI serialization) for network connectivity

IP Layer | Universal connectivity to global IP infrastructure

Figure 2–11 Basics of Internet Small Computer System Interface (iSCSI).

industry research—should guarantee iSCSI will succeed as a storage transport. However, networking technologies succeed based on provision of a transition path. The same applies for iSCSI, where the transition path may occur from internal server storage to iSCSI SANs, parallel SCSI devices to iSCSI, or enterprise Fibre Channel storage to iSCSI SAN.

Adoption of new technologies occurs most frequently with those likely to gain. With iSCSI, that would indicate adoption first in mid-size to large cor-

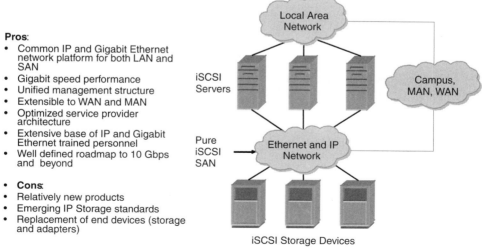

Figure 2–12 Pure iSCSI storage networks.

porations that have already deployed a Fibre Channel SAN; recognize the benefits of direct access, networked storage infrastructures; and need the ability to scale to large deployments across geographically dispersed locations. This profile often accompanies a significant storage budget that could be considerably trimmed in cost and complexity savings introduced by an IP-centric approach.

For a pure iSCSI storage network, no accommodation is made for Fibre Channel. More specifically, the iSCSI specification, as ratified by the IETF, makes no reference to Fibre Channel. That protocol conversion is outside the purview of the standards organization and left completely to vendor implementation.

Several mechanisms exist to enhance current Fibre Channel SANs with IP. Optimized storage deployment depends on careful analysis of these solutions, attention to control points within the architecture, and recognition that aggressively embracing IP networking can lead to dramatic total cost benefits. These considerations are covered in Section 2.6.5, "Enhancing Fibre Channel SANs with IP."

2.6.3 SAN GUIDANCE: Comparing Ethernet/IP and Fibre Channel Fabrics

With the introduction of IP storage as a capable storage network transport, many comparisons have been drawn between the two technologies. For fair comparison, one must recognize that Fibre Channel and Ethernet are both Layer 2 networking technologies virtually equivalent in performance. They both provide point-to-point, full-duplex, switched architectures. It is very hard to differentiate networking technologies with these common characteristics. Therefore, the speed and feed comparisons between Fibre Channel and Ethernet are largely irrelevant.

However, Ethernet is the largest home for the Internet Protocol, and IP ubiquity dramatically expands fabric flexibility. The equivalent in Fibre Channel would be the FCP, but since that works only on Fibre Channel fabrics, it can't compete with IP as an intelligent packaging mechanism. With that in mind, the Table 2–1 depicts some fabric differences.

Fibre Channel SANs function well in data center environments and are useful for massive Fibre Channel end-device consolidation. But for reasons identified above, Fibre Channel requires complementary technologies such as IP and Ethernet to help integrate storage into overall corporate cost and management objectives.

TABLE 2–1 COMPARISON OF FIBRE CHANNEL AND ETHERNET/IP FABRICS

	Pure Fibre Channel Fabric	Ethernet and IP Fabric
Distance	Approximately 100Km, including DWDM	Unlimited
Size limitations	Fabric switch limit of 239	Unlimited
Network performance	Equivalent (point-to-point, full-duplex, switched)	Equivalent (point-to-point, full-duplex, switched)
Transport	Fibre Channel, DWDM	Ethernet, ATM, Packet-over-SONET, T-1, T-3, DS-3, DWDM
Fault Isolation	Not available; single fabric solution	Protection via autonomous regions
Positioning	High performance	Network convergence
Total cost of ownership	Independent to SAN	Integrated with corporate IP networking
Network management	Independent	Integrated to IP
Network reach	Data center, Metro SAN	SAN, LAN, MAN, WAN

2.6.4 Host Bus Adapters and Network Interface Cards

Regardless of the networking interconnect, servers and storage devices need methods to take data from the CPU or the disk drives out to the wire. Servers use HBAs or network interface cards (NICs) for such functions, and storage subsystems use controllers. Both types of devices are functionally similar. Frequently, end-system connectivity gets inappropriately mixed in with network connectivity to describe SANs, but the two are fundamentally different. With the ability to do wire-speed conversion within networking fabrics between different cabling and protocols, end-system interconnects and network fabrics need not be identical.

With the dramatic differences between traditional IP-based LAN traffic using NICs and traditional storage-based traffic using Fibre Channel HBAs, it helps to clarify how these fit with new IP storage adapters, such as iSCSI. In the traditional IP case, TCP/IP segmentation resided in the host application layer. When the server wanted to send information out on the wire (link layer), it would have to segment the file into smaller frames that would be sent to the NIC driver layer. The driver layer had the simple task of relaying those packets to the wire. With large files, however, the host-based process of parsing the information into smaller units consumed considerable CPU cycles—and ultimately led to poor performance.

Fibre Channel-based HBAs compensated for this inefficiency by moving the data segmentation directly to the card and letting the card do the heavy lifting of converting to smaller frames for the link layer. This freed CPU cycles for application processing and created a highly efficient mechanism for moving data out to the wire.

A combination of these two approaches results in the efficiency of the Fibre Channel approach, through a process called TCP/IP offload. TCP/IP offload can be used for network based servers using TCP/IP, including iSCSI or NAS. The processing for data segmentation once completed in the host now moves to the card, freeing CPU cycles. Also, the data comes out of the server directly to a TCP/IP and Ethernet link using iSCSI, providing native access to IP networks and the corresponding universal reach. IP storage can run on traditional IP NICs through software drivers, but the CPU utilization will be high and could impact application performance during operating hours. During off-peak times, when CPU cycles are available, this approach may be sufficient.

IP storage adapters can be further categorized by the types of offload mechanisms. At the basic level, all IP storage adapters employ some form of TCP/IP offloading. Further, some adapters will offload the iSCSI process from the host as well. The intricacies among these implementations require examining several features during evaluation. First and foremost, IP storage adapters should provide wire-speed throughput with CPU utilization of less than 10 percent. This guarantees that even in times of peak processing, the adapter will perform without consuming more that 10 percent of the available CPU resources. Additionally, features like integrated storage and network traffic processing on a single card should be evaluated. Even if such features aren't used all the time, common interface cards for network and storage connectivity cut redundancy costs dramatically. For example, two integrated cards could operate together, one in network mode the other in storage mode. If one fails, the other takes over in both modes. While performance may be impacted, the cost savings for redundancy likely far outweigh that trade-off. Finally, dual-pathing and link aggregation of multiple adapters may be required for high-performance, mission-critical applications. These features should be present in IP storage adapters. Figure 2–13 diagrams the basics of traditional IP network, traditional storage, and new IP storage adapters.

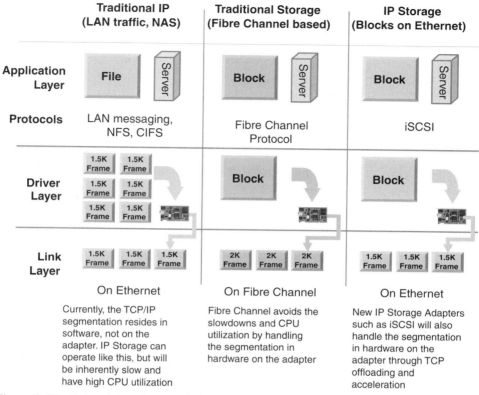

Figure 2–13 Network interface cards, host bus adapters, IP storage adapters.

2.6.5 Enhancing Fibre Channel SANs with IP

Critical decisions face storage and networking professionals as they try to balance Fibre Channel storage and SAN investment with IP networking investment. The buildup of two incompatible switched, full-duplex, point-to-point networking architectures simply cannot continue long term. It behooves everyone in the organization, from the CIO to storage managers, to question maintaining separate, independent networking topologies based on different technologies, such as one based on Fibre Channel and one based on Ethernet.

Traditionally, there has been a distinct separation between networking groups and storage groups within corporate IT departments. Some storage groups have claimed that networking technologies cannot support their requirements and that independent storage traffic requires special networks. The reality of the situation is that IP and Ethernet technologies have supported storage traffic for some time (in file-level formats), and recent innovations such as iSCSI provide block-level transport as well. Going forward, networking professionals interested in an overall view of the IT infrastructure will benefit from a closer look at storage, and vice versa for storage professionals.

Whether or not the merging of Fibre Channel and IP technologies meets certain organizational structures is largely irrelevant. Market forces behind the integration of these technologies are upon us, and savvy technologists and business leaders will embrace this dynamic change.

2.6.6 Making Use of the IP Core

Enhancing Fibre Channel solutions with IP starts through an understanding of the IP core. This part of the network provides the most performance, scalability, and intelligence to facilitate the Internet-working of any devices. Equipment used in the IP core can include routers, chassis-based enterprise Ethernet switches, and optical networking equipment using standard Ethernet or DWDM. Other networking technologies include ATM, Frame Relay, and SONET, all of which have mature mechanisms for handling IP transport.

At the edge of the network reside Fibre Channel devices, including servers, storage, and Fibre Channel SAN switches and directors. This equipment provides access to Fibre Channel devices, specifically end-device aggregation, and the fan-out of storage ports.

In order to make use of the existing IP core, which spans from enterprise, to campus, to metropolitan area networks (MANs) and wide area networks (WANs), an IP storage distribution layer integrates the Fibre Channel devices. This intelligent mechanism for protocol conversion enables Fibre Channel to extend its reach and capabilities in ways that it could not accomplish single-handedly. The basics of this model are shown in Figure 2–14.

2.6.7 Linking Fibre Channel to Fibre Channel with IP

The most common initial deployments for Fibre Channel using IP include remote replication for large Fibre Channel disk subsystems and linking two Fibre Channel SANs across IP, otherwise known as SAN extension. In the first case, IP storage switches or gateways front-end each Fibre Channel subsystem, providing Fibre Channel access to the disks and IP and Ethernet connectivity to the network. Typically, a subsystem-based replication application (such as EMC's SRDF, Hitachi's TrueCopy, HP/Compaq's DRM, XIOtech's REDI SAN Links) then operates on top of this physical link. Across a pair of subsystems, one will assume the initiator status while another assumes the target status, and the appropriate data is replicated through synchronous or asynchronous mechanisms.

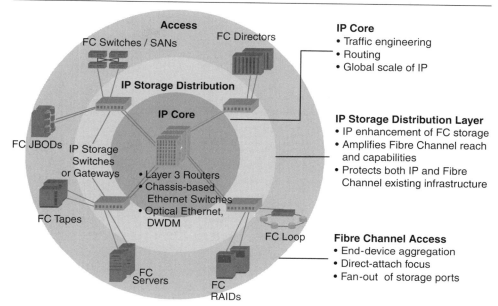

Figure 2–14 Using IP to enhance Fibre Channel.

Similar architectures exist that may also include Fibre Channel SANs, such as switches and directors. Those Fibre Channel SAN islands can also connect via IP using IP storage switches or gateways. Both of these options are shown in Figure 2–15. Servers and storage within each SAN can be assigned to view other devices locally as well as across the IP connection.

The benefits of these architectures include the ability to use readily available and cost-effective IP networks across all distances. Typically, these costs can be an order of magnitude less than the costs associated with dedicated

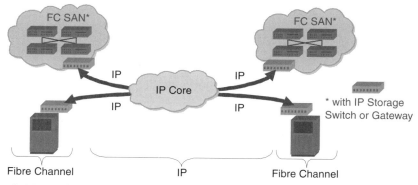

Figure 2–15 Mechanisms for linking Fibre Channel SANs and devices with IP networks.

dark fiber-optic cabling or DWDM solutions required by pure Fibre Channel SANs. Also, adoption of IP technologies within the core prepares for the addition of native iSCSI devices.

2.6.8 Integrating iSCSI with Fibre Channel across IP

The addition of iSCSI devices means that more of the connection between initiators and targets can be IP-centric. Storage planners gain tremendous flexibility and management advantages through this option, maximizing the use of IP networking and localizing the Fibre Channel component to the attachment of storage devices.

Using iSCSI devices with native IP interfaces allows the devices to talk to each other across any IP and Ethernet network. However, iSCSI makes no provision for Fibre Channel, and the conversion between iSCSI devices and Fibre Channel devices must reside within the network. This protocol conversion process typically takes place within an IP storage switch or gateway that supports both iSCSI and Fibre Channel. It can also take place in a server with specialized software or even within a chip that is embedded in a storage subsystem, as shown in Figure 2–16.

For a single device-to-device session, such as server to disk, most multiprotocol products can easily accomplish this task. However, when considering more sophisticated storage device-layer interaction, such as device-to-device interconnect for remote mirroring or SAN extension/interconnect, the protocol conversion process may have more impact on the overall operation. Since iSCSI and Fibre Channel have separate methods of SCSI command encapsulation, the various "states" of each storage session differ between the implementations. And while in a perfect world, the conversion process should not

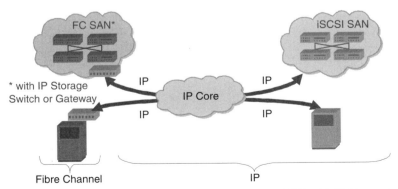

Figure 2–16 Mechanisms for linking Fibre Channel SANs to iSCSI with IP Networks.

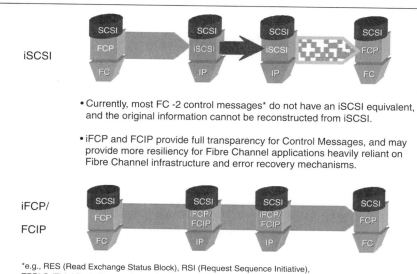

iSCSI

- Currently, most FC -2 control messages* do not have an iSCSI equivalent, and the original information cannot be reconstructed from iSCSI.

- iFCP and FCIP provide full transparency for Control Messages, and may provide more resiliency for Fibre Channel applications heavily reliant on Fibre Channel infrastructure and error recovery mechanisms.

iFCP/

FCIP

*e.g., RES (Read Exchange Status Block), RSI (Request Sequence Initiative), TPRLO (Third Party Process Logout), RSS (Read Sequence Status Block)

Figure 2–17 iSCSI and iFCP/FCIP to connect two Fibre Channel end nodes.

affect the overall integrity of the transaction, there is no practical way to preserve complete integrity across two translations (Fibre Channel to iSCSI and iSCSI to Fibre Channel). Therefore, using iSCSI to interconnect two Fibre Channel disk subsystems or two Fibre Channel SANs adds unnecessary risk to the overall system, particularly when considering the storage error conditions that must be kept in check. This is shown in Figure 2–17. Mitigating this risk requires a complementary approach to iSCSI, embracing the IP network, and aiming for a transition path to pure IP SANs.

2.7 IP SAN Protocols

Throughout 2001 and 2002, the IP storage industry spent considerable time addressing the underlying protocols for IP storage. The SNIA IP Storage Forum *(www.ipstorage.org)*, an industry group within the SNIA, provides valuable informational and educational materials on IP storage, including the protocols. The standards ratification process for IP storage is conducted by the IETF *(www.ietf.org)*, the same organization that has standardized and ratified the protocols relating to IP and the Internet.

The three IP storage transport protocols currently under consideration by the IETF reflect unique strategies for block data over TCP/IP networks. They are iSCSI, iFCP, and FCIP, shown in Figure 2–18.

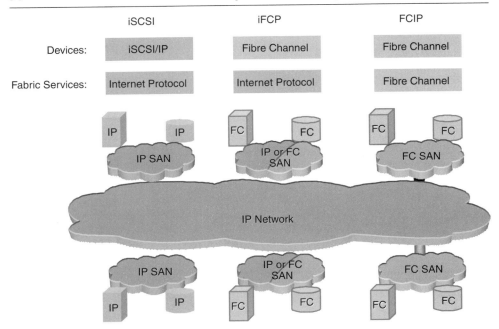

Figure 2–18 Protocol options for IP storage.

The technologies fall into two categories:

- The Fibre Channel over IP (FCIP) protocol is a Fibre Channel perpetuation strategy for linking Fibre Channel fabrics over distance. FCIP has minimal IP content facilities, since its aim is not to replace Fibre Channel with IP but simply to facilitate further deployments of Fibre Channel fabrics via IP tunneling.

- The Internet Fibre Channel Protocol (iFCP) and Internet SCSI (iSCSI) protocols, by contrast, are IP strategies for supplementing or replacing Fibre Channel fabrics with Gigabit Ethernet and IP infrastructures.

This basic distinction between Fibre Channel and IP strategies reveals fundamental assumptions about market directions and the solutions that customers may deem most viable. As a Fibre Channel strategy, FCIP assumes that current Fibre Channel fabrics are appropriate for data center SANs and that IP is only required to accommodate distances that exceed the capabilities of native Fibre Channel. Both iFCP and iSCSI make the opposite assumption. iFCP and iSCSI address the limitations of Fibre Channel fabrics for both data center and remote SAN connectivity. Since iFCP and iSCSI are native IP solutions for storage end devices, Fibre Channel fabrics are no longer required. The iFCP protocol is designed to support Fibre Channel end devices, and it substitutes an IP infrastructure in place of Fibre Channel. It also has the capability to incorporate existing Fibre Channel hubs and switches, if present. The iSCSI protocol ultimately replaces both storage end devices and the storage transport with IP technology. Thus while FCIP represents Fibre Channel perpetuation, iFCP represents migration transition from Fibre Channel to IP SANs, and iSCSI represents the ultimate goal of homogeneous IP storage networking.

As native IP storage protocols, iFCP and iSCSI are complementary. The iFCP protocol addresses the current SAN market in which both server platforms and storage devices use Fibre Channel interfaces. The current HBAs, Fibre Channel RAIDs, JBODs, and tape subsystems enjoy a much higher degree of interoperability and stability than Fibre Channel fabric switches. The iFCP protocol enables these Fibre Channel end systems to be joined over an IP network, both for data center applications and for wide area requirements. It offers customers the option of using familiar and more manageable Gigabit Ethernet switches and IP routers to build enterprise SANs. This allows SANs to be more easily incorporated into mainstream data communications implementation and management. Aside from overcoming the complexity and interoperability issues of Fibre Channel fabrics, iFCP enables customers to start building IP SANs today. By attaching current Fibre Channel end systems to IP networks, IP storage switches supporting iFCP (and iSCSI) create a foundation on which data center, metropolitan, and wide area storage applications can be built over time. This foundation is the common architecture that will support iSCSI end devices as well.

While iFCP provides the migration transition path from present to future SANs, the iSCSI protocol is the enabling technology for homogeneous IP SANs. The development of iSCSI storage NICs and iSCSI interfaces on storage and tape devices will allow customers to treat storage as just additional nodes on the network and to fully utilize the functionality of IP networks for storage. As with iFCP, leveraging IP and Gigabit Ethernet technology for the SAN fabric allows iSCSI to implement advanced services for storage, such as quality of service levels and encryption of storage data. As iSCSI products based on Gigabit and 10 Gigabit Ethernet come to market, customers will be able to synchronize their requirements for network messaging and storage backbones, and deploy a common network infrastructure for a variety of application needs.

It is worth noting that iSCSI affords customers the option of building native iSCSI solutions without relying on other technologies. Customers can build iSCSI SANs or use iSCSI devices alongside NAS storage.

While Fibre Channel-based storage currently represents the upper layer of the enterprise market, sustained adoption is a market reality. Customer awareness for best of breed Fibre Channel storage deployment options combined with best of breed IP and Ethernet storage networking will drive the adoption of native iSCSI. Customers will always gravitate to solutions that are more familiar, more manageable, and more easily supported. Use of iFCP in IP storage switches or gateways allows customers to minimize their Fibre Channel exposure and maximize benefits of mainstream IP networking. Products based on iSCSI will take this transition a step further by creating iSCSI SANs connected to IP networks. In combination, iFCP and iSCSI solutions thus take customers from where they are today to where they need to be tomorrow.

2.8 Chapter Summary

The Storage Architectural Landscape

- Storage devices now comprise more of the total enterprise IT budget than servers.

- SANs and NAS provide networked storage options and are complementary.

- New IP SANs allow geographic freedom through reach of IP networks.

2.1 Storage Building Blocks

- Basic building blocks include operating systems, file systems, volume management, and storage devices (disks and LUNs).

- SNIA shared storage model helps outline a variety of storage architectures on a single framework.

- SNIA shared storage model helps IT professionals plan for corporatewide storage solutions, enabling greater efficiency.

2.2 Internal Storage/Server-based storage

- Internal storage quickly became a bottleneck in large computing environments and migrated to a variety of external storage.

2.3 External Storage (JBOD, RAID, Tape, Optical, Other)

- JBODs are just what the name says and require additional functionality in the host or network to be scalable and highly available.

- RAIDs enhance performance through striping and provide fault tolerance through mirroring and parity checks.

- Combinations of RAID levels provide mission-critical storage availability to servers and applications.

- Tape drives and libraries provide lower cost per megabyte than disk, but require more time for backup and retrieval.

- Optical storage provides cost in between disk and tape with more resilient media than tape.

- Solid-stage storage is used in niche, high-performance configurations.

2.4 Direct-Attached Storage

- DAS extends server life by providing additional storage capacity.

- DAS can offload some server-based storage functions to the device, such as RAID.

- DAS has high performance but does not scale, offers limited sharing, and can represent a single point of failure.

2.5 Network-Attached Storage

- NAS delivers networked storage but at the file layer, representing a higher level of abstraction.

- NAS uses TCP/IP networks for connectivity.

- NAS works well for file-related applications like corporate file sharing and Web serving, but cannot deliver the performance and scalability for block-oriented applications like databases.

2.6 Storage Area Networks

- SANs deliver the performance and block access of DAS with the network flexibility of NAS.

- First-generation SANs were built with Fibre Channel and delivered giga-bit performance, additional scalability, resource sharing, and distances to tens of kilometers.

- Fibre Channel has interoperability between end systems (servers and storage devices), but multivendor switch interoperability is still awkward.

- Pure IP SANs using iSCSI take advantage of longstanding IP and Ethernet networks.

- New IP storage adapters combine the best of traditional IP networking cards with Fibre Channel HBAs to deliver TCP/IP offload for high throughput of IP storage.

- IP SANs deliver unified management, common technology with corporate networks, ability to use trained personnel, and built-in extension to MANs and WANs.

- IP SANs require multiprotocol capabilities to integrate with existing Fibre Channel infrastructure.

- IP storage switches and gateways integrate Fibre Channel storage and Fibre Channel SANs with IP networks.

- IP storage switches and gateways provide conversion capabilities between iSCSI and Fibre Channel for unified, multiprotocol SANs.

2.7 IP SAN Protocols

- The three IP storage transport protocols are iSCSI, iFCP, and FCIP.

- iSCSI and iFCP are IP strategies for supplementing or replacing Fibre Channel fabrics with IP and Ethernet infrastructures.

- FCIP is a Fibre Channel perpetuation strategy to connect Fibre Channel fabrics over distance.

- Multiple protocols are required because iSCSI makes no provision for Fibre Channel.

- Fibre Channel-to-Fibre Channel communication is handled by either the iFCP or FCIP protocols.

- Using iSCSI to link two Fibre Channel systems can result in lost states and poor error recovery.

3 The Software Spectrum

Across nearly all aspects of enterprise technology, purchasing processes have shifted from hardware-centric decision making to identifying best platforms for software and applications. Servers have essentially become commodity-driven compute engines, amassed in such volume and density that they simply become processing power enclosures. Networking equipment can easily be strung together, but only the effective monitoring and management of that information highway can tap the potential of its capabilities. Similarly with storage—while having ample space always makes solving storage problems easier, effective use of storage resources requires sophisticated organizational monitoring and management systems.

Chapter 2, "The Storage Architectural Landscape," covered the benefits of networked storage architectures from a hardware perspective and the means to deploy effective infrastructure to accommodate torrents of corporate data. This underlying equipment, however, also must be shaped with effective organizational systems that allow data managers to minimize their ongoing administration of the infrastructure and maximize the utilization and efficiency of the overall system. Storage management software helps IT professionals accomplish this task and is the focus of Chapter 3.

With ongoing administration and operation costs far exceeding acquisition costs for storage infrastructure, IT decision makers must account for this imbalance while charting their storage networking roadmap. Careful examination of storage software components can help identify crucial costs early in the deployment phases, resulting in long-term savings. While the concepts of storage management may seem foreign at first, the underlying mechanisms boil down to simplifying organizational and administrative tasks related to storage. Keep in mind that data storage space is just another corporate asset that requires efficient mechanisms to realize maximum returns. As the overall amount of data storage increases, and the ability to assign dedicated personnel decreases, effective software tools emerge as the only viable means for corporations to gain control of their information assets.

3.1 Framework for Storage Management Software

The end-to-end equation for storage management software involves numerous components, functions, and product categories. This seemingly complex spectrum of terminology and definitions often leads to unnecessary confusion about the role and objectives of storage management software. Business and technical professionals alike will be well served by a breakdown of storage management categories into a coherent framework, as presented in the following sections. By starting with the basic functional needs and translating those into required actions (as assisted by software applications), IT professionals can create effective storage software deployment strategies.

3.1.1 The Need for Storage Management Software

Businesses face an increasing array of challenges to manage storage infrastructures. First, IT professionals must manage a dazzling array of hardware and networking components that provide the underlying platform for storage. The sheer number of devices far outstrips the capacity of a single individual or group to keep track of them. Second, storage professionals must provide capacity and associated services across a variety of applications, from databases, to email, to transaction processing. Again, keeping track of these requirements and the business fluctuations requires some degree of automated assistance. Finally, all of this must take place with 24/7/365 availability and the capability for immediate recovery in the event of any failure.

These business requirements mandate the automation of the storage management process. Using software tools, storage professionals can effectively manage and monitor their infrastructure, provide capacity and services for application requirements, and guarantee uptime through high-availability configurations with built-in disaster recovery mechanisms. These are the core components of storage management software.

3.1.2 User View of Storage Management Software Components

To accomplish their objectives, storage professionals require assistance in three primary areas for effective storage management—infrastructure management, transaction management, and recovery management—outlined in Figure 3–1. Infrastructure management provides visibility to the entire architecture and the ability to make adjustments to the underlying platforms. As

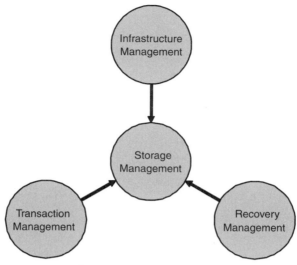

Figure 3–1 Core components of storage management.

storage moves from direct-attached to networked models, an administrator's visibility extends far beyond the traditional purview. Software tools for SAN management and storage resource management provide visibility and reach across the entire infrastructure.

Transaction management represents the application focus storage administrators must maintain to effectively serve the organization. Tools for data coordination, such as volume management or NAS file services, help implement storage resources for applications. Once in place, storage policy man-

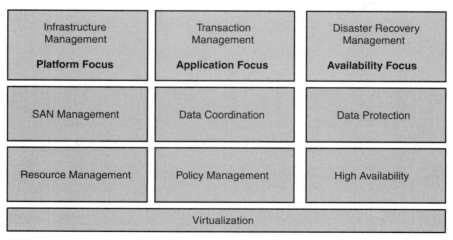

Figure 3–2 Software elements of storage management.

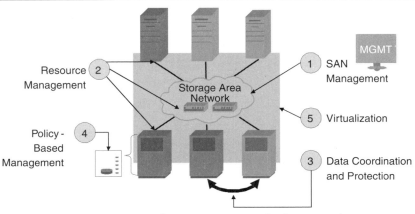

Figure 3–3 Storage management software components in the enterprise.

agement helps ensure that resources are appropriately dedicated, monitored, and managed in a dynamic storage environment.

The availability focus comes in the form of disaster recovery management through data protection. Whether through backup applications or sophisticated real-time replication, storage professionals can guarantee uptime through the use of these software applications.

Virtualization touches several aspects of the storage management infrastructure. The core principal of virtualization separates physical and logical storage, allowing for a variety of infrastructure, transaction, and recovery functions. The physical placement of virtualization in Figure 3–2 symbolizes that virtualization in and of itself provides limited functionality. However, that functionality facilitates many higher level processes outlined in the model. These are more specifically detailed in Section 3.8, "Virtualization."

3.1.3 Piecing Together Storage Management Software

Figure 3–3 shows where certain storage software functions reside from the architectural view. The following sections cover each area in more detail.

3.2 Storage Network Management

Because networked storage infrastructures are required for optimized storage deployments, the corresponding storage network management, or SAN management, takes on critical importance. Today, customers have a choice of SAN management software that can come directly from SAN switch vendors, array vendors, server vendors, or third-party software companies that integrate directly with SAN hardware.

Storage networking implementers will benefit from careful attention to this decision. While SAN management software from equipment vendors typically offer greater functionality and features, a third-party SAN management solution can provide configuration tools and diagnostics across multi-vendor solutions.

Most SAN management applications operate with an independent set of interfaces that drive control through that application. Efforts are underway in industry organizations like the Storage Networking Industry Association (SNIA) to standardize on common methods for storage network management to facilitate greater interoperability between applications. Ultimately, this will provide user flexibility to use multiple applications for SAN management and the ability to more easily shift between applications.

These standardization efforts fall underneath the overall framework of Web-based Enterprise Management, or WBEM. Within this framework, the Common Information Model (CIM) establishes a standardized means to organize storage network–related information, such as product information characteristics of a SAN switch or disk array. Within these overarching framework models are a set of specific means to exchange information between devices and applications, such as Extensible Markup Language (XML), Hypertext Transfer Protocol (HTTP), and Simple Network Management Protocol (SNMP).

3.2.1 Discovery

The first step towards effective SAN management begins with device discovery. The basic process involves the identification of storage network devices within a storage fabric. For end devices such as HBAs or disk arrays and tape libraries, the initial connectivity and boot process establishes the login to the SAN fabric, typically through a SAN switch. The SAN switches become the initial repository of device information and can then share this data with SAN switch management applications or third-party applications.

Typically, all devices within a SAN have an Ethernet/IP interface dedicated to management. Each device has a specific IP address and communications to other devices or to centralized management agents via an SNMP using Management Information Base (MIB). MIBs are basic frameworks that allow applications and devices to share device-specific information. There are standard MIBs, such as MIB-II, with information that pertains to all devices, such as interface status for a specific port. Hardware vendors also typically provide vendor-specific MIBs that cover unique product features.

Using a combination of information from SAN switches, which have device information through the login process, and direct access to devices through the Ethernet and IP interfaces using SNMP, management applications have a wide array of information to provide to administrators on the general status of devices within the storage network. From this initial discovery process, more sophisticated management, such as manipulation of the storage network, can occur.

3.2.2 Zoning and Configuration

Storage networks create connections between multiple servers and storage devices using a variety of interconnect mechanisms from a single switch or hub to a complex mesh of switches that provide redundancy for high availability. The universal connectivity of storage devices to a common playing field provides tremendous flexibility to architect storage solutions. However, having that connectivity doesn't necessarily mean that one would want every storage device to be able to see every other storage device.

Managed communication between storage devices helps administrators balance the agility of universal accessibility with the business needs of resource allocation, segmentation, security, and controlled access. This managed communication begins with a process of zoning and configuration.

Let's use a simple example of a Windows server and a UNIX server on the same storage network, with two separate disk units (JBOD-A and JBOD-B—each with two individual disks) and one tape library. A typical zoning and configuration application is shown in Figure 3–4. On the right side of the diagram is a list of devices, including the individual disks, tape library, and servers (identified by their HBA interfaces). On the left side of the dia-

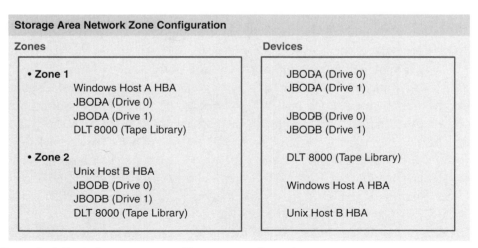

Figure 3–4 Typical storage networking zone configuration.

gram is a list of zones. Placing devices in a particular zone ensures that only other devices within that zone can "see" each other. SAN switches enforce the zoning through different mechanisms based on the worldwide name (WWN) of the storage device or on the port of the switch to which it is attached. For more detail on zoning, see Section 3.2.3, "SAN Management Guidance: Hard and Soft Zoning."

In this example, the administrator has separated the disk units for the Windows and UNIX hosts. This avoids any conflicts of one operating system trying to initialize all of the visible storage. However, the tape library has been placed in both zones. To avoid potential conflicts, this configuration would need to be accompanied by a backup software application that can manage the access to the tape library, ensuring access by only one host at time. Sharing the tape library allows its cost to be distributed across a greater number of servers, thereby servicing more direct backups.

3.2.3 SAN Management Guidance: Hard and Soft Zoning

Zoning applications typically operate in two types of device modes: hard zoning and soft zoning. Hard zoning, also referred to as port-based zoning, means that all of the devices connected to a single port remain mapped to that port. For example, three drives on a Fibre Channel arbitrated loop may be allocated via a specific port to Zone A. If another drive is assigned to that loop, and it attaches through the same specified port, it would automatically appear in Zone A.

Another zoning mechanism, soft zoning, or WWN zoning, uses the unique Fibre Channel address of the device. In IP or iSCSI terms, the device has a Worldwide Unique Identifier (WWUI). With soft zoning, devices may be moved and interconnected through different SAN switches but will remain in the same zone.

Hard zoning offers more physically oriented security, while soft zoning offers more flexibility through software-enforced zoning. For very large configurations, customers will likely benefit from the intelligence of soft zoning coupled with the appropriate security and authentication mechanisms.

3.2.4 SAN Topologies

In addition to zoning devices in a SAN, some applications offer the ability to visualize the SAN in a topology view. A sample SAN topology is shown in Figure 3–5.

SAN topology views can serve as effective management utilities, allowing administrators to quickly see the entire storage network and to drill down to

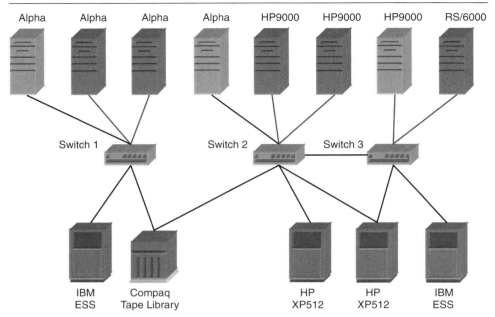

Figure 3–5 Topology view of a storage area network.

device levels. In some cases, it may be easier for administrators to assign and allocate storage capacity using topology managers.

SAN topology views also provide more visibility to the network connectivity of SANs. While a zoning and configuration tool helps clarify the communication relationship between storage devices, topology managers help clarify the communication means between storage devices. Specifically, topology managers can show redundant connections between switches, redundant switches, and the available paths that link one storage device to another.

3.2.5 Monitoring

Monitoring allows storage administrators to keep the pulse of the storage network. This includes the general health of the SAN hardware, data activity levels, and configuration changes.

Event and error tracking is used to keep logs of the activity within a storage network. SAN management applications track events such as device additions, zone changes, and network connectivity changes. These logs keep detailed records of SAN activity and can serve as useful tools if problems occur. With hundreds or thousands of SAN configuration operations taking place on any given day, the ability to go back in time to analyze events is invaluable. Similarly, error logs help diagnose the root cause of potential failures within a SAN. Minor errors, such as an unsuccessful first login to a SAN switch may not mean much as a stand-alone event, but a pattern of such errors can help administrators rapidly analyze and repair potential problems in the SAN.

Storage administrators can use alarms and traps to help effectively monitor the storage network. A trap is a set threshold for a certain variable that triggers notification when reached. For example, a trap can be set for a SAN switch to send an alarm when the temperature of the box reaches a "red zone." Such traps are helpful because a problem may not be directly related to failures within the equipment. For example, a broken fan would automatically send an alarm, but if someone placed a large box next to a data center rack, prohibiting airflow, a temperature gauge would be the only mechanism to ensure preemptive awareness of overheating.

SAN management traps typically integrate with large enterprise management systems via SNMP. By tying into these larger software systems, SAN alarms can be directed to the appropriate support staff through existing email, paging, or telephone tracking systems.

Perhaps the most important monitoring component for progressive deployment of storage networking infrastructures is performance. Performance monitoring can be tricky. Ultimately, organizations measure performance of applications, not storage throughput. However, the underlying performance of the SAN helps enable optimized application performance.

Since storage networks carry the storage traffic without much interpretation of the data, SAN performance metrics focus on link utilization, or more specifically, how much available bandwidth is being used for any given connection. An overengineered SAN with low utilization means excess infrastructure and high costs. An overworked SAN with high utilization means more potential for congestion and service outages for storage devices.

3.2.6 SAN GUIDANCE: Protocol Conversion

As outlined in Chapter 2, three transport protocols exist for IP Storage: iSCSI, iFCP, and FCIP. For iSCSI to Fibre Channel conversion, a key part of storage network management, IT professionals can use the framework in evaluating product capabilities. Not all IP storage switches and gateways provide full conversion capabilities. For example, some products may support iSCSI servers to Fibre Channel storage, but not vice versa.

Additionally, storage-specific features for applications like mirroring or advanced zoning capabilities between IP and FC SANs may affect protocol

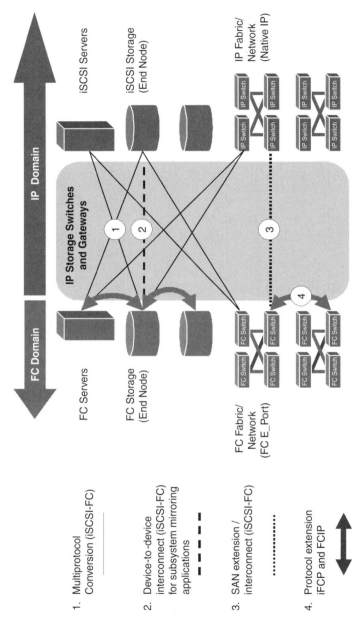

IP Domain

FC Domain

IP Storage Switches and Gateways

iSCSI Servers

iSCSI Storage (End Node)

IP Fabric/ Network (Native IP)

IP Switch

FC Servers

FC Storage (End Node)

FC Fabric/ Network (FC E_Port)

FC Switch

1. Multiprotocol Conversion (iSCSI-FC)

2. Device-to-device interconnect (iSCSI-FC) for subsystem mirroring applications

3. SAN extension / interconnect (iSCSI-FC)

4. Protocol extension iFCP and FCIP

Figure 3–6 Type of IP and FCP conversion.

conversion capabilities. This type of connectivity, items 2 and 3 in Figure 3–6, should be specifically examined in multiprotocol environments.

For Fibre Channel to Fibre Channel interconnect across an IP network, such as item 4 illustrates, the iFCP and FCIP protocols are more suitable because of their ability to retain more of the FCP layer.

3.2.7 Hard Management

Appropriately titled by its frequency of implementation, as opposed to the implementation challenge, is the physical documentation of SANs. No matter how much software is deployed or how detailed the visibility of the applications, nothing protects a business better than clear, easy-to-follow policies and procedures. Obviously, this is more easily said than done, and often the primary challenge in disaster recovery scenarios lies in understanding the design guidelines used by SAN architects. If these architects leave the company or are unavailable, the inherent recovery challenges increase dramatically.

Documenting SAN deployments, including a set of how-to instructions for amateur users, serves as both a self-check on implementation and an invaluable resource for those who may need to troubleshoot an installation sight unseen. At a minimum, items for this documentation would include applications used, vendor support contacts, passwords, authorized company personnel and contact information, backup and recovery procedures, and storage allocation mechanisms.

In conjunction with documenting storage administration policies and procedures, proper cabling and labeling of storage configurations can dramatically save time and effort in personnel costs—one of the largest components of the operational IT budget.

3.3 Storage Resource Management

Storage resource management (SRM) is the second component of infrastructure-focused SAN management. While storage network management (SNM) focuses primarily on the connectivity and combinations of storage devices on a network, SRM focuses on the individual devices and the ability to see and modify those devices from a central location. SRM may also be referred to as device management, an appropriate term, given the focus, and an easy way to distinguish from SNM. The primary benefit of SRM is the ability to make more effective use of the resources within an organization, specifically storage capacity and resource efficiency, as outlined at the end of this section.

For clarification purposes, we divide SRM categories into devices and subsystems. Devices are those elements within the overall storage infrastructure that provide access to storage, while subsystems house the actual disk or tape media.

3.3.1 Device Management

In the device category, SRM looks remarkably similar to SNM. Devices under an SRM application may include HBAs, switches, and routers. The SRM application provides a unified view of these devices and the ability to make some changes. In many cases, the SRM application will simply point to the device-specific management interface embedded within the product.

Device management features of SRM include discovery, topology mapping, and configuration planning. These tools provide SRM applications the information to help find potential problems and recommend solutions. Zoning is typically not included in SRM packages.

The primary difference between device management across SNM and SRM applications is the integration with additional multivendor infrastructure. For SRM applications, the visibility typically extends deeper into the subsystems category.

3.3.2 Subsystem Management

SRM features shine when used in large installations of disparate storage subsystems that require centralized administration. In these environments, an SRM application takes a logical view of the storage configuration and provides administrators a clearinghouse to receive information and implement changes.

SRM applications discover storage within the overall infrastructure and provide logical-to-physical maps of storage utilization, such as which servers are using which storage. Further, SRM applications identify operational file systems and file-level detail of such storage. For block-based storage, SRM locates volume groups and provides volume mapping visibility within and across subsystems.

This level of detail can be used by storage administrators to understand asset allocation and identify usage patterns across applications, departments, and individuals. From this viewpoint, administrators now have the required knowledge to drive decisions about optimized storage use within the organization. This leads to the establishment of policies such as quota management, covered in Section 3.5, "Storage Policy Management."

Even with storage resource management focused on the subsystems side, LUN and RAID creation and modification still remain within the subsystem.

These features may be accessed through centralized interfaces; however, this basic level of disk aggregation can be effectively accomplished only by the subsystem vendor.

3.3.3 Resource Efficiency

SRM information allows administrators to see the efficiency of their storage resources, such as the amount of storage used compared to the total amount available in the array. This top-level view helps quickly pinpoint overutilized or underutilized storage, allowing administrators to appropriate respond. Additionally, SRM views of the data itself can provide efficiency clues. For example, closer examination of file data may reveal rampant file revision propagation or an absurdly large collection of .mp3 or video files. Once this information is collected and examined, administrators can appropriately respond.

Identifying which servers and applications address which storage helps match the logical and physical pictures. If the accounting department is using 75 percent of the capacity of an array in another building, it may make sense to have that array located within the accounting department yet still available through the storage network to the rest of the organization.

3.3.4 Capacity Planning

Using historical information from SRM applications, specifically trend analysis, administrators can plan for storage capacity more effectively. With visibility into the actual data, including the types of files and applications related to growing volumes, SRM applications can plot and chart areas of future storage growth. Based on such information, administrators can make more accurate decisions based on more than a simple look at the total number of terabytes within the organization.

In addition to helping predict future capacity needs, SRM can help administrators make use of existing capacity, thereby minimizing new storage purchases. For example, the duration for saved email archives can be weighed against the cost of new capacity.

3.3.5 Integration with Other Storage Management Applications

For SRM to be truly effective, the monitoring functions must be incorporated with other functions of storage management, such as data coordination, protection, and policy management. Administrators can begin with basic questions such as the type of storage data, primary users, usage habits, access times and durations, and storage location. From there, policies and actions can be put in place to maximize efficiency, cap reckless data accumulation, and automatically provision and protect storage as needed.

3.4 Data Coordination

At the center of the data storage software infrastructure, the data coordination functions perform the task of coordinating data access between applications and storage subsystems. These underlying operations serve other storage management functions, such as data protection, policy management, and resource management. In general, the coordination functions sit closer to the movement and organization of the data.

The data coordination functions are transaction-focused areas of storage management. Acting as the interface between applications and subsystems, the primary operations include file services for NAS and volume management for block-accessed storage. In both cases, storage consolidation allows administrators to make the most of the infrastructure through storage pooling or aggregation to a common application presentation. The basic outline of these functions is shown in Figure 3–7.

3.4.1 File Services for NAS

File services, or file systems, provide users with the basic functions of

- A naming scheme for files and directories that enables organization of data for multiple users and applications.

- Authorization for access and modification control that includes a breakdown of creating, reading, and writing operations.

- Storage allocation that coordinates with volume management functions to determine where files may reside.

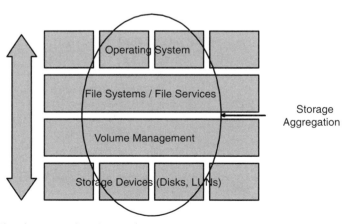

Figure 3–7 The data coordination path.

File services provide applications a simpler and easier mechanism to access blocks of disk-based storage. By abstracting the working unit of storage from a disk block fixed in size and location, a file system allows applications to work with files that can be stored across multiple disk blocks and locations through the use of volume management. This facilitates file transactions such as varying the file size, creation and deletion, shared identification and use of file data across multiple users, and access and modification control.

Many early computing applications—particularly those in the mainframe world and those focused on databases—were designed to attach directly to disk storage that was accessed in blocks. Today's computing environments rely heavily on the ability to store and retrieve data in file-based formats. File systems may be used directly by operating systems to maintain information such as what parameters should be used to start the machine, including modules to load and network services to initiate. Once the operating system is running, it may continue to use files to keep information temporarily available but out of memory or to log events that occur during the normal course of operation.

The more common understanding of file systems is for the applications themselves. In these cases, applications use files to hold parameters specific to their requirements, common modules also used by other applications, logs on application-related transaction information, and ultimately the data itself.

The file services function can reside throughout the data storage infrastructure. All host operating systems provide their own file systems, and many provide multiple file systems tailored to different needs of media. In addition, specialized file systems can be added to existing host operating system platforms to provide enhanced functionality. On the server, a network file system like NFS of CIFS maps application-level file system operations into transactions over the network with NAS filers. In turn, NAS filers use a variety of internal file systems to hold the file objects that they service. As a specialized server for file-based storage access, NAS provides scalability benefits in multiuser, dynamic-growth storage environments. New systems take file services one step further by providing them within storage networking fabrics. Often referred to a *NAS head*, by providing file access in the front and block access (volume management) in the back, these devices provide an additional level of fabric flexibility.

3.4.2 Volume Management

Volume management provides operating systems a means to aggregate disks and LUNs into logical storage units called volumes. Volumes can be directly accessed by operating systems, which may be the case with database applications, or through file systems. In either case, each volume can be made up of a set of disks and LUNs that are connected to the appropriate host, directly or through a storage network.

With a software management layer for volumes between the host and storage subsystem, specific features can be offered to the administrator. The volume management layer allows for the creation of dynamic disks, which then enables the logical manipulation of a group of dynamic disks. This disk group can be used to support one large logical volume, or software-based RAID may be implemented.

Additional features of volume management include modification of dynamic disks within the group, access and control features of hosts to volumes, and the ability to redirect data requests across volumes for failover.

Volume management provides users with the basic functions of

- A naming scheme for volumes made up of LUNs that enables organization of data for assignment to multiple hosts and applications.

- Storage allocation that coordinates with file system or database management functions to determine where files or databases may ultimately reside.

3.4.3 Storage Aggregation

Using file services and volume management, the overriding benefit of these software tools is that they provide an abstraction layer between applications and disks. This provides consolidation capabilities for aggregating file or volume presentation. In a homogeneous environment, file services can bind multiple volumes to a file system, and volume management binds disks to a volume. Another benefit is the ability to provide file or record-locking, or both, across multiple servers.

The basics of virtualization rely upon the storage aggregation capabilities of file services and volume management. For definition purposes, we focus on virtualization primarily in heterogeneous environments, including a variety of device types as well as vendors, covered in Section 3.8, "Virtualization."

Storage aggregation delivers configuration flexibility to storage administrators, providing the ability to layer more sophisticated storage management, such as policy management, within the configuration.

3.5 Storage Policy Management

An effective storage management operation needs storage policies to control and enforce the use of resources. While SRM provides a view of storage devices and the ability to change specific device features, policy management takes a wider approach across the infrastructure to define, implement, and enforce a set of rules between users, applications, and storage.

This section focuses on the basic elements of storage policy management within the technical storage networking context. Chapter 11, "Managing the Storage Domain," takes a more global view of the corporate oversight of storage resources from an organizational perspective.

First and foremost, storage policies help administrators overcome the unending growth of storage resources within the organization. From the enterprise to departmental to personal storage, such as workstations and laptops, administrators need automated mechanisms to set usage rules and provide service levels required throughout the organization.

Basic storage policies (see Figure 3–8) can be broken into the following groups:

■ Security and authentication policies ensure the proper access and manipulation of the data.

■ Capacity and quota management policies ensure measured allocation across multiple users.

■ Quality of service policies guarantee service levels for both the storage itself and the access to that storage.

3.5.1 Storage Policy Cycle

Storage policies have a continuous cycle with stages, outlined in Figure 3–9. The exact definition of stages may vary slightly among organizations, but the important common characteristic is the ongoing process improvement built into the cycle.

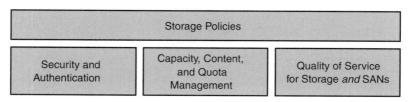

Figure 3–8 Storage policies.

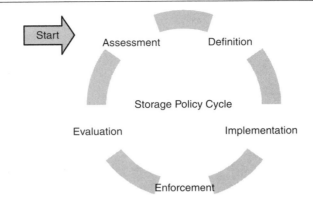

Figure 3–9 Storage policy cycle.

Assessment involves observing usage and performance patterns to determine areas for improvement. One example might be an application whose data set continues to grow exponentially, reducing the amount of available storage for other applications sharing the same storage. The definition stage requires identification of the anomaly's root cause and a method to solve it. Implementation comes through setting a rule or policy within the software infrastructure. Depending on the cause, effect, and desired results, setting a policy may occur in more than one component of storage software. Enforcement takes place when the desired actions are achieved through the rules. Careful monitoring provides data for evaluation of the set policy and the ability to begin the cycle again with any required modifications.

In many ways, an active storage infrastructure with a broad mix of users, applications, and resources is like an evolving ecosystem. Cause-and-effect relationships rarely remain isolated, and administrators must track implemented policies to watch for unintended effects. Appropriate monitoring through the use of SRM tools, will provide adequate notification for administrators to adjust accordingly.

3.5.2 Capacity, Content, and Quota Management

Every organization aims to maximize the use of resources, and SRM along with storage policies help accomplish that goal. Examples of policies in action include capacity, content, and quota management.

Capacity management involves optimization of storage space on a given device, such as a RAID array, or within a volume. In an ideal world, all devices would operate at or close to 100 percent capacity. However, the reality of our dynamic computing environments dictates otherwise. Unpredictable spikes in storage demand coupled with the need to have extra real-time capacity available means that 100 percent utilization can actually be counterproductive.

The optimal utilization percentage depends on device and storage cost, application needs, and costs of adding more physical capacity. For example, for a high-end RAID array with relatively expensive storage, the optimal utilization might be around 90 percent with 10 percent reserved for unanticipated peak demand. Less expensive storage might be set with utilization peaks of 60 percent, leaving administrators plenty of leeway for surges in capacity needs before new storage devices become necessary.

On the content side, visibility to the types of data and files can help dramatically reduce storage needs. By examining and categorizing content sources, power consumers in the form of applications or individuals can be identified and contained. For example, the rapid proliferation of MP3 music files might indicate improper use of corporate storage resources. Excessive numbers of large files (image, CAD design) with similar names and underlying data structures could be the result of saving inordinate copies, which might be satisfied with a less expensive storage mechanism, such as tape archiving.

Quota management, after identifying storage content by source and data type, allows administrators to pinpoint and curtail unnecessary consumption. This may apply to corporate users from engineering to administration, or to key applications. Of course, quota management requires a set of rules and guidelines that fit with organizational priorities in concert with IT priorities. A cap on engineering storage capacity that impacts development schedules might require adding to new storage purchase budgets. On the other hand, capping resources for email storage might compel individuals to be more conscious about their consumption without impacting productivity.

3.5.3 Security and Authentication

Security for storage (also see Chapter 9, Section 9.5, "Security for Storage Networking") begins by identifying threats and then implementing solutions to address them. Some of these threats and solutions are outlined in Table 3–1.

TABLE 3–1 STORAGE SECURITY THREATS AND SOLUTIONS

Potential Threat	Solution
Is the entity accessing the storage whom he or she claims to be?	Authentication
Does the entity accessing the storage have the right clearance?	Authorization
Is the data being read or shared unintentionally?	Privacy
Is the data subject to unintentional or malicious modification?	Integrity

Enforcement of these storage security solutions occur throughout the storage management chain, depending on the software in place. While the implementation of these solutions can vary, the objectives remain the same. For example, authentication can be set within the file system, identifying access at the user level, or this function can take place within lower layers of the infrastructure, such as the network fabric. Storage security therefore requires a multifaceted approach across the entire data management chain, from user access, to device access, to device management.

The most basic form of storage security is the physical isolation of the storage environment. Fibre Channel-based storage networks provide some physical security because the technology is separate from more common corporate IP networking. In the early days of Fibre Channel, storage administrators viewed this physical isolation as a feature—the rest of their networking colleagues were unable to understand and meddle with their setups. More common availability of Fibre Channel equipment no longer guarantees such independence.

LUN masking determines which disk drives (or logical unit numbers) are seen by servers. LUN masking can be enforced by HBAs, switches, or storage array controllers. Modification of LUN masking requires password-protected access to the configuration utility. Zoning by port or WWN via SAN switches is one form of LUN masking.

The use of IP networking technologies for storage also delivers a set of well-defined security mechanisms. Virtual LANs (VLANs) and access control lists (ACLs), common in mainstream IP networking, can be used to segment and isolate traffic between end points or network areas of an IP storage network. Existing IPSec functions, such as authentication and data encryption, which are defined in IETF specifications, can be used with IP storage networking. For example, virtual private network equipment can be used between two IP storage switches or gateways to deliver encrypted IP storage traffic between two SANs.

3.5.4 Storage Encryption

While encryption has long been used as a security mechanism for IP networks, that capability has been largely absent from conventional SANs, partly based on the historical lack of support for Fibre Channel encryption. Recent product introductions now make possible Fibre Channel encryption along with the associated management tools required to administer encryption keys.

While security tools such as zoning, ACLs, and authentication address storage access security, they do not address the security of the data payload. In order for the payload to be protected, it must be encrypted with a key that locks (and unlocks) the original data structures. Encryption keys for 3DES (one of the most secure forms of encryption) are made up of 168 bits.

Encryption can be implemented in software and located within Fibre Channel equipment or specialized encryption hardware. Current implementations typically use hardware-based encryption to guarantee high throughput rates. A number of configurations can be deployed to guarantee data security at the payload level. Even if an unauthorized user were to access the

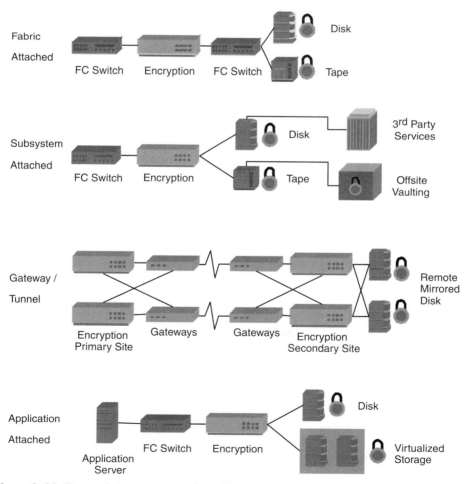

Figure 3–10 Types of storage encryption. *(Source: NeoScale Systems)*

data, it would be useless without the key. The basic configurations are shown in Figure 3–10. In addition to these solutions, users can encrypt data at the file-system level before entrusting it to the storage subsystem.

In a fabric attached deployment, storage encryption takes place within the storage network, allowing multiple storage devices to be protected. All storage that resides behind the encryption device requires key authentication for data access. Simpler configurations such as subsystem attached encryption allow data to be moved to third-party service providers or offsite vaulting with security guarantees. Data that ended up in the wrong hands while being moved offsite would still be protected. A gateway or tunnel implementation allows data to be encrypted at the payload level while traversing MANs or WANs. Application-attached encryption restricts the protection to those applications requiring the highest level of security.

Of course, in any implementation, key management determines the accessibility and recoverability of encrypted data. IT professionals considering payload-level encryption will need to keep keys in multiple secure locations, including legal offices and other venues that guarantee protected access. Loss of a key results in permanent data loss.

3.5.5 Quality of Service for Storage and Storage Area Networks

Quality of service applies to end-storage devices as well as the storage transport, and both must be considered for end-to-end service guarantees. For end-storage devices, quality of service refers to the availability of the storage media—for example, the RAID level. Mission-critical applications require storage devices that have RAID levels set for maximum availability combined with remote mirroring for business continuity in the event of a disaster. Less critical storage may operate sufficiently with RAID levels that provide less availability in favor of increased performance and use tape archiving as a backup mechanism. This provides cost savings with more usable storage per RAID device, forgoing the remote mirror for recovery by using tape.

Storage professionals should assign storage quality of service requirements to individual applications. These service levels can be implemented through storage management software to create an enterprisewide policy. The exercise alone of matching applications to storage service levels will create a useful framework for balancing availability and cost factors. Carried through to the purchasing decisions of new storage devices, this type of framework clearly demarcates the need for high-end, midrange, or entry-level storage devices.

Quality of service also applies to the storage transport, or the storage network. In this case, the interconnect between storage end systems must be adequately provisioned for mission-critical applications. This can apply to allocated bandwidth, multipath availability, or even balancing the long-distance transport across multiple carriers.

Figure 3–11 shows an example of bandwidth prioritization through the use of VLANs and traffic prioritization. Here, the backup of an online transaction processing (OLTP) database needs priority over a less critical backup of corporate files. No matter when the database backup begins, it will be granted the appropriate bandwidth to complete its backup operation within a designated time window.

3.5.6 Storage Paths

Storage network administrators may also choose to guarantee dual, redundant paths for specific application to storage connections. This practice is often referred to as path management. New software packages with this feature use storage network topology information to create a map of available connections between servers, fabric switches, and storage devices. Criteria such as dual, redundant paths or 2Gb/s Fibre Channel links can be specified in order to meet availability and performance needs.

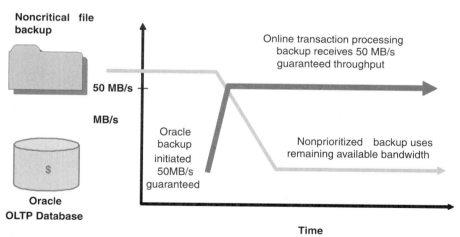

Figure 3–11 Storage transport quality of service.

Attention to storage paths ensures that applications not only have the appropriate data capacity, but also the appropriate service-level transport for data access.

3.5.7 Departmental Segmentation and Accounting

Storage policy management translates to several organizational policies to help assign storage costs. For example, departments can be easily segmented to provide accounting charges based on storage use. Storage administrators can assign storage in terms of both capacity and quality of service, offering options to individual departments and their specific requirements.

Software automation carries this one step further by allowing dynamic changes with minimal manual reconfiguration. For example, capacity can be automatically added on the fly for specific users. Billing systems can then track allocation and keep department heads aware of their capacity usage and expected internal expenses. This focuses attention on storage capacity requirements of the departments through clear, bottom-line financial metrics, eliminating gray areas of infrastructure requirements and allocation.

3.6 Data Protection

Data-protection software, from coordinating tape-based backup to real-time disk replication, defends corporate data assets. Through a range of mechanisms that deliver onsite and offsite data copies at various time intervals and across multiple media formats, corporations mitigate the chance of data loss while striving to provide continuous availability. For most companies, the costs of data loss far outweigh the costs of data protection. As such, they invest millions of dollars per year on data protection techniques such as those described in this section.

The primary decisions for data protection compare cost to availability. In this case, availability refers to both the time taken for the backup operation and the time needed to restore the data set in the event of a disaster. Figure 3–12 outlines the position of several data-protection schemes based on their cost and availability measures.

For most organizations, the redundancy built into storage architectures spills into the data-protection implementations as well. For example, many companies implement more than one data-protection technique, such as combining tape-based offsite backup with onsite snapshot copies to disk. This gives them near instant recovery onsite as well as the insurance of an offsite recovery if needed.

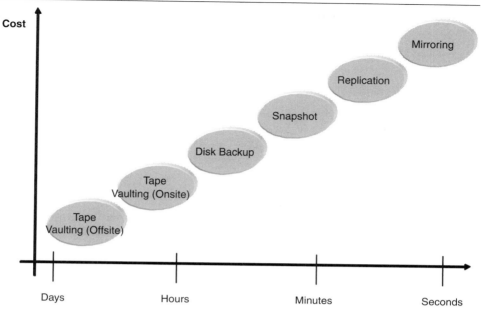

Figure 3–12 Cost-availability trade-off.

3.6.1 Tape-Based Backup

Tape archiving is often relegated to the low end of the totem pole of backup technologies. While falling disk prices have made disk-based backup solutions more attractive to a larger segment, tape still fills a valuable need. Density alone makes tape an attractive choice for large backup operations—tape library capacities measure in hundreds of terabytes compared to disk array units in tens of terabytes. Additionally, the flexibility of removable tape media cartridges for both onsite and offsite storage adds another level of protection. Today's IP storage networking options may soon impact transport of tape cartridges. Why bother with moving them between buildings or sites if the data can be easily sent over an IP network? Even with that capability, it may still be more effective to have a tape library for archiving due to device and media capacity.

Storage networks enable sharing of tape libraries among multiple servers, including NAS filers, as shown in Figure 3–13. This type of configuration also requires software to manage access to the tape library, preventing multiple servers from simultaneous access. Backup packages like Veritas NetBackup, Legato Networker, CA Brightstor, and IBM Tivoli for Storage provide the features for managing tape libraries in shared environments, including schedule modules to perform backups at the appropriate intervals, such as daily, weekly, or monthly.

In SAN configurations with shared tape libraries, the backup software resides on a backup application server that manages the control information with the individual servers. With clearance established, the backup server grants access to the appropriate server and allows a direct link to the tape library. This process, often referred to as LAN-free backup, facilitates faster backup operations than do more traditional data paths for shared tape libraries through the LAN.

Tape libraries also serve as a useful complement to NAS. Even though NAS delivers file-based storage through its front end, the back end of a NAS system often has a block-based Fibre Channel connection that can be networked to a tape library for block-based backup of the NAS unit. This type of solution provides economical archiving of NAS data and may also operate simultaneously with NAS replication across multiple filers.

Server-free backup (Figure 3–14) is another technique used in conjunction with tape backup, although it can also be used with disk backup. In server-free implementations the data path is completely offloaded to the storage devices, freeing servers to focus on application processing. Server-free backup solutions take advantage of the same LAN-free designs implemented

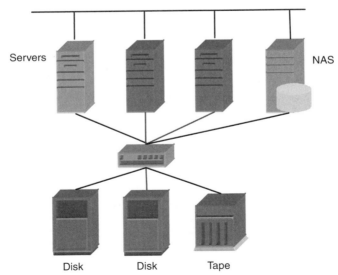

Figure 3–13 Consolidated tape backup across servers and NAS.

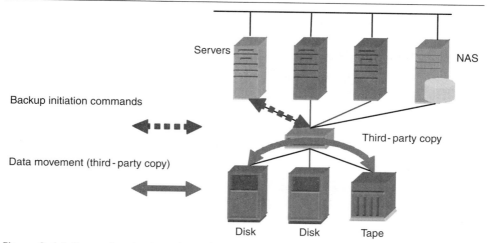

Figure 3–14 Server-free backup through third-party copy.

with SANs but also use data-mover agents that reside in the storage fabric to facilitate disk-to-tape or disk-to-disk data paths.

The data-mover agents employ a third-party copy command called extended copy. This can run off of a fabric-based storage device such as a router or appliance. The backup application server initiates a command to the data mover, and the data mover then assumes control of the copy operation until complete. The ability to conduct a high-speed, image-level backup free of server intervention builds a scalable backup infrastructure. Key benefits include more backup operations within a fixed window, simpler administration, reduced server load, and faster restores.

3.6.2 Disk Backup and Recovery

Disk-based backup ranks high on the simplicity scale but equally high on the required capacity scale. Specifically, a single disk-based backup will double the required disk storage capacity. This may be on top of disk capacity required for RAID features. In the extreme, an organization may find itself with only 25 percent usable capacity of total terabytes owned. This can be a significant cost when compared to tape archiving.

Aside from capacity considerations, disk solutions eclipse tape for achieving short backup and restore windows. For applications requiring guaranteed availability, disk-based solutions are the only mechanism for secure, rapid recovery.

Because of these cost, availability, and performance dynamics, permutations of disk copy, such as point-in-time and snapshot copy as well as replication and mirroring, come into play.

Many disk-backup solutions leverage internal RAID functions built into subsystems. This allows for multilayered redundancy to protect against disk failure, mirror failure, unit failure, and in the case of remote facilities, infrastructure failure.

3.6.3 Point-in-Time and Snapshot Copy

Point-in-time and snapshot copy solutions address the capacity requirement concerns of disk backup while providing short restore times. Point-in-time copies, as the name implies, isolate time-stamped copies of data at regular intervals and provide the ability to revert to those images in the event of application or data failure.

The first point-in-time copy includes the entire data set, doubling the storage capacity requirement. Thereafter, only changes to the data set are copied at regular intervals. Administrators can choose to initiate and maintain multiple point-in-time copies so recovery can roll back to the appropriate data set. These intervals can measure from minutes to hours to days.

With an updated copy available at all times, the recovery process with a point-in-time copy occurs almost immediately. Instead of attempting to restore the database, users are simply redirected to the last stable copy.

Snapshot copies operate in a similar fashion to point-in-time, but with the slight difference that the snapshot volume merely tracks incremental changes with pointers back to the original data set. Like point-in-time, snapshots can be created at regular intervals to provide rollback capabilities in the event of failure. However, snapshots do not replicate the original data set. Therefore, they don't require the upfront capacity increase, although additional capacity is required to maintain the snapshot information. This will vary based on the amount of data changed at each interval and the interval or snapshot frequency. The additional capacity required for a snapshot copy correlates to the amount of original content that must be saved before incremental changes are made.

Like point-in-time, snapshot copies provide quick recovery in the event of disaster, since no restore is required. But snapshot copies alone cannot protect against all disasters, since the copies still point to the parts of the original data set, and a physical storage failure could invalidate several logical snapshot copies. For a complete disk-based backup solution, snapshot would require the addition of replication or mirroring to protect against physical storage failure or site disaster.

3.6.4 Hierarchical Storage Management (HSM)

Serving a data-protection function and also a space optimization function, hierarchical storage management (HSM) helps storage administrators balance the cost per megabyte with the retrieval time of varying storage media. The conventional business driver behind HSM was the relative high cost of disk compared to the relative low cost of tape, coupled with varying types of data and service levels within the organization (see Figure 3–15).

For example, a mission-critical e-commerce database must be instantly accessible at all times and must have mirrored or replicated copies available in the event of disaster and disk backup for fast restore. On the other end of the spectrum, large CAD files for products that have been discontinued probably don't merit the same availability, yet designers are reluctant to discard the data—they want it available if needed. This second example fits perfectly with HSM principles: to take less critical data that doesn't require immediate access times and move it to more economical storage, such as tape. In the event that the design team resurrects a particular product, the CAD files could be transferred back to disk during the production cycle to facilitate faster access times.

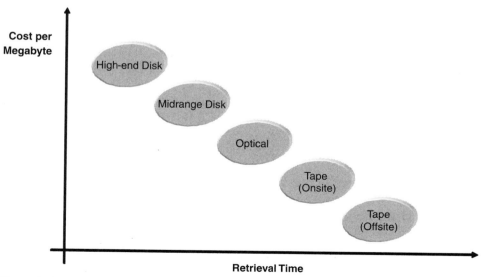

Figure 3–15 Comparisons of media technologies: disk, optical, tape.

With disk costs dropping precipitously, HSM can be applied to disk-only environments as well. For example, mission-critical information might reside on high-end Fibre Channel disk drives, while less critical information could be stored on much less expensive serial Advanced Technology Attachment (ATA) drives.

HSM software manages this entire process, allowing administrators to set guidelines and storage categories that determine when and where files and volumes are stored. Automated HSM policies identify files that haven't been accessed recently, maintain a pointer at the original location, and then move the actual data to less expensive media. This migration process happens transparently to users, requiring only a quick restore when the file is accessed, if ever.

The concepts of HSM have been a part of enterprise storage strategies for many years. Today, with new SAN architectures and the explosive growth of data, applying HSM principles through specific HSM packages or other storage management software can lead to significant cost savings in storage capacity purchases.

3.7 High Availability

3.7.1 Mirroring and Replication

Mirroring and replication solutions go beyond the protection mechanisms of point-in-time and snapshot copies by providing continuous real-time availability. These solutions do not provide for incremental rollbacks and therefore are frequently coupled with point-in-time and snapshot solutions for such functionality. Mirroring and replication deliver the highest levels of data availability across local and remote geographic distances.

Although they have similar objectives, mirroring and replication have different implementations. With mirroring, each copy of the data is identical, and one can be substituted for the other at any time. Further, applications see complete consistency at all times between the two copies.

Implementing mirroring requires that each write operation be written and confirmed by both mirrors before the application can continue. This insures that at each incremental change in the data, both copies remain identical. Mirroring implies that the connection between the primary and secondary copy remains intact. Any temporary outage in that link is interpreted as a failure of the mirror.

Replication can take place in synchronous or asynchronous mode. Synchronous mode is more similar to mirroring in that the I/O must be written and confirmed by both copies before proceeding. However, synchronous replication can handle temporary network outages and store updates between the primary and secondary location until the link is restored, upon which the updates continue. Applications can detect this update latency and may be temporarily put on hold until the synchronization resumes. These parameters, such as timeouts, can be tuned to discern between a network glitch (measured in single seconds) and all-out failure (measured in tens of seconds). A failure would render the replication incomplete and initiate the appropriate recovery procedures.

With asynchronous replication, applications receive I/O completion confirmation only from the primary copy, allowing continued operation without waiting for additional confirmation from the second copy. The replication process managed between the two disk arrays allows them to be out of step or for the second copy to complete its I/O command one or two steps later. This allows the application to run at full speed with less I/O latency, but also mandates keeping track of the outstanding I/O commands between the primary and secondary copies in the event of failure. In that case, the second copy would only be valid once the log of incremental updates was written and confirmed.

Looking at mirroring, synchronous, and asynchronous replication together, each has its own strengths depending on performance and geography. True mirroring is best suited for local, controlled environments where the likelihood of a network failure between the two mirrors is extremely low. This often means that mirroring takes place within a single disk array, eliminating network interference as a potential way to break the mirror. Mirroring also offers applications the highest read performance of these options.

Trading time for distance, or performance for remote disaster recovery storage, synchronous mirroring would be the next choice. Here, applications may detect some latency, but the remote storage provides data protection benefits not delivered with a local mirror. Since synchronous mirroring requires completion of both primary and secondary I/O operations, the network link must have reasonable performance and quality of service. Asynchronous replication stretches the balance between time and distance one notch further. Though the primary application will operate in real time without having to wait for secondary I/O completion, the incremental gap in out-

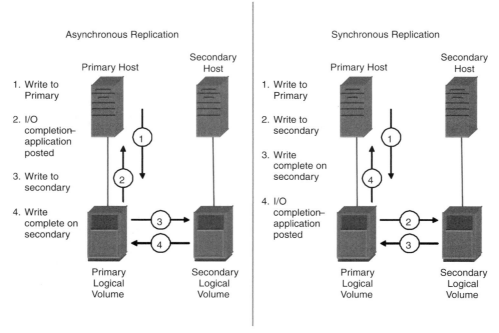

Figure 3–16 Comparing asynchronous and synchronous replication.

standing commands between the two copies adds some time in the event of recovery.

Vendor implementations of remote mirroring and replication include

■ Hitachi Data Systems TrueCopy

■ EMC Symmetrix Remote Data Facility (SRDF)

■ XIOtech REDI SAN Links

■ HP SANworks Disaster Recovery Manager

The basic functionality of remote replication is shown in Figure 3–16.

3.8 Virtualization

Perhaps no other area of storage management has gotten as much attention as virtualization. One explanation is that no other area of storage management has effectively covered such a wide variety of functions under one banner. For better or worse, virtualization has cast its shadow far and wide, positioned by many companies, large and small alike, as the panacea to solve all storage problems.

The rise of virtualization as a hot storage topic may be more indicative of customer pain than technological innovation. Storage management has become increasingly complex as users balance features, functions, and vendors in a myriad of combinations. In fact, the dizzying array of options would send any rational human being towards a solution that can "virtualize" the pain away.

Looking more closely into what makes up virtualization, we see that many features bundled under this banner have been prevalent in enterprise storage management for years. Therefore, we will define virtualization by looking at what it does as opposed to what it is.

3.8.1 Basic Concept of Virtualization

In its simplest form, virtualization presents heterogeneous storage homogenously. More specifically, it provides a mechanism to aggregate different storage devices into a single storage pool that can be parsed and allocated through central administration. This process creates a presentation layer of logical views of physical storage devices that can come from multiple vendors.

This basic concept is shown in Figure 3–17A. In this environment all of the storage devices are virtualized into a common pool that can be distributed across the application servers accordingly. Administrators no longer need to know how each storage device is configured, where it is located, or what the capacity or utilization may be. Since all capacity gets lumped into a common pool, the virtualization engine will take care of the rest. In this respect, virtualization simplifies storage management by inserting an abstraction layer between the storage and the user assignment of that storage.

However, the reality of the situation is quite different. Aggregating storage into a single pool works well when devices share common characteristics and can be treated equally. In practice, organizations maintain a wide variety

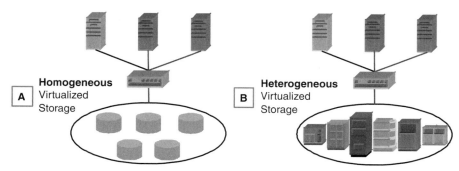

Figure 3–17 Virtualization in homogeneous and heterogeneous environments.

of equipment that translates into unique capacity, performance, and functionality characteristics for each device. Therefore, the representative environment will more likely be similar to that in Figure 3–17B.

In this case, value-added features of each storage device may be lost in the virtualization process, hampering some of the initial goals. For example, some storage devices may have disk drives and RAID sets configured more for speed than availability. Simply aggregating such devices into a larger pool of available storage reduces their value and contribution. To address this issue, some vendors implement storage classes within the virtualization process. However, taken to the extreme, each device, or group of homogeneous devices, would be in its own class, thereby restricting the capability to create an aggregated pool of storage.

Freedom to choose among storage devices and to substitute one for another has been a driving force behind virtualization. The ability to break the lock-in of one particular vendor by substituting another compels customers to evaluate such solutions. Stepping back, that may represent just a shift of the vendor lock-in from the storage device vendor to the virtualization vendor.

By virtualizing storage, the virtualization engine facilitates storage flow to and from the devices and represents a central clearinghouse for this information. Placing a variety of storage devices within an aggregated pool, front-ended by a virtualization engine, implies that the virtualization engine controls access to the entire pool. Further, consider the processing involved with the recovery of one of the devices in a virtualized pool. Of course, backing up may be simple enough, with the various devices feeding into a single stream to a consolidated backup device such as a tape library. But what about the restore? The virtualization engine must remember where each piece of data resided and return it to its initial location. While this may be technically feasible, the time and processing required to complete such an operation makes the recovery of virtualized storage ominous.

The reality leads one to understand that control points within the infrastructure matter and must be examined closely. Chapter 4, "Storage System Control Points," takes a detailed look at this subject.

3.8.2 Separating Virtualization from Data Coordination and Protection Functions

Virtualization functions have been a part of data storage infrastructures for many years, and they will continue to be. Reactions to virtualization in the storage networking industry frequently boil down to debates about definition rather than function.

In fact, the core aspects of virtualization are the same as data coordination functions like volume management. Veritas Software has delivered this functionality in its volume manager and file system products for years, allowing administrators to create virtual file storage or volumes from LUNs of varying arrays. Typically, Veritas Volume Manager (VxVM) or File System (VxFS) implementations do not span virtual volumes across multivendor environments. But no technical reasons exist to prohibit such use. New virtualization solutions have taken this simple concept one step further and focused on volume management across heterogeneous environments.

Data-protection functions such as backup and mirroring are frequently, and mistakenly, bundled as virtualization solutions. These storage applications do send virtual volumes across local or remote networks, and may rely on underlying virtualization techniques. But bundling these data protection functions into a single virtualization basket only confuses an already misunderstood technology.

3.8.3 Areas of Virtualization Deployment

Basic virtualization functions can be deployed across layers in the enterprise storage environment, including host, fabric, and subsystem. These are illustrated in Figure 3–18 and compared in Table 3–2. Pros and cons exist within each of these areas, and a myriad of implementations are offered by different vendors.

The most common form of virtualization is host-based and has been present in enterprise configurations via volume management and file system applications. The advantages of this approach include support for heteroge-

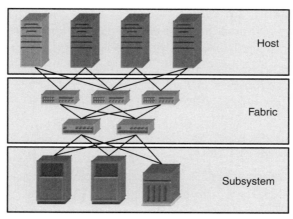

Figure 3–18 Areas of virtualization deployment: host, fabric, and subsystem.

neous environments, ease of installation, and delivery of APIs to applications. However, host-based implementations run in software, thereby consuming CPU cycles that could otherwise be used for application processing. Additionally, each host must be configured independently for its own logical disk volumes, which leads to scalability limitations. With each host importing independent LUNs, the LUNs cannot be easily shared across multiple hosts.

Subsystem-based virtualization provides greater performance than host-based implementations through the use of best-of-breed RAID technologies and optimized caching. However, subsystem-based virtualization often applies to only a single array. Some vendors have implemented virtualization capabilities that easily span multiple disk arrays. However, subsystem approaches are vendor-specific and unlikely to exploit features across a variety of vendor platforms.

Fabric-based virtualization comes in two methods that can reside in different areas of the fabric. Figure 3–19 helps clarify the dimensions and effects. The two types, in-band and out-of-band, refer to the placement of the virtualization engine in relation to the data path. In the case of in-band, the engine intercepts all I/O commands and redirects them to the appropriate resources. All command requests and data pass through the engine. This limits overall performance to the performance of the in-band device.

With out-of-band virtualization, only command information is passed through the virtualization engine. Once the required meta-information for storage is shared with the initiator, that initiator has direct access to the storage device. This provides the highest level of performance. Essentially, an out-of-band virtualization engine introduces the right host to the right device, then gets out of the way.

Both types of virtualization can reside within different areas of the fabric. One platform for fabric-based virtualization is within appliances. Appliances are frequently rack-mounted Windows or Linux PCs that have a few additional storage ports on PCI cards. These devices provide simplicity, ease of installation, and low cost. An appliance not specifically designed for network may impact performance.

An alternative approach to appliance-based is switch-based virtualization. Switch-based virtualization overcomes speed limitations by using a network-centric platform designed for wire-speed throughput. By placing functionality directly within the switch and providing switch-to-switch redundancy, this approach offers a more scalable architecture. Switch-based

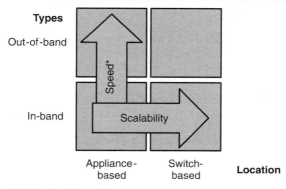

Figure 3–19 Types of fabric virtualization.

virtualization eliminates the need for more devices in the data path, delivers faster reactions to network-related events, acts as a central configuration control for zoning, and assists in better path management.

3.8.4 Understanding the Multivendor Virtualization Game

Looking back at the features of storage management, one can easily be overwhelmed by the laundry lists of features required by enterprise storage deployments. Storage software aims to automate as much of the process as possible, but still leaves a heavy burden on the shoulders of the storage administrator. Virtualization helps alleviate that burden by masking lower layer functions of the storage management chain and presenting clear, intuitive interfaces for tasks like storage allocation and data protection. By doing so, virtualization engines firmly demarcate areas of control within the infrastructure. They serve as central distribution points that dictate the look and feel, as well as the performance and reliability, of the entire configuration.

With standards emerging for this sector, multivendor virtualization solutions may one day be a reality. In the meantime, it is unlikely that these solutions will operate in lock step, and more probable that segmentation and isolation of solutions will take place. Unfortunately, this is exactly the problem that virtualization tried to solve. Segmentation will likely take place based on areas of intelligence, and customers have options to react accordingly. For example, within the subsystem layer, it would seem unlikely for large storage subsystem manufacturers to provide similar feature sets across other vendors' products. Figure 3–20 shows that the interoperability challenge spans the horizontal host, fabric, and subsystem layers. Recognizing

TABLE 3–2 HOST, FABRIC, AND SUBSYSTEM VIRTUALIZATION

	Definitions	**Benefits**	**Limitations**
Host	Volume management or file-system services that reside in software on the host. Software intercepts I/O commands and redirects to the appropriately mapped storage devices.	Support for heterogeneous targets. Delivers API to applications.	Configuration per host. Performance scaling. LUNs imported by host prohibit sharing.
Fabric	Network-based handling of I/O requests from host. Commands are redirected to mapped physical storage. In-band virtualization engines reside in the data path handling both redirection and data flow. Out-of-band virtualization engines reside outside the data path and maintain metadata for redirection, but data flow remains device-direct. Virtualization engines can reside in stand-alone appliances or within network switches.	Centralization of storage administration. Offloading from servers (compared to host approach) offers CPU cycles for applications. Simple support for heterogeneous environments.	Vendor-specific storage features not applicable to complete environment. Appliance approach not scalable. In-band approach requires massive processing power to avoid impacting data path.
Subsystem	Target-based services that map sets of drives to logical volumes presented to hosts.	Best of breed RAID 0,5 Higher performance than host approach. Scales to multiterabyte capacity. Subsystem cache delivers high I/O throughput.	Administration on per-target basis. Vendor-specific storage features not applicable to complete environment. No path awareness.

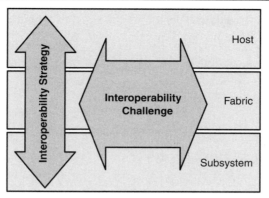

Figure 3–20 Interoperability strategies and challenges for virtualization.

the market forces that inherently present such challenges, strategic options for balancing multivendor solutions should focus on the vertical access across areas of intelligence. For example, it is common to support host-based volume management software along with SAN switches and intelligent subsystems. Each layer has the ability to perform some virtualization functions and can be used to balance other areas in the food chain. This approach helps balance both control points and vendor lock-in, and ultimately reduces total ownership costs.

3.9 Chapter Summary

The Software Spectrum

- Purchasing processes are shifting from hardware-centric decision making to identifying best platforms for software and applications.

- The underlying hardware must be matched with effective software management systems.

- Storage software helps administrators effectively get control of their storage domains.

3.1 Framework for Storage Management Software

- Storage management breaks down to infrastructure management, transaction management, and recovery management.

- Infrastructure management has a platform focus and includes SAN management and resource management.

- Transaction management has an application focus and includes data coordination and policy management.

- Recovery management has an availability focus and includes data protection and high availability.

3.2 Storage Network Management

- SAN management provides network-centric administration features.

- Discovery identifies all devices within a storage fabric.

- Zoning and configuration determines which storage devices can access and modify each other.

- Zoning can take place through port-based (hard) or WWN (soft) mechanisms.

- SAN topologies serve as a useful tool for mapping physical layouts of storage.

- Monitoring keeps administrators aware of the general health of the SAN.

- Protocol conversion takes place in the SAN between Fibre Channel and IP transports.

- Different device types (iSCSI and Fibre Channel) and device attachment methods (direct or via a SAN) require different protocol conversion mechanisms.

- Documented storage policies and procedures, including cabling and labeling of devices, helps speed recovery in the event of disaster.

3.3 Storage Resource Management

- Storage resource management helps centralize control of storage devices.

- SRM applies to HBAs, SAN switches and routers, and storage subsystems.

- Subsystem efficiency can be tracked through SRM and can aid in capacity planning.

3.4 Data Coordination

■ Data coordination takes place through file systems and volume management.

■ File systems deliver abstraction between logical volumes and files.

■ Volume management delivers abstraction between disks/LUNs and logical volumes.

■ File systems and volume management aggregate storage resources to common presentation layers.

3.5 Storage Policy Management

■ Storage policies use information from resource management to enhance efficient use of storage.

■ Policies include security and authentication; capacity, content, and quota management; and quality of service for storage and storage networks.

■ Storage policies are implemented and maintained through an ongoing process.

■ Capacity management optimizes the use of existing storage resources.

■ Security and authentication policies guarantee privacy and data integrity.

■ Quality of service features enable delivery of guaranteed resources.

3.6 Data Protection

■ Data protection schemes present various cost-availability tradeoffs.

■ Tape backup delivers low–cost-per-megabyte storage with low speeds and long restore times.

■ Tape cartridges provide flexibility for onsite and offsite storage.

■ With SANs, tape libraries can be shared across the infrastructure, including backup for NAS.

- Disk backup has a high cost per megabyte with high speeds and short restore times.

- Point-in-time and snapshot backup tools enable sequential rollback to restore databases to predisaster or precorruption states.

- Hierarchical storage management helps minimize total storage costs by moving infrequently accessed data to lower cost media.

3.7 High Availability

- For guaranteed uptime, disk backup solutions require mirroring or replication, or both.

- Mirroring provides the highest availability via instant restore times.

- Synchronous and asynchronous replication trade restore time for distance and enable remote backup solutions for site-specific disasters.

3.8 Virtualization

- Virtualization is often misunderstood due to bundling of other storage software features in the term.

- Basic virtualization is the homogeneous presentation of heterogeneous storage.

- Data-protection features like backup or availability features like mirroring and replication can reside on top of a virtualization layer.

- Virtualization can be deployed across host, fabric, and subsystem layers.

- Options exist for customers to balance storage control points through different virtualization deployments.

4 Storage System Control Points

Storage networks are fueling a rapidly adapting architectural model for storage. Today's storage infrastructure continually adapts to keep pace with application deployment and data creation. Innovative applications and the sheer amount of information stored shift processing bottlenecks throughout the system. Bottlenecks often arise when systems are architected based on the rich experience of yesterday's requirements with imperfect knowledge of how those requirements will evolve over time. Both entrenched storage vendors and enterprising upstarts aim to alleviate processing bottlenecks through the use of pioneering technologies deployed as storage system control points.

The simple split between servers and storage, or initiators and targets, implies a need for network connectivity. The introduction of a storage network allows previously restricted storage functions to operate across this split to provide an end-to-end solution. A complete understanding of these storage functions, potential areas for deployment, and best practices for optimized solutions allow administrators to properly architect storage infrastructures.

Chapter 4 begins by outlining the basic storage services required to build a robust, resilient data storage repository. By starting with the basic storage functions, we keep our fulfillment objectives in mind rather than simply talking about the control points abstractly. Classified as storage service deliverables, these functions include capacity, performance, availability, recovery, security, and manageability.

A look at the historical evolution of storage helps clarify where storage functions and associated intelligence have resided in the past and potential areas where they will reside in the future. Although the hype for new technology may cause us to believe that we face a completely new set of circumstances, technology transformations follow historical patterns, many of which apply to storage. Examples in distributed systems and routing apply to the evolution currently taking place in storage networking. Understanding the history of storage evolution and its technology cycles helps us understand today's challenging environment and prepare us for future decision making.

Ranging from the simplest to most complex storage networks, functions and intelligence reside within three basic system areas—host, fabric, and subsystem. Looking at specific storage functions, we examine the pros and cons of where they reside and why. The dramatic changes underway come from the ability to place intelligent storage services in the fabric. Fabric-based solutions bring fluidity to storage network control points.

Networking plays a crucial role as the link between hosts and subsystems. Brokering all storage transactions, traditional interconnects historically set finite boundaries on storage control points. Today, the convergence between I/O technologies such as Fibre Channel and networking technologies such as Ethernet shatter previous conventions of storage design. With an ever-increasing amount of data looking for a means to get from A to B, and a corresponding requirement to heavily invest in storage fabrics, choice of storage interconnects can dramatically affect total cost of ownership and return on investment.

4.1 Storage Service Deliverables

The logical breakdown of storage intelligence and its geographic placement within the overall storage infrastructure mandates categorization. As a starting point, we define six basic storage functions, or services, required to provide enterprise-class storage solutions. Those services include manageability, capacity, recoverability, performance, security, and availability.

Note that virtualization is not specifically called out as a service itself. Due to the numerous uses of the term, we employ the classic virtualization definition in our framework. That definition—to abstract heterogeneous storage homogeneously—can be part of one or more associated services. That abstraction may be across multiple disk drives, volumes, or storage arrays. However, the associated services, not the abstraction layer, determine the customer value..

Chapter 3, "The Software Spectrum," outlined overall storage management features across three focal points: infrastructure, transactions, and disaster recovery. That framework fits with our storage services, as shown in Figure 4–1.

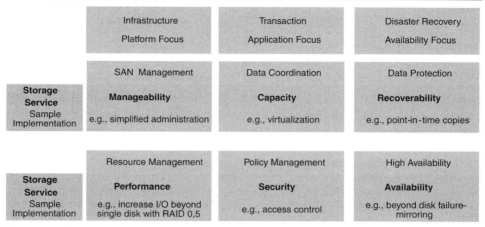

Figure 4–1 Storage services within the storage software landscape.

4.1.1 Storage Service Definitions

The basic services in Figure 4–1 define the storage portion of the service. The overall group is therefore focused on lower layer activities that extend up to volumes, but not necessarily including file systems. The services set supports any combination of platforms for block-based, file-based, or object-based storage. Since the services are independent of the storage platform, we can evaluate service offerings across almost any platform or network type.

- **Manageability**—As expected, manageability ranks high on the list of required services. With installations becoming ever more complex, management of the storage infrastructure consumes larger portions of the overall operating budget. Users strive for manageability through simplified administration, configuration, monitoring, and repair. Today storage system management spans servers, HBAs, SAN switches, subsystems, and tape libraries. Each can have its own interface and method of management communications, causing unnecessary complexity.

- **Capacity**—The capacity service falls into two categories—LUNs and volumes. Ultimately, the storage service deliverable is a volume made up of LUNs, which in turn comprise one or more disk drives. With simplified SAN deployments, volumes typically reside within a single array or enclosure. Today, with volume aggregation capabilities available in the network, "virtual volumes" may include capacity gathered from a range of drives or arrays.

- **Recoverability**—Even with highly available configurations, the potential for data corruption exists. Whether recovering from a dropped packet or a corrupted database, the ability to rapidly return to a steady and operational state determines overall deployment availability. Upon encountering data corruption or system failure, point-in-time copies facilitate one way to return to order. With lower-level recovery issues, such as a dropped packet, protocol exchanges in the networking layer recover accordingly.

- **Performance**—Performance services encompass methods to boost storage throughput or transaction benchmarks with available resources. One example is RAID 0 functionality to create volumes. By striping data across multiple disks, the effective I/O throughput increases. Other performance-enhancing measures might be to use 2-Gb/s high-speed Fibre Channel networks to boost throughput between high-end servers and storage.

- **Security**—The deployment of a storage network requires access and control mechanisms across the infrastructure. In direct-attached systems, the physical security of the data center may have been sufficient. With wider storage distribution across the enterprise, storage administrators need the ability to actively monitor and control access to valuable storage resources and prevent these resources from being used to further compromise the system.

- **Availability**—Protecting environments from sudden configuration changes, high-availability services facilitate rapid changeover to alternate active computing engines, including storage. One common form of availability is RAID 1 functionality, effectively mirroring data across two devices. In the networking world, multicasting provides similar capabilities, allowing one packet to be sent to two or more destinations.

By categorizing storage services, we can evaluate sample implementations and placement within the overall storage infrastructure. Implementations vary across hardware and software, but more specifically traverse previously cordoned areas now open with the reach of storage networks. Storage services can be provided through host-based applications running on servers, within network implementations running on appliances or switches, or within target subsystems such as RAID devices. The areas of storage intelligence and potential hardware platforms are shown in Figure 4–2.

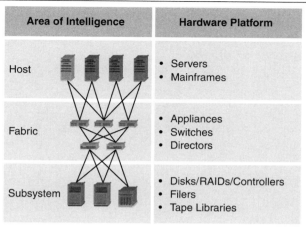

Figure 4–2 Potential storage services locations.

4.2 Brief History and Evolution of Storage

Before delving into potential storage services locations within the overall infrastructure, it helps to have some context to the evolution of computing and storage architectures stretching back several decades. A look back in time across compute platforms, storage platforms, and the logical and physical interaction highlights that all roads point toward distributed systems. This is made possible by advances in storage devices, access technology, and storage software.

4.2.1 The Mainframe Era

The 1950s and 1960s witnessed rapid technology adoption in high-growth industries such as banking, airline travel, medical diagnosis, and space exploration. These industries required fast access to large amounts of data for transaction-intensive business processes, and mainframe architectures filled that need.

The independence of data storage can be linked to IBM's delivery of the first tape drive in 1952 and the first 2,400-foot tape reel in 1953. At the time, it was a cost-effective means to store large amounts of data over a long period of time. With increasing density every year, IBM's 2,400-foot reel tape remained the standard until the introduction of the half-inch tape in 1984. While tape was good for storage, it was slow for access. Transaction-intensive business processes required picking a needle out of the haystack in minutes. The answer came in 1956 from a team of IBM engineers in San Jose, California. The 305 RAMAC (Random Access Method of Accounting and Control) could store five million characters (five megabytes) of data on 50 disks, or the equivalent of 62,000 punch cards. This was the first device available that could go directly from point A to point B on a disk without reading the information in between.

The 1960s brought higher density disk storage, one head per disk, and airborne heads that allowed for faster access to more data. It also introduced the Cyclical Redundancy Check (CRC), which is an algorithm that allows a system to automatically check itself for errors and to correct some of these errors. Tape drives learned to "read backwards," a method still used today for increasing tape performance.

Storage access for mainframes was direct-attached with a limited number of storage nodes, with devices located next to mainframes within a data center. This centralized architecture worked well for the mainframe applications served.

In the 1970s the innovation of the Winchester disk drive and floppy disk enabled data portability and began the slippery slope of migration of data from the mainframe. At the same time, industry visionaries such as Ken Olsen at Digital Equipment Corporation (DEC) proposed that a series of smaller networked machines, called minicomputers, could accomplish the same tasks as IBM's larger mainframe computers.

4.2.2 Minicomputers and Clustering

In October 1977 the first VAX prototype came off the production line. VAX was a 32-bit minicomputer that also enabled DEC's VAX strategy of clustering several smaller computers together to form a huge network. DECnet was the initial networking technology proposed and delivered for VAX clusters, but in 1979 Ethernet, a system developed by Bob Metcalfe at XEROX's Palo Alto Research Center (PARC) had gathered more supporters. That year XEROX, DEC, and Intel launched their Ethernet networking plans.

Minicomputers and clustering broke the centralized lock between storage and mainframes, and alternative approaches such as DEC's VAX clusters provided choices beyond those offered by IBM. However, IBM still dominated the R&D landscape for new technologies, especially storage, and created the Plug-Compatible Market (PCM). IBM retained over 90 percent of the market because it owned the connection control points upon which disk storage architectures were built. Aftermarket competitors were forced to follow IBM's lead, which usually meant they were 12 to 18 months behind Big Blue in introducing new products.

Even with IBM's market stronghold, the appearance of minicomputers and clustering began to decentralize storage. Users now had options to develop specific data stores for nonmainframe applications. This enabled choice but also led to the breakdown of centralized storage management. However, the cost advantages of avoiding mainframe storage outweighed the unforeseen consequences of decentralized storage architectures. Without the ability to see how complex this decentralization could become, it continued and picked up speed with new advances in disk storage. such as RAID (Redundant Array of Inexpensive Disks).

In 1987 IBM and the University of California at Berkeley jointly patented the first RAID device. RAID accelerated data access and, more importantly, introduced the concept of redundancy in computer systems for reliability. RAID systems were the impetus for the next growth stage in storage, allowing manufacturers to deliver performance and availability that had previously been achieved only through expensive large-platter disk systems dominated by IBM. The most cited case of this exploitation is EMC's capture of IBM's disk storage market through the 1990s.

While the famous RAID paper brought forward a common language for describing functions like striping or mirroring across multiple disk drives, the technology prospered with the ability to place large amounts of RAM in front of cheap disks and imitate high-performance mainframe boxes. The RAM allowed instant write acknowledgments and aggressive caching for read performance. It is no coincidence that EMC and other array vendors grew out of the memory market. In fact, one of the first disk products was called an Integrated, Cache-Based Disk Array.

4.2.3 Client-Server Computing

The increasing popularity of client-server computing in the 1990s launched the deployment of midrange servers throughout the enterprise, with each group having its own storage. Server storage evolved from direct-attached RAID systems to networked storage systems based on the introduction of Fibre Channel.

All major server vendors began to offer storage choices, and independent storage vendors also offered their own storage arrays optimized for specific needs. This migration to open systems, spurred by the adoption of interconnects such as Fibre Channel, ultimately led to the creation of independent storage islands. Typical customer configurations might include a small cluster of application servers with a small Fibre Channel network connected to one vendor's storage solution. For example, the enterprise resource planning (ERP) software often ends up on a completely different set of servers and storage devices from the customer resource management (CRM) software.

As storage for each application grew separately, the growth in the personal computer market meant that more and more storage was split among application servers and users' desktops and laptops. Data production activities such as office automation (word processing, presentations, email) or data-intensive applications such as computer aided design often resided outside of the application server's storage. This split storage deployment caused an excessive cost through redundant storage deployments and difficult administration.

4.2.4 Distributed Web, Application, and Database Servers

Recognizing the storage investments made to keep up with digital information and the increasing portion of corporate spending on data management, both vendors and users now aim to consolidate systems to maximize resources. Distributed servers for Web services, applications, and databases are possible through the use of sophisticated networks, including load balancers and "application aware" switches. Similarly, storage through intelligent storage networks can be located almost anywhere on a global network supporting hundreds, if not thousands, of nodes.

The ultimate goal of maximizing storage resources requires delivery of virtual storage pools, as provided by storage capacity services. Also required are the other primary storage services of manageability, recoverability, performance, security, and availability. Operating in concert, these services reside throughout the larger distributed system of servers, networks, and storage devices. In Section 4.3, "Placing Storage Intelligence," we examine optimized locations for a variety of these storage services.

Figure 4–3 outlines the overall shift to distributed architectures across computing and storage platforms. Whereas previously storage could not join the distributed playing field, the advent of storage networks and services permits this type of participation. Just as computing architectures have moved to distributed scalable models, so will storage.

4.2.5 Scalability

All services must scale across three dimensions: size, speed, and distance. Scalability allows users to grow configurations without changing design parameters because of that growth. Size can be classified as the number of nodes in a network, such as servers, switches, and storage devices. Speed refers to the processing speed of the overall systems, such as application I/O operations per second, as well as the component bandwidth such as 2-Gbps Fibre Channel or 10-Gbps Ethernet. The ability to cover metropolitan, national, and

Computing Architecture	Mainframes	Minicomputers and Clustering	Client-server	Distributed Web, App, DB servers
Storage Access	Direct	Cluster	Small network	Global network
Storage Nodes	< 5	5–10	10–1000	> 1000
Storage Architecture	Centralized	Decentralized	Split	Distributed
Storage Capacity	Tape, RAMAC	Large disks and RAID	Storage islands	Virtualized storage pools
Storage Location	Data center	Data center and beyond	PCs and application servers	Anywhere

Figure 4–3 Historical trends across computing and storage infrastructure design.

global reach for applications requiring business continuity and disaster recovery mandates scalability in terms of distance as well. See Figure 4–4.

4.2.6 Building More Scalable Routers

History has shown that distributed systems boost size and throughput scalability, particularly in networking applications. Consider initial routers' internal design compared to today. The first generation of routers had centralized

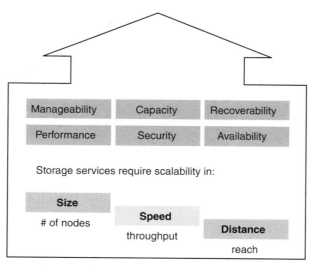

Figure 4–4 Storage services require size, speed, and distance scalability.

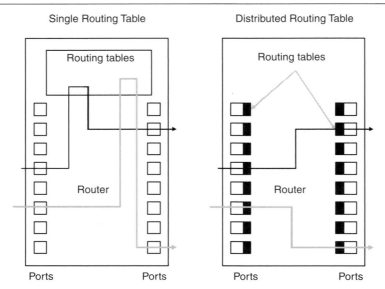

Figure 4–5 Routers progressed from single to distributed tables for greater speed and performance.

routing tables. All data entering the router went through the single routing table, in effect creating a processing bottleneck. By distributing routing information directly to each port, decisions could be made independently, releasing the central processing bottleneck. While the central processor is responsible for the overall implementation, each port operates with a Forwarding Information Base (FIB) based on a forwarding table from the central processor. This architecture enables greater throughput across a larger number of nodes.

In effect, a router is a network within a chassis. As such, one would expect networking of any devices, including storage nodes, to benefit from the distributed architecture demonstrated on the right of Figure 4–5.

4.2.7 Network-Based Storage Services

Applying storage networking to the evolution of routing, the natural conclusion is a migration towards distributed architectures to boost scalability. The introduction of a switch between two storage end nodes breaks open the traditionally isolated path and presents openings for new solutions. From a storage networking perspective, these solutions come from intelligence previously residing in the host or target but now delivered through network-based platforms.

As with routing, early deployments for network-based storage services used a single location model for implementation. When the services engine

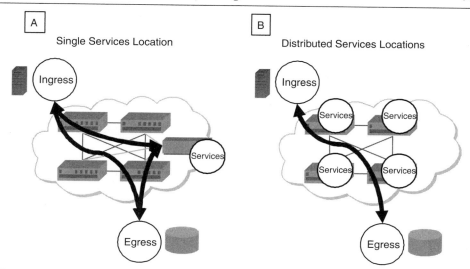

Figure 4–6 Using distributed storage services for optimized deployments.

resides outside the data path, more traffic exchanges take place between the end nodes by default. As shown in Figure 4–6A, a single services location model requires communication between ingress, egress, and services nodes. In this example, the ingress and egress end points are likely storage nodes such as server HBAs or disk arrays. Adding a distributed model to the configuration, much as routing added distributed functions to ports, facilitates simpler communication between ingress and egress points on the network. The direct path is shown in Figure 4–6B.

By distributing services information, each node on the network is empowered to carry out the requested operations between any ingress and egress points. This configuration guarantees the maximum efficiency of high-speed network connections specialized for storage. This streamlined approach is demonstrated in Figure 4–7.

4.2.8 Network Choices for Storage Services

The introduction of a multipoint architecture, or network, into the storage domain provides choices for services locations and functions. Given the trends in changing applications, user requirements, and equipment adaptation, services will continue to shift based on processing bottlenecks. For a variety of markets and applications, location optimization will be unique.

Separating services between hosts and targets implies a functional split; however, moving services from either the host or target domain into a third

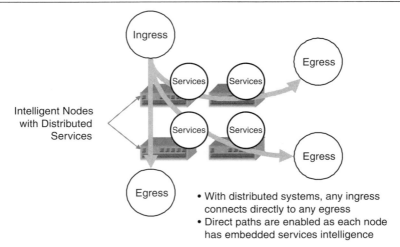

- With distributed systems, any ingress
  connects directly to any egress
- Direct paths are enabled as each node
  has embedded services intelligence

Figure 4–7 Optimized network flow through distributed services.

network location represents another breakthrough. It is far simpler to set up an exchange between two end nodes than it is to add a third location. With two nodes, each node knows that any data received is from the other node. With three nodes, the identification process grows by an order of complexity. But, once the third node is established, the identification and communication infrastructure building blocks are in place to scale to n (any numbers of) nodes. This is the communications model deployed in mainstream networking today for use across the Internet, the world's largest network. Storage networking is also moving to n node scalability and is likely to follow the same model.

4.3 Placing Storage Intelligence

Placing storage intelligence and accompanying services depends upon application requirements, cost points, network utilization, and preferences. For each service category, certain implementations might work better in one area than another. While the rapid pace of change makes hard and fast guidelines challenging, certain storage services location make more sense than others. Using a few implementation examples across services categories, we show how host, fabric, and subsystem methods differ.

4.3.1 Intelligent Storage Delivered

The first storage subsystems provided a relatively simple means of protecting data on nonvolatile media. Demand for storage beyond what could be effectively delivered by tape spurred the introduction of plain vanilla disk systems. The invention of RAID algorithms dramatically changed the picture and launched both performance and intelligence improvements in storage functionality. In the case of RAID 0, performance improvements resulted from striping data across multiple disks and generating higher overall throughput that any single disk could generate independently. With RAID 1, mirroring functionality enabled intelligent redundancy mechanisms to boost overall system availability.

With DAS, host and target implementations competed with one another to offer additional RAID services. Depending on the cost/performance trade-offs, location of RAID functionality varied between hosts and targets. While all RAID functionality could be accomplished via host-based software, RAID 0 and 5 (striping and striping with parity) were best placed in the target due to the compute-intensive nature of these algorithms. Even though RAID 0 and 5 could run in host-based software, the required CPU processing cycles were likely to take away from application performance. Today, even with many host-based volume management software packages offering RAID 5 functionality, this feature is almost never turned on due to the performance impact. RAID striping functions have therefore found a comfortable and largely uncontested home within the storage subsystems themselves.

Staying with the direct-attach model, RAID 1 (mirroring) could reside in either location—host or target. However, when the host has to maintain two copies, it must generate twice the I/Os, and the application waits for both to complete. A three-way mirror would triple the I/O traffic. The same applies for target-based RAID 1—it must handle twice the I/Os. Host-based RAID 1 does offer a tight coupling with applications and can easily control the behavior of the service, but at the penalty of handling double the traffic.

The build-out of a storage network changes the optimal location of RAID 1 services. Fortunately, many scenarios in storage networking can benefit directly from longstanding techniques applied in traditional data networking. For example, multicasting protocols—essentially an *n*-way mirror—attempt to replicate data as close as possible to the receiving end nodes. A host-based mirroring implementation in a storage network would therefore be the worst implementation when applying multicasting techniques. Replicating data at the source is the most inefficient use of network connections. By pushing the replication closer to the end nodes, the total amount of network traffic decreases, maximizing network efficiency. This basic effect is shown in Figure 4–8.

A network implementation of mirroring minimizes the number of copies in the network, thereby maximizing network efficiency. The overall goal focuses on optimizing the host to network to target connections. In the case

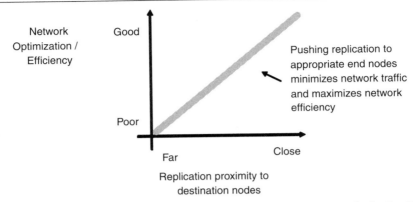

Figure 4–8 Optimizing network efficiency by pushing replication towards destination nodes.

of the cost per port, a server-based HBA or subsystem-based controller port is typically far more expensive than a network port. Reducing the load on an HBA or controller implies less need for additional end-node ports that can be more economically substituted with network ports.

Simplifying the model, Figure 4–9 shows how both host-based and target-based mirroring applications require twice the amount of HBA or controller traffic, leading to the use of additional network segments to complete

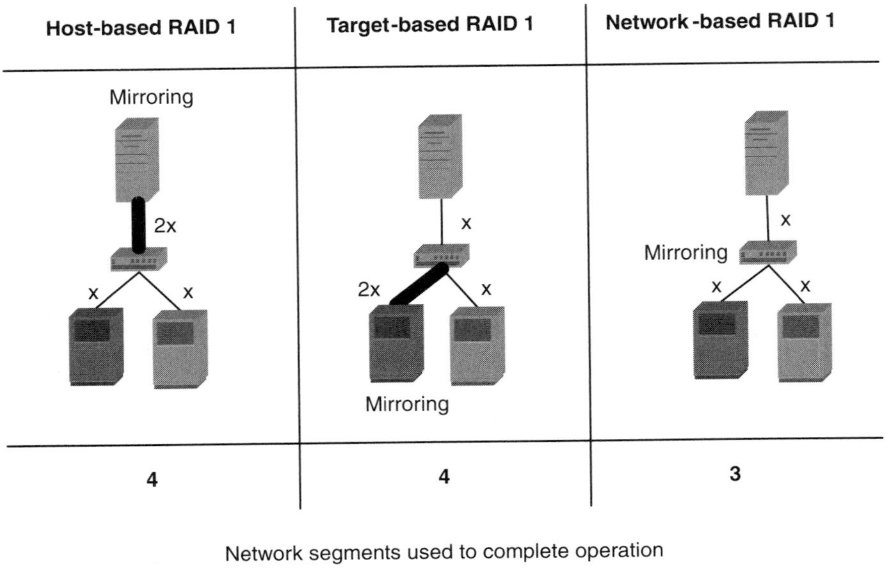

Host-based RAID 1	**Target-based RAID 1**	**Network-based RAID 1**
Mirroring		
2x	x	x
x x	2x x	Mirroring x x
	Mirroring	
4	4	3

Network segments used to complete operation

Figure 4–9 Simplifying network usage models with network-based storage services.

the operation. A network-based RAID 1 implementation, however, is optimized to push the replication to the midpoint between the receiving end nodes, thereby minimizing the overall network traffic. While the difference in this model may appear negligible, consider a storage network with dozens of switches and hundreds of end nodes. The ability to migrate mirroring functionality to the optimal midpoint between receiving end nodes can have a dramatic effect on network efficiency.

4.3.2 Managing Attribute-Based Storage

In complex, heterogeneous storage environments, customers increasingly want to manage storage based on storage attributes. Rather than identifying a storage device based on its manufacturer and model number, the attributes more relevant from a management perspective include type of storage, protection level, access paths, and recovery capability. This approach to storage management becomes a reality when those attributes are managed within the network, as the network has the best mechanisms to deliver storage attributes to management packages. These mechanisms include the following:

- **Visibility**—By its very location between hosts and targets, the network has better visibility to end nodes. Since all end devices must log in to the storage network, the network by default knows the location (to the port level) of each storage device. A host implementation would need to query each end node within the network to determine its exact location. The network also knows the device type through the login process.

- **Access and Topology**—Acting as the interconnect between hosts and targets, the network knows the optimal paths between end nodes, has the ability to determine new routes, and can map the physical topology of the network.

- **Reactive Capability**—With complete end-node visibility and knowledge of access paths and topologies, the network is best suited to determine reactive action to errors in storage operations.

Take the example of a storage target that isn't responding to a host request. Without network-based storage services, the host has no knowledge of why the target didn't respond. It doesn't know if the link went down, or the disk was corrupt, or if something else happened within the network. The recovery action can be timely and expensive waiting for an HBA to time out before responding with an error to the application. That error might provide little knowledge of the condition besides "no response."

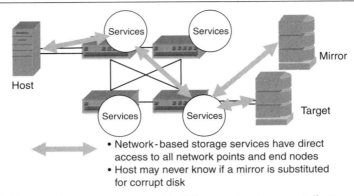

Figure 4–10 Network-based services provide full access to storage attributes.

With an intelligent storage network, the network knows how to identify the problem immediately. For example, it can separate disk errors from network errors, and coupled with intelligent services such as RAID 1, it could substitute a mirrored disk for a corrupt disk without the application's knowledge. Figure 4–10 shows how distributed network services provide "one-hop" access to all nodes in the configuration.

4.3.3 Locations for Additional Storage Services

The emergence of sophisticated networking devices for storage provides a new platform for storage services. Some services, such as dynamic multipath hosting and application coordination, will likely remain as host-based for the foreseeable future. Others, such as LUN creation through disk aggregation and RAID 0/5 will likely remain target-based due to CPU requirements and network optimization. But the majority of storage services can be well served via distributed network locations. Figure 4–11 outlines the categories of storage services, implementations, optimal locations, and reasons.

The gravitational pull of storage services into the network is taking place for a number of reasons. In many cases, the increasing size of storage network configurations makes the network location an optimal delivery point. Additionally, new market entrants can offer the same functionality as host-based and target-based implementations at a fraction of the cost. As industry margins continue to shift towards value-added software, we are likely to witness a free-for-all across host, fabric, and target implementations to capture a larger portion of the overall storage services spectrum. With vendors chasing after the same IT storage budget, each will need to capture as much of the pie as possible.

	Implementation	Optimal Location	Reasons
Manageability	• Attribute-based storage • Application coordination	• Network • Host	• Visibility, access, knowledge, reactive capability
Capacity	• LUN creation • Volume	• Target • Host, network, target	• Disk aggregation • Resizing most easily at host
Recoverability	• Packet recovery • Point-in-time copy • Disk error	• Network • Network • Target or network`	• Proximity • Minimize copy traffic • Recovery speed
Performance	• RAID 0,5 • Data movement	• Target • Network	• Balance target throughput with network • Minimize usage
Security	• Access control	• Network	• Knows ingress, egress points
Availability	• RAID 1 • Dynamic multipath hosting	• Depends: network location optimizes bandwidth • Host	• Similar to multicasting • OS integration

Figure 4–11 Optimal locations for storage services.

4.4 Building Blocks of Distributed Systems

Section 4.3 outlined several advantages for using network connectivity to deliver storage services. As shown, the only true means to deliver scalability is through the use of distributed systems across some type of networked infrastructure. Recognizing this fact, we examine how some of the fundamental thinking behind storage has changed.

The basic building blocks of distributed systems go back to early computer design and the separation of primary computing functions such as memory, CPUs, storage (I/O), and networking. Each function serves a distinct purpose yet is an integral part of the complete system. The basic functions are shown in Figure 4–12.

For quite some time, memory and CPU capabilities and speed far outstripped that of I/O and networking. The doubling of processor transistors

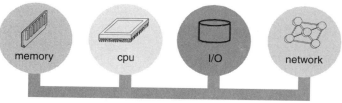

Figure 4–12 Primary computing functions.

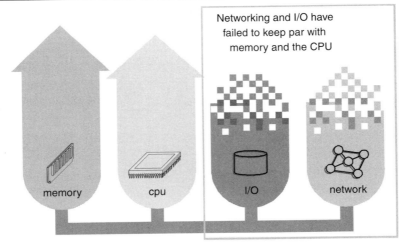

Figure 4–13 The gap between computing resources.

every 18 months, as identified by Moore's law, and the rapid advances in memory density kept these components ahead of the relative technology curve. The most frequent bottlenecks to system processing stemmed from the I/O and networking components. This led to server-centric solutions in which I/O and networking needs were sacrificed in order to enhance overall system performance. For example, the solution may have relied only upon DAS to fulfill throughput needs. Alternatively, network replication may have been restricted to overnight hours due to limited bandwidth. This gap is shown in Figure 4–13.

Following the silicon chip lead established by processors, complementary advances in networking technologies helped level the playing field across computing resources. Within the last five to ten years, interconnect technologies such as Fibre Channel and Ethernet have reached speed and performance levels that more closely match those of CPU and memory capabilities. In addition, the lines between I/O and networking are getting blurrier through the proliferation of NAS and block IP storage technologies.

These factors contribute to two shifts in thinking about networking and storage strategies. First, I/O and networking have outgrown previous performance limitations. Second, the underlying technologies are converging to the point where they can now be treated more equally. This shift is outlined in Figure 4–14.

Equal treatment of storage and networking brings us back to the original breakdown of core computing functions—memory, CPU, I/O, and networking. The most scalable and efficient computing solutions are those that effec-

Prior Thinking

Current Thinking

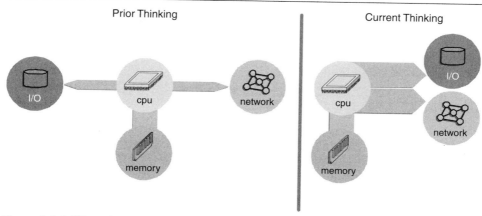

Figure 4–14 I/O and networking increase speed and converge architecturally.

tively balance and utilize these resources. Distributed systems enable these kind of solutions. The key to going forward is to determine the optimal methods of building the larger distributed system, the communication between the resources, and a means for overall management.

Since networking is the essential glue for any distributed system, we take a closer look at how network control points impact storage networking and I/O in Section 4.5.

4.5 Network Control Points

The storage network, or fabric, acts as the primary intermediary between traditional host and target storage services implementations. Coupled with the introduction of intelligent devices, the network itself becomes a control point of the overall storage infrastructure. In the past, many have referred to the network as nonintelligent plumbing that was largely irrelevant. This may have been true when intelligence resided on either the host or the target. However, with the network now providing increasing levels of storage services, it can no longer be ignored.

Improvements in network technology, such as the introduction of Gigabit Ethernet, coupled with the ability to put block-based storage on IP networks, dramatically shift the network landscape and have serious ramifications on storage control points. In the past, network interconnects were separated by overall bandwidth, distance capabilities, and scalability as measured by the number of nodes on the network. Figure 4–15A shows how the interconnects split across interprocessor communication, I/O, LANs, and

WANs. Distance is on the X-axis, node scalability on the Y-axis, and bandwidth represented by circle size.

The introduction of Gigabit Ethernet and technologies such as iSCSI enables Ethernet to accomplish the same kind of functions previously limited to SCSI and Fibre Channel, as shown in Figure 4–15B. The importance of this shift cannot be underestimated. For the first time, an interconnect technology not dominated by the storage community is encroaching on traditional storage territory. It is likely that the storage community, once isolated by the self-directed nature of its interfaces, has yet to fully grasp the consequences of this network convergence. Given Ethernet's ability to grow, scale, and adapt to a wide variety of environments, its capabilities are likely to cover all of the I/O space in time, as shown in Figure 4–15C. This doesn't mean that traditional I/O technologies will disappear, but rather that the playing field in terms of features and performance will be leveled to the point where the average customer would not know the difference.

The networking community, however, has rapidly embraced the evolutionary nature of Ethernet and is already adapting to Ethernet's ability to move to the MAN and WAN space, especially with the introduction of 10-Gigabit Ethernet, as shown in Figure 4–15D.

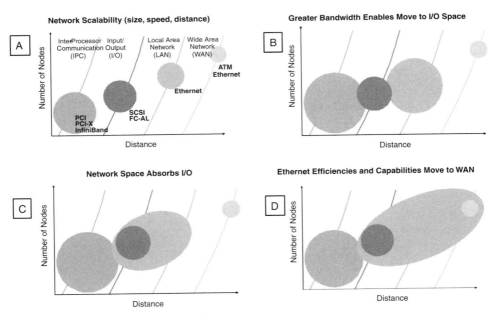

Figure 4–15 Leveling the interconnect playing field.

Vendors and customers likely to prosper in storage will recognize the adaptive path of networking technologies and embrace the change. Others will futilely resist and grapple to sustain alternative storage-focused interfaces, continuing to invest in their propagation by developing incremental, yet ultimately insufficient, technology improvements.

4.6 Balancing Multivendor Configurations

Customers intent on influencing long-term decisions for their storage networking configurations must adapt to technology changes and understand the control points of the infrastructure. The networking shifts represent two parallel changes to traditional concepts of storage. First, the ability to place intelligence within the network, as opposed to hosts or targets, provides an alternate control point to balance traditional vendor lock-in. For example, target-based mirroring and replication functions may now reside within the network, offering a choice to conventional host-based or target-based implementations.

The other change underway relates to the shift from conventional Fibre Channel–only storage networks to those that involve a combination of Fibre Channel and Ethernet networks. Consider the following scenario. With Fibre Channel–focused configurations, subsystem vendors were largely beholden to work with the relatively few number of Fibre Channel switch vendors in order to deploy complete end-to-end solutions. The introduction of IP and Ethernet as an alternate storage interface removes the need for such a partnership. For example, a large subsystem with an iSCSI interface need no longer connect to a Fibre Channel switch.

The implications of these choices have ripple effects for large configurations, particularly in the case where value-added storage services make up a significant portion of the complete solutions. As mentioned earlier, with multiple vendors grappling to sustain profit margins, each will attempt to bundle more and more storage services into their offerings. Therefore, it is likely that a customer would be able to install replication technology across host, fabric, and subsystem platforms. The collection of available choices will force price erosion across storage services and also drive a combination of competition and "co-opetition" among storage vendors.

To date, most of the discussion about competition in the storage networking industry has taken place within each layer of the configuration—for example, host-based software (Veritas and Legato), fabric (Cisco, Brocade, and McDATA), or subsystems (EMC and HDS). In these scenarios, seem-

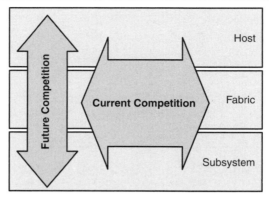

Figure 4–16 Balancing multivendor configurations.

ingly organized industry partnerships have emerged only to be split at a later date when the participants could not bring the partnership to fruition.

Additional partnerships have been formed across layers of the storage chain, but these too are in jeopardy as storage services and intelligence migrate between layers and put virtually all alliances at risk. For example, vendors that previously focused only on storage interconnects within the fabric will likely expand to offer storage services such as replication. This will put them in direct contention with vendors offering target-based replication services. How these alliances evolve is open for debate, but no one can deny that market forces will expand future competition between storage vendors across host, fabric, and subsystem layers. These forces are outlined in Figure 4–16.

4.7 Chapter Summary

Storage System Control Points

- Storage networks allow the movement of storage intelligence across the entire infrastructure.

- Storage intelligence or services act as solution control points.

- Historical architectures help present a picture of the future.

- There are pros and cons for storage services residing within host, fabric, and subsystem layers.

- Networking plays a crucial role and should not be relegated to plumbing.

4.1 Storage Service Deliverables

- Storage services fit into the overall framework for storage software, including infrastructure, transactions, and disaster recovery.

- Services include

    - Manageability (e.g., simplified administration)

    - Capacity (e.g., virtualization)

    - Recoverability (e.g., point-in-time copies)

    - Performance (e.g., increases I/O performance beyond single-disk performance)

    - Security (e.g., access control)

    - Availability (e.g., beyond disk failure with mirroring)

- Categorization helps clarify locations.

4.2 Brief History and Evolution of Storage

- A broad historical perspective across compute and storage platforms reveals a trend toward distributed systems.

- The mainframe era represented high-cost, single-vendor, centralized storage.

- The minicomputer and clustering era delivered multinode storage access for decentralized storage.

- The client-server era led to split storage architectures between data centers, departmental servers, and desktops.

- Distributed Web, application, and database servers require distributed storage in virtualized storage pools.

- All storage services must scale in terms of

    - Size (e.g., number of nodes)

    - Speed (e.g., throughput or I/Os per second)

    - Distance (e.g., geographic reach)

- First-generation single-table routers were replaced with more scalable, higher performing distributed systems.

- A router is essentially a network within a chassis.

- Similar design principles of distributed services apply to storage.

- Intelligent nodes with distributed storage services facilitate scalable, high-performing systems.

- An intelligent storage network leaves options for storage services locations.

4.3 Placing Storage Intelligence

- Storage services locations depend upon application requirements, cost points, network utilization, and preferences.

- No hard and fast guidelines apply; however, certain storage services make sense in some areas over others.

- RAID 0/5 as compute-intensive operations tend to do well when located within the subsystem.

- RAID 1 (mirroring) is similar to network multicasting.

- Multicasting algorithms suggest replication as close as possible to the receiving nodes to minimize network utilization.

- With RAID 1, network-based mirroring is the optimized deployment for the best network utilization.

- Additional network ports can offset server HBA or subsystem controller ports.

- Network ports are often less expensive than end system HBA or controller ports.

- Attribute-based storage is best delivered by network-based storage services.

- Network location for storage services allows for

    - Visibility

    - Access and Topology

    - Reactive Capability

4.4 Building Blocks of Distributed Systems

■ Distributed systems have proven to be the most scalable solutions.

■ Core computing functions include memory, CPU, I/O, and networking.

■ Traditionally, memory and CPU functions outstripped I/O and networking.

■ I/O and networking advances put building blocks on even ground.

■ Interconnect advances (Fibre Channel and Gigabit Ethernet) allow I/O and networking to keep up with memory and CPU performance gains.

■ I/O and networking similarities converge, leading to architectural overlap and consolidation.

4.5 Network Control Points

■ Storage network or fabric is the disintermediary between traditional host and target storage services implementations.

■ Interconnects have traditionally been separated by bandwidth, node scalability, and throughput.

■ Gigabit Ethernet, 10 Gigabit Ethernet, and iSCSI allow Ethernet and IP to encroach on the storage-dominated interconnect landscape.

■ Ethernet also is moving into the MAN and WAN.

■ Cost and management advantages will force network consolidation.

4.6 Balancing Multivendor Configurations

■ Fluid, services-based storage networks allow for easy migration of storage services across host, fabric, and subsystem layers.

■ Conventional view of competition focused within each layer.

■ New competition is across each layer where host, fabric, and subsystem will compete to offer value-added services and a broader product portfolio.

■ Users can balance both within and across layers.

5

Reaping Value
from Storage Networks

The competitive business climate demands increasing data storage capabilities ranging from availability and recovery, to capacity management, to vendor aggregation. Multiprotocol storage networks serve all of these requirements in the form of block-based SANs or file-based NAS. As an enabling platform, networked storage naturally assumes a greater role in the cost and control of the overall storage infrastructure. Chapter 4, "Storage System Control Points," covered the control aspects of the storage fabric, outlining the areas of intelligence for storage services and the importance of balancing the fabric layer with the host and subsystems layer. This chapter covers the cost component of the storage networking layer by looking at the strategic reasons to combine both defensive and offensive measures and the value achieved by doing so across a common networking platform.

The Internet took the world by storm. The mad dash to put anything and everything digital onto a single network, whether for educational, government, commercial, or experimental reasons, led to data storage requirements and capacity not previously anticipated. Today, many commercial elements of the Internet have reworked business models and adjusted storage capacity requirements. Have you noticed all of the storage capacity restrictions on "free" Web site services, such as online photo sharing and Web-email boxes? Have you noticed how many times you are offered a chance to "upgrade" to the monthly fee option with more storage? Managing storage on the Internet, or for that matter, on any networked environment, includes capital and operational costs that hit the bottom line.

In industries where storage availability and protection drive revenue-generating businesses, the networked storage budget grows as a function of the overall operating budget. To harness these costs and drive ongoing returns from the investment, companies must broaden the metrics for measuring returns. This comes through merging defensive strategies like data protection with offensive strategies like platform consolidation.

5.1 Balancing Offensive and Defensive Strategies

The race to digitized information, which requires 100 percent uptime guarantees, coupled with the world political climate, has driven the role of defensive storage strategies in almost every medium to large corporation. Data storage availability and protection have become the hot topics of the last five years, serving to keep applications up and running, and to restore capabilities at hand if needed in the event of a site disaster. From a budgetary process, these requirements often fly through approval processes compared to other requests. Few executives are willing to tolerate the costs associated with downtime for e-commerce-related business or the costs of losing critical business information that cannot be recovered.

Given this preoccupation with data protection, the build-outs in many organizations have focused on these defensive approaches. Networked storage environments, as the very backbone of data availability and protection mechanisms, are often categorized under this umbrella. In many cases, this provides for adequate project justification. But companies that consider only a defensive approach to storage networking cannot reap the full benefits provided by this infrastructure.

Offensive strategies for storage networking fit hand in hand with defensive strategies but also further maximize the value of a networked storage environment. By looking beyond traditional concepts of data protection to entirely new methods for handling storage, offensive strategies help companies "change the game" and uncover opportunities for operational agility and flexibility that directly impact both capital and operational costs. The primary advantage of a dual-pronged approach to SAN deployment is that the underlying principals of the networked storage environment are similar across both strategies. For example, the same SAN plumbing used to facilitate more efficient backup operations also fits effectively within the larger context of corporate networking, particularly with the flexibility of IP SANs.

Offensive and defensive strategies often overlap. Depending on individual corporate planning processes, the lines between offensive and defensive approaches may vary. Even with a potential gray zone between strategies, the model helps IT professionals evaluate options beyond those traditionally considered for SANs. Figure 5–1 outlines some general distinctions between offensive and defensive strategies.

Defensive Strategies	Offensive Strategies
• Risk management	• Operational agility and flexibility
• Short-term cost savings	• Medium - to long-term cost savings
• Focus on current assets	• Focus on current and future assets
• Conventional platforms	• Emerging platforms
• Data Preservation	• Enhance enterprise market position

Figure 5–1 Comparing defensive and offensive storage networking strategies.

With defensive strategies, cost savings frequently relate to short-term objectives, typically the greatest pain points in the process. For example, a company unable to complete regular backups due to excessively long backup windows may adopt a SAN to alleviate the problem. In the race to solve such pressing issues, other considerations may be left out of the picture. For example, will the backup solution also help with storage consolidation? Is it replicable at other offices and locations? Does it fit with requirements for off-site storage in addition to simply reducing the backup window? These questions generally fall into medium- and long-term savings categories associated with offensive strategies.

Asset focus also differs between approaches. The defensive approach focuses on maximizing the use of existing assets, such as extending the life of a tape library by sharing it across multiple servers or using storage resource management to help grab additional capacity from inefficiently used RAID devices. The offensive approach looks at both current and future assets, such as what devices are likely to be part of the infrastructure over time, how they will be managed, and what the best options are for building an infrastructure to accommodate them. For example, balancing a combination of current block-accessed SAN devices with new file-accessed NAS devices requires a platform consolidation approach that is best achieved with a common networking infrastructure such as Ethernet and IP.

Platform choice differs between offensive and defensive approaches. Defensive strategies lean towards conventional platforms, taking incremental moves towards SAN deployment. The typical scenario is a company that has several Fibre Channel servers with DAS devices that moves towards a Fibre Channel SAN. While this deployment will provide SAN benefits, such as higher availability and more efficient backup operations, it still leaves gaps for solutions such as remote backups and integration with NAS. An offensive approach would be to move towards an IP storage network. This leapfrog step provides all the benefits of a SAN, but also gives the ability to keep all the Fibre Channel servers and storage devices with a SAN primarily based on IP networking. While IP as a SAN platform may fall in to the "emerging" category in the storage world, IP and Ethernet have longstanding maturity and robustness from decades of use in the networking world.

5.1.1 Risk and Total Cost of Ownership

Along the lines of comparing deployment approaches, another view of offensive and defensive strategies looks at overall storage growth affecting risk and total cost of ownership (TCO). The proliferation of data storage capacity coupled with the corporate requirements to maintain effective storage management increases both risk and TCO. From a risk perspective, the increase in the amount of data translates into exposure to potential loss. For example, companies relying on customer databases to deliver products and services face potential revenue loss if that information is lost or becomes unavailable. The primary concern for that operation is data protection and availability to reduce the amount of risk.

Increases in the total amount of storage also drive up the TCO. TCO typically includes the capital equipment acquisition costs plus the operational costs over a fixed time period. Companies that try to maintain traditional storage architectures, such as DAS, in the face of ballooning capacity requirements quickly find themselves in a never-ending race to add more storage to more servers while watching management and administration costs skyrocket. In this case, storage network deployment facilitates more rapid expansion of new storage capacity without directly impacting individual server or application operation. With the flexibility of a networked infrastructure in place, total costs decline.

Figure 5–2 shows the effects of storage growth on risk and TCO. In both cases, storage networking strategies—offensive and defensive—help corporations mitigate these effects.

The clear distinction between the approaches is used primarily as a thought framework for the chapter. Certainly, there are defensive approaches that reduce TCO and offensive approaches that reduce risk. However, by separating these two driving forces, IT professionals can more effectively position the project justification and return on the investment when considering storage networking deployment.

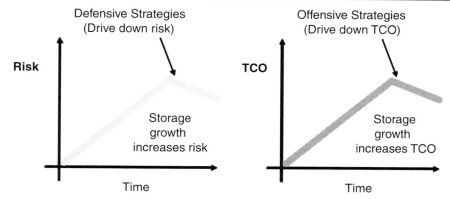

Figure 5–2 Storage growth increases risk and total cost of ownership.

5.2 Primary Defensive Strategies

This section covers several defensive approaches to networked storage. The objective is to show how the inclusion of a network topology for storage facilitates cost savings and return on investment, primarily from the standpoint of minimizing risk. In the case of defensive strategies, we define risk both in terms of potential data loss as well as the financial and human capital risk associated with managing storage, specifically budget reduction risk and reliance on storage administrators. Defensive approaches to network storage are part of an optimized storage deployment foundation, yet in isolation cannot provide the full benefits for long-term strategic deployment. The defensive approaches covered here also lead to the additional returns of offensive approaches in the following section.

5.2.1 Data Availability

High-availability SAN topologies reduce downtime for mission-critical applications by providing fully redundant paths between server-based applications and storage. For fully redundant configurations, dual paths ensure that loss of equipment or a network connection will not affect operation of the system or application uptime. With DAS, the simplicity of the connection made achieving redundancy straightforward. On the server side, redundant host bus adapters (HBAs) could be connected to dual cables leading to dual controller ports on the storage device. Since servers and storage devices typically reside within the data center, and more frequently within one or two adjacently located racks, the risks involved with connection loss are minimal.

Introducing a network to the architecture quickly doubles the number of interconnects between servers and storage, and requires more careful attention to the deployment of redundant paths. Let's take the case of a simple SAN, as shown in Figure 5–3. In this example, each server has dual HBAs that each connect to a separate SAN switch. Similarly, each storage device has dual controller ports that also connect to separate SAN switches. By zoning primary and alternate paths between the servers and storage devices, any failure in a server, HBA, SAN switch, or storage device can be overcome by using the alternate redundant equipment. There is no single point of failure in the architecture, which thereby enables maximum uptime for mission-critical server applications, keeping them running and generating revenue around the clock.

Once in place, the basic storage network infrastructure can be easily expanded beyond a couple of switches to incorporate dozens of switches around a central core. In the case of Fibre Channel SANs, director-class switches with up to hundreds of ports are deployed in the core. These directors provide high-availability features such as hot-swappable power supplies and cooling systems, redundant control processors, interchangeable modules for a variety of interconnects, and capabilities for nondisruptive firmware upgrades. They also support features to create large, scalable fabrics such as zoning, trunking, and end-to-end configuration of the storage network. The overall design of large director-class switches addresses unplanned downtime through these high-availability features. Additional serviceability features, such as redundant memory for firmware images, and a variety of diagnostics tools to monitor the health and operation of the SAN guarantee the maximum amount of uptime for the overall configuration.

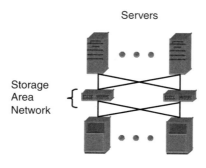

Figure 5–3 Data availability through redundant paths in a simple SAN.

Figure 5–4 shows the deployment of two director-class switches at the core of the storage network. These could be Fibre Channel directors, the more conventional approach to designing SANs. Gigabit Ethernet switches also could be used that support similar features of Fibre Channel directors, but do so using the mature platform of Ethernet and IP. This type of IP core fabric deployment is covered in the offensive strategies section on this chapter.

Similar to the simple diagram in Figure 5–2, redundant directors ensure that any server has access to any storage device regardless of equipment failure within the configuration. Multiple directors can be trunked together using 1-Gbps or 2-Gbps Fibre Channel. Alternatively, higher-speed connections such as new 4-Gbps or 10-Gbps Fibre Channel could be used for greater performance.

The previous examples covered data availability primarily from a local topology. Today's enterprises require availability that spans more than one geographic location. Fortunately, the network storage platform lends itself to such configurations, as outlined in the following sections.

5.2.2 Availability and Protection with Remote SAN Topologies

Today's around-the-clock business environment demands guaranteed data availability and protection that cannot be offered in single-site solutions. The potential for site disruption, natural or unnatural, requires that all organizations maintain remote site configurations of their mission-critical storage and applications. Once in a networked configuration, storage can be easily extended to remote sites. In the case of a pure Fibre Channel network, remote sites can be up to 10Km away with dedicated Fibre Channel connections or up to 100Km with dedicated fiber-optic extensions such as Dense

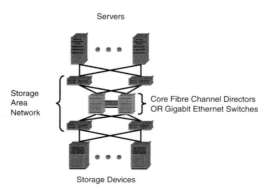

Figure 5–4 High availability through director-class switches and scalable fabrics.

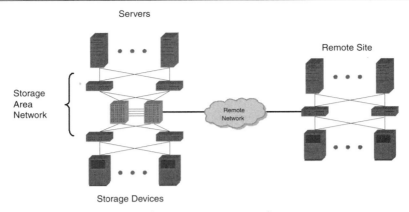

Figure 5–5 Incorporating remote sites to storage networks.

Wave Division Multiplexing (DWDM). With IP networks, SANs can be extended to virtually unlimited distances. Figure 5–5 illustrates a sample remote storage configuration.

Through the use of clustering and storage mirroring software, the remote site serves as a guaranteed backup in the event that the primary site becomes unavailable. Applications can continue to run, and customers can continue to be served, thus avoiding costly downtime. These are the primary drivers for remote storage configurations today, which frequently fall into the disaster recovery category. However, this incomplete picture leads corporations to lose additional SAN value in not fully realizing the power of the networked platform. Recognizing that availability and protection are only first steps to optimized deployment, companies can achieve greater returns on their storage investment and benefit from longer term strategic savings. This chapter covers these options under offensive strategies.

5.2.3 Data Availability and Remote Site Storage User Diagram

Figure 5–6 shows a sample configuration where IP switches are used to create a highly available core, and a remote site is connected directly to that core via an IP network. Centralization on an IP platform allows users to consolidate network technologies across local and remote topologies.

5.2.4 Budget Reduction and Human Capital Protection

Defensive strategies go beyond data risk to address the business risks of dealing with limited budgets and constraints on human capital, specifically trained storage professionals. Almost every IT manager struggles with the "do more with less" mandate permeating corporate landscapes. But not every department has exponential storage growth requirements like the IT

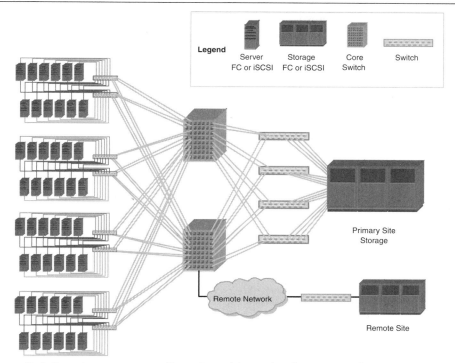

Figure 5–6 Sample customer configuration with a redundant core and remote storage.

group. "Do more with less" combined with exponential workloads lends to precarious corporate competence.

Budget reductions for IT professionals and storage managers present insurmountable obstacles with traditional storage infrastructures such as DAS. For example, with DAS, each storage device must be manually configured to work with each server. Since the storage devices typically are only available on a server-by-server basis, the configuration process can be time-consuming. Storage devices covering different models or different vendors may require specific skill sets beyond those of a single administrator. This leads to a direct relationship between the amount of storage in the overall configuration and the number of storage administrators. In fact, based on average storage growth rates, even keeping budgets at constant levels constitutes a budget reduction.

Figure 5–7 shows how a SAN dramatically reduces the storage management costs associated with DAS. By networking storage devices together and providing centralized storage management, a single administrator has the ability to manage a greater amount of storage from a single console. Further, all of the required storage functions, such as backup, archiving, and consolidation, can be initiated via centralized software functions.

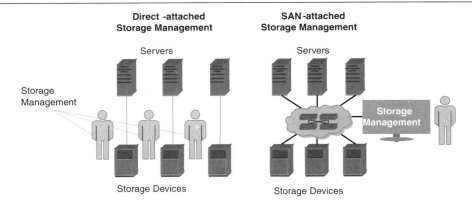

Figure 5–7 Storage networks facilitate storage management savings.

Storage networks help IT professionals grapple with escalating storage capacity and management requirements by minimizing the financial exposure to budget fluctuations. Additionally, the functionality of a storage network and the ability to automate many of the standard software functions helps IT managers and directors deal with staffing issues such as turnover and difficult-to-fill positions. By providing centralized functionality with greater automation, the entire IT department can accomplish more with less. This largely defensive strategy guarantees that user demands are met within the confines of corporate operating restrictions.

5.3 Primary Offensive Strategies

Effective storage strategies ride on the recognition that networked storage goes well beyond a set of required functions. Transitioning from the mindset of "We need this to protect our business" to "We have an opportunity to exploit a competitive advantage within our industry" means that technology deployment and business strategy meet to provide tangible, cost-saving benefits to the bottom line. Adopting an offensive mindset is the first step to realizing these gains.

Recent developments in the rapid progression of storage networking have made competitive advantage openings wider than ever before. Specifically, the merging of traditional network architectures, such as those based primarily on Ethernet and IP, with traditional storage architectures, such as those based on Fibre Channel and SCSI, has created enormous opportunities between requirements, capabilities, and solutions. The ability to connect traditional storage devices with common IP networks creates an entirely new distribution mechanism for storage. The power of that distribution mechanism cannot be underestimated, especially since IP networking represents the single greatest electronic distribution network in the world today. Granting ever-increasing data storage capacity access to that new distribution system fosters entirely new methods of handling data storage and management.

Companies that recognize IP networking as a new distribution mechanism for storage can rapidly transform their infrastructure and business processes to take advantage of it. The equipment exists today to seamlessly migrate from conventional storage architectures to those that embrace IP as a distribution mechanism. The resulting confluence of storage and networking, and the consolidation between the two, serves as the starting point for offensive storage strategies.

5.3.1 Storage Agility through Scalable, Flexible SANs

5.3.1.1 MEETING UNFORESEEN DEMAND SANs provide operational agility for storage through scalable, flexible architectures. Once servers and storage are networked, that network can grow and change with varying business and technical needs. One example of SAN scalability is the rapid expansion of new capacity. In the previous section on budget protection, we discussed defensive approaches to containing storage capacity costs through SANs. In the offensive view, rapid expansion, such as adding near-instant capacity growth to a successful e-commerce application, can be accomplished through a storage network. In a direct-attached approach, where each server has its own captive storage, adding new storage might require adding new server HBAs and new storage devices. Both of these time-consuming processes might require that the server be offline for the reconfiguration period. With a SAN, available capacity from underutilized storage devices could be reassigned as needed. Alternatively, a new storage device could be added to the SAN nondisruptively and quickly assigned to the appropriate server.

The ability to deal with unforeseen business changes mandated by underlying technology shifts makes storage competence and agility an integral part of any IT organization. Not only will networked storage solutions allow for added capacity, as described in the previous example, but they also allow for rapid deployment of applications on new server platforms. Either side of the network (servers or storage) can be tailored to fit the appropriate business needs. This growth and realignment capability ensures that unpredictable business requirements are met.

5.3.1.2 PROVIDING EQUIPMENT CHOICE SANs offer storage flexibility by being able to assign any storage to any server. Many administrators use this flexibility for storage consolidation applications, such as connecting

a variety of disparate servers to uniform, centralized storage or creating pools of heterogeneous storage that can be assigned to individual applications. In either case, the underlying network architecture allows administrators to substitute one storage device for another, providing freedom to choose among equipment providers.

This is not to say that all storage devices are created equal. The internal design of a storage array or tape library can vary dramatically from one vendor to the next. For disk arrays, this might include the type of drives used, the size of the disk cache, or the capacity of an internal switching backplane. These characteristics directly impact the storage speed and reliability, resulting in some devices that can't easily be swapped for another. Yet the storage fabric linking servers to devices provides flexibility to substitute storage devices among each other, especially if they are within the same category of performance and feature characteristics.

This device flexibility provides an offensive approach to vendor management, allowing heterogeneous storage within a single configuration and providing more customer control. If one type of disk array becomes too expensive or can't provide the feature set required, another can be added without having to reconstruct the entire configuration. So, in addition to solving short-term storage consolidation needs that may be defensive in nature, customers build in an offensive approach to long-term vendor management with the installation of a storage network.

5.3.2 Network Centralization

Network centralization is the epicenter of offensive approaches to storage deployment. The ability to utilize the world's largest electronic distribution data network for storage implies that enormous discontinuities in current practices can be realigned accordingly. Specifically, companies that have DAS or Fibre Channel SANs can begin to focus on methods to handle data storage that leverage the global IP network.

In the early part of this decade, the storage networking industry debated the merits of different interconnect technologies, primarily IP and Ethernet as compared to Fibre Channel. While Fibre Channel has proven an effective edge interconnect for storage devices and SANs, it simply cannot compete with IP and Ethernet on a global scale. This discussion was covered in more detail in Chapter 2, "The Storage Architectural Landscape." More important than the technology is the size and scope of the industries at hand. IP and Ethernet have dominated corporate networking for years and served as an effective mechanism for LAN clients to talk to servers and NAS clients to talk to NAS servers. These applications have been well served with IP and

Ethernet, and the networking component has provided more than adequate performance, reliability, security, and flexibility.

With today's technology, customers have the opportunity to add storage networking to the larger network landscape of IP and Ethernet. From a storage perspective, this is likely to begin by linking Fibre Channel SANs across IP networks. Whether they are local, campus, metropolitan, or wide area networks, Fibre Channel SANs can be connected across IP networks to provide greater distance and scalability than pure Fibre Channel scenarios. Since almost every organization has an IP network in place, the extension of Fibre Channel SANs across this existing infrastructure makes business sense compared to deploying additional, separate Fibre Channel storage networking infrastructure for SAN connections.

New IP Storage switches allow storage networks to be built with IP cores, yet still retain compatibility with Fibre Channel devices. These configurations also have a natural extension to IP networks, further enhancing the value of that common technology infrastructure across a variety of networking and storage applications. Finally, the deployment of iSCSI servers and storage devices with native IP connections allows direct access to the IP network and the ability to exploit that rich and expansive resource.

As shown in Figure 5–87, IP networks provide flexibility and operational agility across all types of data networking and storage networking applications. The benefits of this uniformity can be categorized as follows:

- IP network provides flexibility and operational agility across all installations
- Centralization of network technology reduces management and administration cost

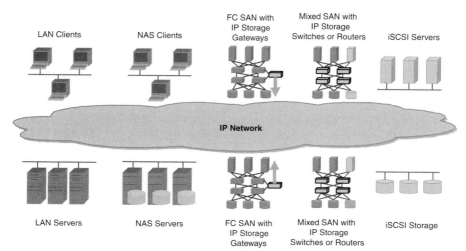

Figure 5–8 IP networking extends across traditional data and new IP storage applications.

Familiar and Ubiquitous IP Networking Technology. IP networks provide low, intangible costs in terms of management, training, and deployment. With years of industry use and the largest installed base in the world, IP networks are more familiar to and easily managed by people than are any other type of network. As such, the tools and training for IP networks are unparalleled in simplicity of use and sophistication, leading to more rapid and cost-effective deployment. The centralization of network technology greatly reduces management and administration cost

Enhanced Functionality. IP networks provide unrestricted topologies that guarantee interoperability across cross-vendor platforms. The industry has delivered advanced routing, management, and security features that power the most demanding of network environments.

Scalability. IP networks provide the utmost in scalability in terms of network size, speed, and distance. Network size is defined as the number of network nodes. Of course, no example comes close to the size of the Internet, the world's largest IP network. Ten Gigabit Ethernet provides the highest speeds available for common networking platforms and is delivered today both as interswitch links and switch backplanes. IP networks reach distances that span the globe, making any geographically point-to-point communication possible.

By adopting the network centralization approach, IT professionals can design architectures that leverage existing staff and technology to dramatically reduce overall cost. This approach embraces the open distribution channels of IP and places storage on the most pervasive networking platform available.

5.3.3 Platform Consolidation

The introduction of IP networking to storage enables consolidation among previously separate architectures of NAS and SANs. Historically, these two storage platforms have operated on completely different networks, with NAS using Ethernet and IP, and SANs primarily using Fibre Channel. As covered in earlier chapters, NAS operates using file-level commands, while SANs use block-level commands. Since both NAS and SAN architectures serve distinct and useful purposes, most companies support both platforms and, in turn, two networking infrastructures.

Stepping back, one can easily see how the build-out, management, and ongoing maintenance of two networks could result in excess equipment purchases and additional overhead for staff, training, maintenance, and support. Without the introduction of block-based IP storage, there was no other choice. To better understand current solutions and the path to platform consolidation, we'll walk through the example beginning with a typical configuration.

In Figure 5–9, the dual fabric of an IP/Ethernet LAN for NAS and a Fibre Channel SAN requires dual management systems, additional hardware, and potentially duplicate staff and training. These two network systems essentially perform the same tasks. Both run point-to-point, full-duplex, switched gigabit traffic, yet they cannot be shared. Additionally, a pure Fibre Channel fabric does not provide a transition path to iSCSI or other IP end systems.

The platform consolidation migration begins by adopting an IP storage fabric, as shown in Figure 5–10. Using IP storage switches or routers, the SAN core transforms to IP and Ethernet while retaining full compatibility with installed Fibre Channel devices, such as Fibre Channel HBAs or storage devices, or with Fibre Channel SANs. This allows existing applications to run without modification, yet prepares for the introduction of iSCSI end systems. These end systems, such as iSCSI HBAs and iSCSI storage devices, now integrate seamlessly into the IP storage fabric, driving more of the end-to-end storage connections to IP.

At this stage in the migration, the customer benefits are numerous. First, a common networking technology platform exists between the LAN and SAN. Even though these two networks might not be fully integrated into a

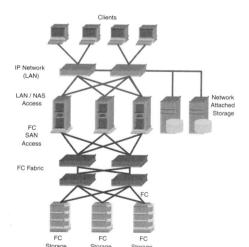

- Dual SAN and LAN / NAS fabrics cost more to install and operate
  - Having IP and Fibre Channel fabrics for storage requires
    - dual management systems
    - extra hardware
    - duplicate staffs and training
- Fibre Channel fabric has no transition path to native IP end systems

Figure 5–9 Conventional Fibre Channel SAN and Ethernet/IP LAN.

single network, they can be managed by common IP-trained staff members and share common IP and Ethernet management software, dramatically reducing overhead costs. Additionally, the introduction of the IP storage fabric provides access to extended metropolitan and wide area networks for a complete range of remote or distributed storage applications.

Carrying the platform consolidation migration through to completion, the Ethernet and IP networks can be combined to form a single, integrated NAS and SAN IP storage fabric. Integrated storage NICs (IS-NICs) running both block-level storage protocols like iSCSI and traditional TCP/IP protocols such as NFS or CIFS make this consolidation possible. Now, using a single fabric, servers have access to SAN and NAS subsystems, either Fibre Channel-based or IP-based. IP storage switches or routers within the fabric assist with iSCSI-to-Fibre Channel conversion when required.

Figure 5–11 demonstrates the complete platform consolidation configuration. Note that the NAS subsystems are now connected directly to the IP storage fabric and can be accessed by servers with IS-NICs or even end-user clients. Similar to the server-based IS-NICs that can access both block-based and file-based systems, the introduction of a consolidated IP storage fabric leaves room for similar storage devices. Hybrid subsystems that can handle both block and file protocols could easily attach to an IP storage fabric and provide a complete range of NAS and SAN services to applications. This greatly alleviates decision turning points for storage administrators considering the benefits of NAS and SAN solutions, eliminating the uncertainty and

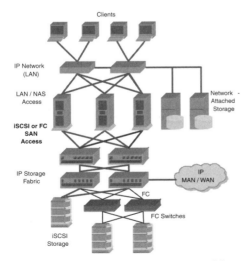

- IP storage fabric complements or replaces FC fabric
  - Functionality identical to that of Fibre Channel switches, but with more flexibility
  - Nonblocking, IP storage fabric provides full support for iSCSI and FC, with wire-speed conversion between the two protocols
- IP storage fabric supports gradual or immediate shift to iSCSI end systems

Figure 5–10 Introduction of IP storage fabric and iSCSI.

providing complete flexibility to tune the configuration to the appropriate platforms.

Server redundancy costs can be cut in half with IS-NICs. Since high-end servers require redundant storage and network adapters, a conventional configuration has two Gigabit Ethernet NICs and two Fibre Channel HBAs. With IS-NICs, full redundancy for LAN messaging and storage traffic can be provided with only two cards. One IS-NIC can run in LAN mode and the other in storage mode. In the event of a failure, a single NIC could cover both functions. Though performance is impacted temporarily during the failure, those costs may be significantly less than providing twice the hardware infrastructure for redundancy.

Many customers wonder about the benefits of NAS compared to SAN and where to invest precious budget allocations. The IP storage fabric coupled with IS-NICs and hybrid subsystems allays those fears through a single investment in IP networks. Let's take an extreme example and say that SANs disappear within 10 years. With an investment in IP storage networking, IP storage fabrics, IS-NICs, and hybrid subsystems, all of that storage equipment could be redeployed to serve NAS-oriented applications. The reverse situation would also hold. In either case, the investment in IP networking infrastructure serves as a flexible, redeployable resource both within an integrated IP storage fabric and within the entire global corporate network. The power of that asset redeployment cannot be underestimated. Companies stand to benefit from extended use of the network assets and the flexibility to redeploy staff as

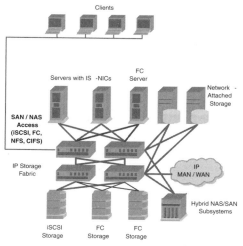

Enhanced Functionality of Integrated SAN and NAS Solution

- Optional use of IP storage fabric for both SAN (block-based) and NAS (filebased)

- IS-NICs provide access for all end systems (SAN, NAS, and LAN clients)

- IP storage switches provide wirespeed, nonblocking IP storage fabric for all IP and Fibre Channel devices

Figure 5–11 Integrated SAN and NAS.

needed to build, operate, and maintain IP networks, whether those networks are used for storage or traditional data applications.

5.3.4 Common IP Network or Common Technology?

Questions are often raised about IP storage networking and sharing storage traffic and data traffic within a common IP network backbone. Some people state that this implementation could lead to congestion bottlenecks. While combining both messaging and storage traffic on a single network is possible, initially a more pragmatic implementation is to segment the IP network infrastructure and move storage and data traffic via different paths. This approach enables customers to protect their investment in IP networking and maximize the efficiencies of moving both types of traffic over a common infrastructure. For example, familiar, standard technologies such as Virtual LANs (VLANs) permit the use of the same network equipment, yet partition the Ethernet network into separate entities.

Common network technology indicates that while deployment may be many physical networks from SAN to LAN to MAN to WAN, the underlying infrastructure is the same, providing benefits such as the use of existing IP networking staff, uniform network management, and common sourcing and maintenance of networking equipment.

Figure 5–12 shows an IP storage fabric in conjunction with a Fibre Channel fabric and an IP network backbone. In this example, the storage fabric

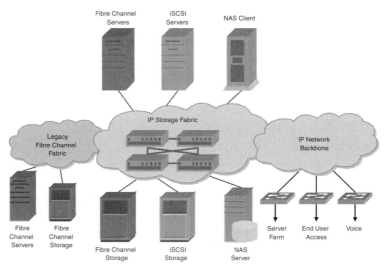

Figure 5–12 Segmenting the IP storage fabric from the IP network backbone.

remains independent from the network backbone that provides server farm, end user, and voice access. This segmentation allows for simplified traffic administration while still retaining the benefits of more IP technology throughout the enterprise.

5.3.5 Multilayered Storage Fabrics

Chapter 2 introduced the concept of a multilayered storage fabric centered on an IP core. Now, incorporating new iSCSI devices and multifunction devices such as NAS/SAN hybrid targets, we expand the model, as shown in Figure 5–13. This highlights the tremendous flexibility of centralizing all storage devices, whether Fibre Channel-, iSCSI-, or NAS-based, on a central IP storage fabric. Storage administrators have a flexible, shared resource that can be partitioned and segmented for each storage platform, yet can also be reallocated as needed. The degree of performance and fine-tuning within the IP core far exceeds the requirements of the average large enterprise customer, leaving ample network capabilities for each platform.

The flexibility of the IP storage fabric shared resource is shown in Figure 5–14. The primary IP storage transports include Fibre Channel devices or SANs connected across an IP fabric, iSCSI devices connected directly to an IP fabric, and multifunction devices, including NAS directly connected to an IP fabric. All three platforms take advantage of robust IP and Ethernet net-

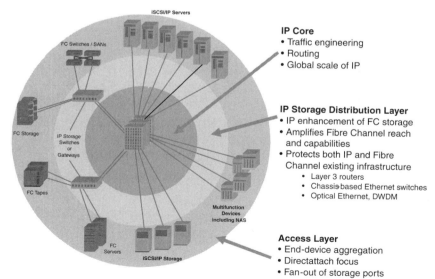

Figure 5–13 Framework for multilayered storage fabrics.

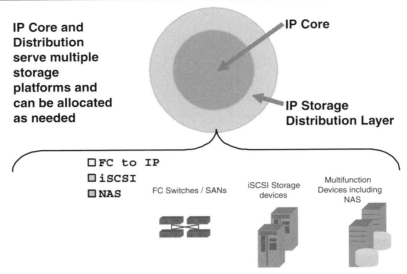

Figure 5–14 Allocating the IP storage fabric among storage platforms.

working features. If one platform emerges as a more economical means to conduct storage operations, administrators can easily reallocate the core network resource as needed to accommodate changes in the underlying storage choices. This flexibility protects significant network spending and ensures platform choice for storage professionals.

5.4 Measuring Returns

Measuring returns on technology investments can be a tricky business. The breadth and depth of large-scale computing projects leaves even the most intricate analysis open for debate. In the preceding sections, we covered both the defensive and offensive approaches to derive value from storage networking investments. Keeping both of these approaches in mind helps to better evaluate and measure the actual returns for individual companies.

This section covers some general guidelines for savings through networked storage, then outlines a couple of useful frameworks to keep both the defensive and offensive approaches at hand for further analysis.

5.4.1 Cost Savings with Storage Area Networks

Calculating returns for technology investments comes down to savings of both operational and capital costs along with incremental revenue from new opportunities. These added-value categories span both defensive and offensive strategies for networked storage. Common customer savings exist through the following:

Lower Costs through Capital Equipment Savings. SANs enable higher disk utilization, extending storage life and postponing new storage purchases. With the flexibility to share storage resources as a pool, administrators can use previously wasted excess capacity on under-utilized devices.

Networked resources allows for backup strategies requiring less hardware. For example, where each server may have previously required its own tape drive for backup, networking resources can share tape libraries reducing the amount of total enterprise equipment required.

External NAS extends server life by providing room for applications to grow. Being able to accommodate larger storage capacities and data sets lengthens the usable life of a server and reduces purchasing cost.

Lower Operating Costs through Storage Management Savings. Since personnel costs comprise such a large portion of the ongoing IT budget, reducing intangible costs such as storage management trims operating costs significantly. With networked storage, centralized management eliminates the need for multiple software packages, facilities easier maintenance, and allows each administrator to manage more data.

Reduced Downtime through Availability and Protection. Section 5.2 covered the primary defensive strategies including clustered configurations for networked storage enabling reduced downtime to keep mission-critical revenue generating applications running around the clock. Additionally, from a data protection standpoint, SANs facilitate a host of backup and recovery options such as onsite or offsite mirroring in the event of a disaster.

Operational Agility through Flexible, Scalable Architectures. Section 5.3 covered the primary offensive strategies, including savings from the rapid capacity expansion model, and the consolidation across multiple vendors, providing more purchasing control and equipment choices to end users.

Use of IP networking technology also adds considerable offensive-focused strategies for operational agility such as the ability to use familiar and ubiquitous IP networks for storage. This prevalent and mature platform has lower intangible costs than traditional Fibre Channel networks, particularly in the areas of management, training, and time to deployment. The IP networking platform delivers enhanced functionality with unrestricted topologies, cross-vendor platforms, and advanced routing, management, and security. Scalability adds to cost savings through the ability to build SANs with large numbers of nodes, high-speed links, and long-distance connections. Most importantly, the investment in an IP fabric is well protected through the options of handling Fibre Channel, iSCSI, or multifunction traffic, including NAS.

5.4.2 Defining Information Technology Goals

The largest returns from IT investments come through correlating cost with business unit priorities. IT managers must keep these priorities in mind when calculating the return on the technology investment (Figure 5–15). The first priority is to defend, support, and expand current business. If the underlying technology isn't supporting existing revenue streams, approximate calculations can determine the amount of lost revenue and justify technology investments.

The second priority, developing new business, can be more difficult to justify, yet it is exactly this skill that can set one company apart from the next. Taking calculated risks on technology investments propels new business that can in turn develop ongoing revenue streams.

Finally, the third priority enhances IT capabilities and expertise. These investments should be made when the economic climate affords the opportunity. Long-term planning helps determine the timing for such investments, as it can take up to a year or more to develop a core set of inhouse skills that will then drive first and second priority investments.

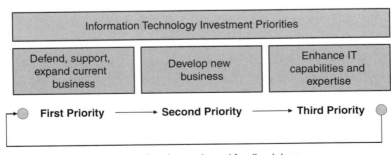

Long term planning cycle and feedback loop
(3d priority can't be ignored, but may have lower spending)

Figure 5–15 Setting information technology business priorities.

5.4.3 Tying Technology Capabilities with Business Processes

Far too often, technical capabilities are developed independent of business process and planning. Because of the ongoing strain on IT organizations, incremental technology investments typically focus on meeting immediate targets for current business functions. This logical step solves short-term needs, but lack of integral communication between the IT department and the business units dooms this relationship to a never-ending catch-up cycle.

Technology and business integration starts from the CEO down. By creating operational *and* strategic links, IT teams accomplish goals of meeting current requirements and designing service offerings that span existing and future needs.

Figure 5–16 outlines a basic framework for new technology offerings across business units. By accomplishing both immediate requirements and longer term strategic needs, the total cost of the technology investment can be amortized across a larger number of business units, generating sizable returns from integrating technical and business functions.

5.4.4 Storage Networking as Competitive Advantage

The intersection of storage and networking represents massive market forces. The data networking market and storage markets each measure in the hundreds of billions of dollars. The surrounding ecosystems add to the end-to-end solutions though applications, service, and diagnostics tools, training efforts, and certifications. This makes the market for networking equipment,

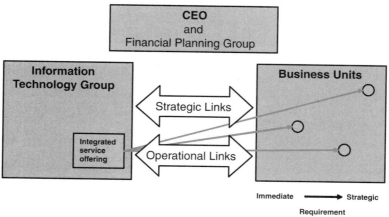

Figure 5–16 Creating strategic and operational links between IT groups and business units.

for example, larger than that of the product shipments alone. Similar market size escalation also exists for storage subsystems.

Regardless of technology merits, pros and cons, personal preferences, or ownership debates, the sheer size of integrating two multihundred billion-dollar markets opens windows of opportunity. Those opportunities come as investments for those tracking public company performance, market direction, and stock price; in terms of new product windows for startups and larger companies filling smaller integration gaps; in terms of cost savings for CFOs looking to negotiate among storage and networking providers; and in terms of competitive advantage windows for IT department to create sustainable advantages.

Companies that operate with mission-critical applications residing on large storage repositories will, by default, need inhouse storage networking expertise. As covered in later chapters, that expertise might be a small team supervising outsourced contracts to an IBM Global Services or EDS-like supplier. Alternatively, that expertise might be a dozen or more talented storage professionals who can construct, operate, and maintain the infrastructure to support business needs. When large market forces collide, those with the greatest inhouse expertise must adopt a strategy to maximize competitive advantage. Today, with the storage and networking markets in the first stage of overlap, those strategies require immediate formulation and deployment.

Figure 5–17 maps technologies to competitive strengths to help companies identify storage competence areas that can be exploited. On the vertical

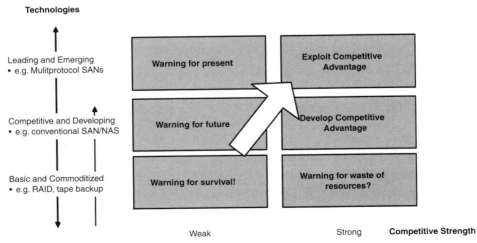

Figure 5–17 Storage technologies and opportunities for competitive advantage.

axis, technologies range from those that are basic and commoditized like RAIDs to leading and emerging technologies such as IP storage networks and mutliprotocol SANs. This simplified chart splits technologies into three categories, but a detailed analysis could include more segments. Competitive strength covers the horizontal axis, ranging from weak to strong, and the technology strategies to exploit competitive advantage fit accordingly.

Companies must place inhouse resources on projects most likely to develop into competitive advantage, while avoiding contributing too much time or effort to commoditized functions. The market windows opening for the storage networking market are wide and will reward those able to seize and exploit advantages of an optimized storage infrastructure.

5.5 Chapter Summary

Reaping Value from Storage Networks

- As an enabling platform, networked storage drives both cost and control of the overall storage infrastructure.

- In industries where storage availability and protection drive revenue-generating businesses, the networked storage budget grows as a function of the overall operating budget.

- To harness these costs, companies must apporach network storage with defensive and offensive approaches.

5.1 Balancing Offensive and Defensive Strategies

- Over the last several years, defensive strategies focused on data availability and protection-dominated storage deployments.

- Even in tight economic times, budgets existed for business continuity and disaster recovery applications.

- These deployments focus only on risk mitigation as opposed to including operational agility.

- Offensive strategies go beyond protection mechanisms to those focused on longer-term strategic storage deployment and TCO.

- Underlying SAN infrastructure enables defensive and offensive approaches.

5.2 Primary Defensive Strategies

■ SANs provide redundancy for higher uptime and availability.

■ SAN switches and directors include high-availability features for fabric resiliency.

■ Core Fibre Channel directors or Gigabit Ethernet switches deliver scalable fabrics.

■ SANs enable remote storage options for added protection and availability.

■ Defensive strategies go beyond data risk to risks of dealing with human capital and trained storage professionals.

■ SANs help reduce storage management costs by accomplishing more with less and reducing the number of administrators.

5.3 Primary Offensive Strategies

■ Offensive strategies look beyond basic functions to exploiting competitive advantages.

■ Merging of storage with networking fosters a new storage distribution mechanism.

■ Offensive thinking harnesses methods to take advantage of the new IP distribution network.

■ SANs provide for rapid addition of new storage capacity to meet unforeseen demand.

■ SANs equalize the storage device playing field, providing more customer control of storage device choices.

■ IP networks have served corporate LAN, MAN, WAN, and NAS applications for years and can now also apply to IP storage networks.

■ Network consolidation on IP centralizes on a common technology resource.

■ IP provides benefits of familiar and ubiquitous technology, enhanced functionality, and scalability in size, speed, and distance.

■ Platform consolidation further supports long-term cost advantages.

- Introduction of an IP storage fabric for Fibre Channel and iSCSI uses common networking components.

- IS-NICs in servers allow for block-based and file-based storage access protocols from single interfaces to an IP storage fabric.

- IP storage networks can be integrated with corporate networks or kept separate via physical or logical segmentation.

- Multilayered storage fabrics provide for all end devices while maximizing use of the IP core.

- With an IP storage fabric, IP cores can be deployed across FC, iSCSI, and NAS platforms.

5.4 Measuring Returns

- Cost savings come from capital and operational expense reductions.

- Added revenue comes from new opportunities enabled by new technology.

- SANs lower capital costs by extending storage life, networking resources to require less hardware, and leaving room for servers to grow.

- SANs lower operational costs through storage management savings, reducing maintenance costs, and allowing administrators to do more with less.

- SANs reduce downtime through defensive strategies such as data availability and protection.

- SANs increase operational agility through flexible, scalable architectures.

- Successful IT groups will tie technology investments to business unit priorities.

- CEO oversight between IT groups and business units assures both strategic and operational links.

- With the hundred billion-dollar storage and networking markets converging, IP storage networking presents opportunities to develop sustainable competitive advantage.

6
Business Continuity for Mission-Critical Applications

Business continuance encompasses several areas of an organization. Some of the factors taken into account when planning for business continuance include risk assessment, location specifics, personnel deployment, network infrastructure, operational procedures, and application/data availability. This chapter's main focus is in the areas related to applications and data availability.

Varying degrees, or levels, of availability can be achieved for applications based on the tools and technologies employed. The levels of availability range from simple disk failure resilience to quick business resumption after a complete data center outage. The tools and technologies range from disk mirroring to sophisticated automated wide area failover clusters. Of course, cost and complexity increase in proportion to increasing levels of availability.

To better understand the levels of availability and the associated array of tools and technologies, we start with the simple case of an application residing on a single server with data on nonredundant DAS and walk through the process of progressively building higher levels of availability for this application.

- Backing up the data on a regular schedule to a tape device provides a fundamental level of availability. In case of data loss due to hardware failure or logical data corruption, the application and data can be made available by restoring from backup tapes.

- Since storage disks have some of the lowest mean time between failures (MTBF) in a computer system, mirroring the boot disk and using RAID storage provides resilience in case of disk failure.

- In the event of a system crash and reboot, using a quick recovery file system speeds up the reboot process, which in turn minimizes the amount of time the application remains unavailable.

- Beyond single-system availability, deploying high-availability and clustering software with redundant server hardware enables automated detection of server failure and provides transparent failover of the application to a second server with minimal disruption to end users.

- RAID storage and high-availability software do not protect applications from logical data corruption. Although data can be restored from backup tapes, the recovery process could be cumbersome and time-consuming. Keeping online point-in-time copies of data ensures a more timely recovery.

- The next level of availability deals with data center outage. This covers the same realm of disaster recovery and disaster tolerance. In the event of a data center outage, replicating data over a WAN to a remote site server ensures application availability in a relatively short time period. This assumes that restoring data from an offsite backup tape is not viable due to the time involved.

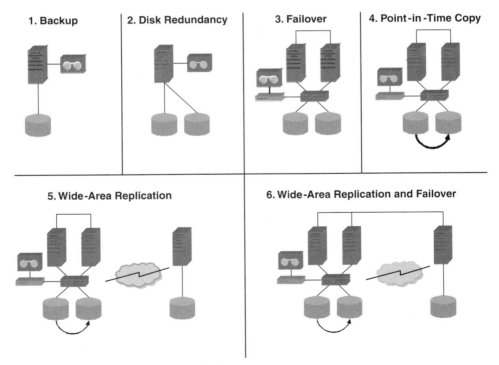

Figure 6–1 Increasing levels of availability requirements.

- Most methods of remote data replication provide a passive secondary standby system. In the event of a primary data center outage, the use of wide-area failover software, which provides failure notification and automated application recovery at the secondary site, ensures a relatively quick and error-free resumption of application service at the secondary site.

These basic levels of availability progress sequentially in Figure 6–1. Fundamentally, providing levels of availability to applications involves managing replicas of data and designing classes of storage for applications and data. Business continuance planning involves identifying key applications; associating metrics with these applications to determine the level of availability required for each application; and implementing tools, technologies, policies, and procedures to attain those levels of availability.

6.1 Assessing Business Continuity Objectives

Anyone even peripherally connected to information technology recognizes that the number of business continuance-level applications has dramatically increased in the last few years. However, the levels of availability required for each application vary dramatically. Assessing each application's availability requirements allows storage and networking administrators to target appropriate solutions.

While assessment of application criticality may be relatively simple for some businesses, in most cases the process can be complex and time-consuming. This is especially true of applications that have evolved over a period of time with nonuniform development processes. Dependency between applications contributes significantly to this complexity. For example, if application A relies on a feed from a database controlled by a separate application B to provide mission-critical information, having complete redundancy for A will be of no use if B is not available. An application itself could physically be running on several servers with their associated storage systems. For example, a client-server ERP application could consist of Web servers, front-end application servers, and a back-end database server. For complex, interdependent application systems, a single individual or group will not likely have complete information to assess the various components' availability needs. In such cases, a cross-departmental internal task force or outsourced third-party business continuance specialist may undertake the assessment project.

Some of the steps to be taken in the assessment process include

■ List all applications.

■ Identify dependencies between applications.

■ Create application groups based on dependencies.

■ Prioritize application groups based on importance.

■ Associate availability metrics for application groups and applications within groups.

Two key metrics that identify the level of availability required for applications and data, especially in a disaster recovery scenario, are recovery time objective (RTO) and recovery point objective (RPO).

6.1.1 Recovery Time Objective

RTO measures the acceptable time for recovery. It poses the question, How long can the application be down?

Cost and downtime implications determine RTO for a given application. There have been several studies on the cost of downtime for specific market segment applications in retail, telecommunications, manufacturing, e-commerce, energy, and financial services. These studies often take into account not just the short-term tangible loss in revenue, but also the intangible long-term effects. While these studies provide useful data, organizations can greatly benefit by performing a thorough assessment customized to their environment.

RTO for an application in turn helps determine the tools and technologies required to deploy the appropriate availability level. For example, if the RTO for a given application is seven days, then restoring from backup tapes may be adequate. If the RTO is a few minutes, wide-area replication and failover may be required in case of a disaster.

6.1.2 Recovery Point Objective

RPO measures the earliest point in time to which the application and data can be recovered. Simply put, how much data can be lost?

The nature of the particular application typically determines the RPO. In case of a major data center outage, it may be acceptable for certain applications to lose up to one week's worth of data. This could be from a human resources application in which data can be reentered from other document sources.

Once again, as in the case of RTO, RPO helps determine the tools and technologies for specific application availability requirements. If, for example, the RPO for our human resources application is indeed determined to be seven days, then restoring from backup tapes may be adequate. However, for a banking application that deals with electronic funds transfer, the RPO is likely to be seconds—if that. In this case, in the event of a data center outage, nothing short of synchronous data replication may suffice.

Sample storage application placements against RTO and RPO are outlined in Figure 6–2.

6.1.3 Factors Affecting the Choice of Solution

Several factors must be considered when determining the criticality and design of business-continuance solutions for specific applications.

- *Appropriate level of availability.* In the absence of tight budget constraints, it still pays to curb the tendency of overengineering a solution. Even if cost is less of a concern, every level of increased availability invariably brings with it another level of increased complexity. Also, solutions designed to provide availability can themselves cause downtime. Consider the example of clustering a database server that really does not require clustering. Bugs in the clustering software and the associated patches could cause an application outage.

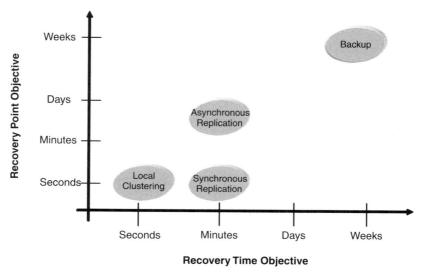

Figure 6–2 Sample storage application placements against RPO and RTO.

■ *Total cost of ownership (TCO)*. Obviously, the TCO of the business-continuance solution should not exceed the potential losses incurred from not having one. Hence, it is important to take into account tangible and intangible costs of the business continuance solution.

■ *Complexity*. When faced with multiple solutions, the least complex usually becomes the most desirable. This is especially true for disaster recovery, since in case of a disaster, personnel with expertise may not have access to systems and applications at the remote site. As such, the simpler solution has a better chance of success.

■ *Vendor viability in the long run*. Viability of the vendor over the long haul should be considered when deploying business continuance solutions. This factor becomes more critical for disaster recovery solutions in which a true test of the solution may not come until a disaster occurs and which might require assistance from the vendor.

■ *Performance impact*. Impact on performance of the application should be evaluated when deploying a business-continuity solution. While it is true that certain solutions can cause degraded application performance, other solutions can potentially enhance performance. Consider, for example, a database in which data is being replicated from a primary server to a secondary server. In several cases, replication will have a negative impact on application performance. Now let us assume that this database is being used for both online transaction processing (OLTP) and reporting. Migrating the reporting function to the secondary server could positively impact overall system performance.

■ *Security*. Deploying technologies to address availability concerns potentially introduces security issues where none existed before. For example, if a business-continuance solution requires that sensitive data for an application be replicated over a WAN, measures have to be taken to provide network security using encryption or other technologies.

■ *Scalability*. Given the realities of explosive data growth, any business continuance-solution considered must scale. Consider, for example, a database being replicated to a remote disaster recovery site using a storage array-based replication technology. Most array-based replication technologies guarantee data consistency on the remote site, as long as all the data being replicated resides within a single array on the primary side. While the database remains within the storage limits of the array, this may be the most optimal recovery solution for that particular database application. However, if data growth causes the database on the primary side to grow beyond the bounds of a single storage array, the solution stops working.

6.2 Availability within the Data Center

In the beginning of this chapter, we touched briefly on various availability levels, ranging from simple backup and recovery to automated wide-area failover. These levels can be split into two categories. The first category outlined in this section addresses business continuity for applications and data within a data center. The second category, discussed in Section 6.3, addresses business continuity across geographically separate data centers.

6.2.1 Backup and Restore

Regularly scheduled data backup ensures a fundamental level of availability for applications. Backups can be used to retrieve an individual file or to rebuild entire servers and restore all the associated data. However, in most cases, restoring data from backups entails a certain amount of data loss. The amount of data lost depends on when the last successful backup was performed and the amount of data change since that backup. The time to restore depends on several factors, including, but not limited to, the amount of data to be restored, the data-backup policies employed, and the backup storage technology and methods used.

Two basic backup types—full and incremental—determine how much data is backed up for a given operation. During a full backup, the entire data set is backed up, whereas an incremental backup stores only data that has changed since the last backup. Full backups obviously involve more time and media than incremental backups. However, restores, especially in the case of an entire system, will be faster with more frequent full backups. Backup policies, driven by availability requirements, dictate the schedules and the types of backup to be performed. Beyond the availability needs, some backup policies may also be determined based on legal requirements. For example, the legal department of a given company may determine that year-end financial data needs to be available for 10 years. This requirement, in turn, could translate to a backup policy that dictates full backups at the end of every year to be retained for a minimum of 10 years.

Despite the emergence of several new data storage and retrieval technologies like CD-RW and DVD, tape still dominates as a backup storage medium. Tape drive speeds and tape storage capacities continue to increase. Tape-based technologies like Super DLT from Quantum; AIT-3 from Sony; and LTO from Hewlett-Packard, IBM, and Seagate enable between 100 to 110 GB of uncompressed data to be stored on a single tape while providing uncompressed transfer rates between 11 MBps and 15 MBps. A fair amount of business-critical data resides in databases, which in general yield good compression ratios. In these cases, it is not uncommon to see the tape storage capacity and drive transfer rates doubled. The increased tape-drive speeds raise backup performance, which puts more load on the IP and primary disk storage networks and also place increased loads on the processing resources of application and data servers. These factors, coupled with shrinking backup windows, have driven backup vendors to develop new backup methods.

In the traditional backup method, data residing on an application host is backed up *through* that host. The host reads data from the attached storage into its memory. It then writes the data out to a locally attached tape drive or to another backup host over a network, which in turn writes it to an attached tape drive. In either case, the application host has to perform the reads and writes required for backup. Other methods of backup have been developed to offload the burden of backup processing from the application host.

One such method, which has been around for a few years, starts with a mirrored copy of the data on the storage system. At the scheduled time for backup, the application is placed in backup mode, all outstanding writes in memory are flushed to disk, and a copy of the mirrored storage is detached. The application is then taken out of backup mode. The detached piece of the mirror represents a consistent point-in-time copy of the data. This mirror copy is mounted and backed up to a separate backup server. Once the backup is complete, the mirror copy is unmounted from the backup server, reattached, and resynchronized with its original copy on the application server. Placing the application in backup mode involves different operations for different applications. In some cases it is done by issuing application commands, while in other cases it could mean shutting down the application. The operation of detaching the mirror copy typically takes a very short amount of time.

Examples of traditional backup, including mirroring examples, are shown in Figure 6–3.

The recent proliferation of SANs has led to the development of server-free backup technology. Using this method, backup data is moved from the

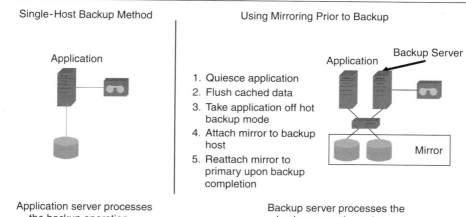

Figure 6–3 Single-host backup method and using mirroring prior to backup.

application host's disk storage to a target tape device over the SAN. This data transfer does not have to go through the application host. At the time of backup, the application is placed in backup mode, and all outstanding writes are flushed to disk. Then, a point-in-time frozen-image copy of the data is made. Frozen images can be accomplished with storage array-based mirror copies, volume management–based mirror copies, or file system-based snapshots. Once a frozen-image copy is complete, the application leaves backup mode and then resumes normal operation. The next step performs a logical-to-physical mapping of the data on disk. Based on this map, a hardware device that can execute extended SCSI copy commands transfers the data to the target tape device. These hardware devices, sometimes referred to as third-party copy devices, include SCSI-to-FC bridges and tape libraries from various vendors.

Regardless of the methods, media, and device technologies used, backup lays the foundation for the business continuance of applications.

6.2.2 Disk Redundancy: RAID

While backups provide an offline method for ensuring a fundamental level of availability, disk redundancy ensures a basic level of online availability. Redundant Array of Inexpensive Disks (RAID) concepts are typically used to achieve disk redundancy. The famous Berkeley paper entitled "A Case for Redundant Arrays of Inexpensive Disks," written by Patterson, Gibson, and Katz in 1987, proposed various levels of RAID for achieving tolerance to disk failures. Although several levels of RAID have been proposed beyond the levels 1 through 5 discussed in the original paper, the most common implementations include levels 0, 1, 3, 5, 0+1, and 1+0. Level 0, where data is striped across a number of disks, does not address redundancy but provides superior performance. Under RAID level 1, data on a particular disk is simply *mirrored* to one or more disks. In other words, the same data is written to multiple disks in parallel. If a disk becomes unavailable, data can be read from and written to the surviving mirrored disks. RAID levels 3 and 5 stripe data across a set of disks and also store parity information that can be used to rebuild data in case of a single disk failure in that set. Levels 3 and 5, however, cannot provide resiliency if more than one disk in a given set becomes unavailable. In terms of performance, write performance of RAID 1 is limited to the speed of the slowest mirrored disk. In most cases, disks with similar performance are used for mirroring, and hence RAID 1 does not typically impose any performance penalties. The parity calculation and, more importantly, the read-modify-write cycle involved with RAID levels 3 and 5 impose performance penalties for writes. However, since data is also striped in these levels, read performance will be better than that of a single disk.

RAID levels 0+1 and 1+0 combine striping and mirroring to achieve levels of redundancy higher than provided by RAID 1, while also benefiting from the performance gains provided by striping. Under RAID 0+1, multiple disks are striped together to form a stripe set, and data is mirrored among two or more stripe sets. If a single disk in a stripe set fails, the entire stripe becomes unavailable. In the case of a RAID 0+1 configuration with two stripe sets A and B, failure of a single disk in stripe set A makes the entire stripe set unavailable, leaving stripe set B unprotected. A consequent disk failure in stripe set B would result in complete loss of access to all the associated data. In RAID 1+0, sets of two or more disks are mirrored to form mirror sets. These mirrored sets are then striped together. As long as each mirror set has at least a single disk available, multiple disk outages will not result in loss of access to the associated data. Hence, RAID 1+0 is considered to be more resilient than RAID 0+1. These distinctions are outlined in Figure 6–4.

RAID is implemented either in storage array hardware using RAID controllers or through host-based volume management software. RAID controllers usually include NVRAM caches in addition to hardware required to implement the RAID logic, while host-based volume managers use host CPU and memory resources. From a performance perspective, RAID levels 3 and 5 implemented in array hardware are generally faster for write operations than is the software implementation. RAID levels 0, 1, 0+1, and 1+0 also benefit from the NVRAM write and read cache provided by arrays. Since we

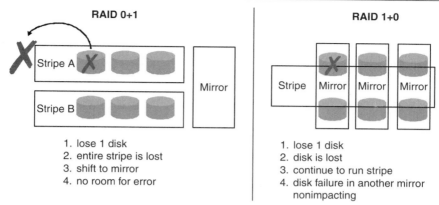

Figure 6–4 Comparing RAID 0+1 and 1+0.

focus on business continuance in this chapter, we examine the availability implications of hardware and software RAID.

Hardware RAID arrays available in various configurations fit a wide range of target markets. While the high-end arrays design out single points of failure, the low-end arrays could be designed with nonredundant components, such as a mirrored NVRAM write cache, or with single power connectors. Most of the high-end array vendors also offer "phone-home" support to proactively monitor and replace failed or failing components before a consequent failure causes a storage disruption.

For applications where the cost associated with high-end RAID arrays cannot be justified, host-based volume managers, using relatively inexpensive low-end arrays or even JBODs (just a bunch of disks), can fulfill availability requirements. Even though high-end arrays include fully redundant components, certain system architectures require that for a given host, data be mirrored for additional redundancy or striped for performance across two high-end arrays. In order to accommodate such architectures, host-based volume managers operate on top of the arrays. Even in cases where a single, fully redundant, high-end array will suffice, a host-based volume manager is also commonly deployed. Reasons for this include administration of logical volumes and volume groups instead of disparate devices with cryptic device names, and migration of data from a given storage array to another for upgrade or other purposes. A more important reason from an availability standpoint is that certain volume managers enable nondisruptive growth of file systems containing application data. Volume managers accomplish this by increasing the size of underlying volumes online using available LUNs provided by the storage array.

Just as backup provides fundamental offline availability, disk redundancy, achieved by deploying RAID storage implemented in hardware, software, or both, provides basic online availability.

6.2.3 Quick Recovery File Systems

A majority of business-critical applications today run on multiple-CPU servers. In the event of CPU failure, most operating systems crash the server and reboot around the failed CPU. In other words, the reboot process fences off the failed CPU. Obviously, during the reboot process, the application running on this server is unavailable. A portion of the reboot process involves checking the file system for consistency. Hence, the time interval for which the application remains unavailable directly depends on the amount of time taken to complete checking all the necessary file systems.

Certain file systems, such as the traditional UNIX file system (UFS), have to perform a complete file system structure check and fix any discovered inconsistencies to recover from a file system failure. For applications with large amounts of data, this could take a significant amount of time. Several file systems available today address this issue by providing *journaled* or *logging* file systems. These file systems record structural changes to the file system in a log or journal. During recovery, the file system consistency-check utility does not have to scan the entire file system, but instead scans only the log and invalidates or completes file system transactions that were active at the time of file system failure. This feature greatly reduces the amount of time required for an application to recover from a system crash and reboot. Bear in mind that even with journaled file systems, certain crash situations could still require a full file system check. Another related feature, available in some products, is the ability to perform checks for multiple file systems in parallel. Applications with a large number of file systems benefit from this time-saving feature. Journaled file systems, preferably with a parallel file system check feature, reduce application downtime by enabling quick recovery after a crash.

6.2.4 Point-in-Time Copies

Logical data corruption, especially in the case of databases, is one of the more common causes of application downtime. Corruption results from application data being lost or altered by sources other than the application, without the application's knowledge. Some causes for data corruption include faulty hardware, bugs in software, and sometimes user or administrator error. Disk mirroring does not help in this scenario, since logical corruption typically is propagated to all the mirror copies. One way to recover applications from logical data corruption is to restore data from backup tapes. However, this can be a time-intensive method, depending on the amount of data that needs to be restored and the available hardware. In most cases the entire application may have to be taken offline during the restore process.

For database administrators, data corruption resulting from partial data block writes, out-of-order transaction commits, accidentally deleted rows, and dropped tables cause major concern. Maintaining a standby database on a separate database server, periodically refreshed by applying transaction logs shipped from the primary database, helps database administrators recover quickly from logical corruption. The standby database represents a point-in-time copy of the primary database. If logical corruption occurs on the primary and is detected in the period between log updates to the standby database, the standby database is quickly promoted to assume the primary role. This dramatically reduces database downtime. Apart from serving recovery purposes, standby databases offload backup and reporting functions from the primary.

Several file systems on the market today provide a snapshot feature allowing an administrator to maintain point-in-time copies. A snapshot represents a frozen image of the file system at a particular point in time. Applications can recover from logical data corruption in a relatively quick manner by restoring data from earlier snapshots or even rolling back all the changes made to a file system since the last consistent snapshot. Most file system snapshot implementations use a copy-on-write mechanism, which does not require twice the allocation of storage space per snapshot. This technique keeps copies of changed file system blocks only since the snapshot was taken. However, maintaining copies of updated and deleted blocks does introduce additional I/O overhead for write operations on the system. It is also possible to keep multiple snapshots for a given file system. The amount of additional storage space required depends on the amount of data change in the file system since the earliest snapshot. Figure 6–5 shows a sample snapshot method.

Yet another method of recovering from logical data corruption is made possible by disk mirrors. Disk mirroring enables point-in-time copies of data at the logical data volume and disk device level. Most high-end storage arrays and certain volume management products provide tools that enable detaching a copy from the mirror set. This copy represents a point-in-time image of block data on storage devices. Unlike file system snapshots, a naïve implementation of disk mirrors can require twice the amount of storage for

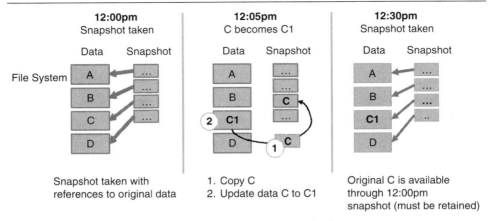

Figure 6–5 An example point-in-time snapshot copy method.

each mirror copy. Hence, in most cases, it is impractical from a cost perspective to keep more than two copies. Since data updates to the primary mirror are not reflected in the detached copies, they have to be periodically synchronized to keep the point-in-time images from lagging too far behind the primary. Data corruption occurring and detected during the synchronization process corrupts all copies being synchronized. Synchronizing two copies with the primary mirror at separate times provides protection against this possibility. Recovery from data corruption involves shutting down the application, unmounting file systems from the corrupt device set, mounting file systems on point-in-time mirror copies, and restarting the applications. The mounting and unmounting of file systems is skipped for certain applications, such as databases, running on raw volumes or devices. In a SAN and in other shared storage environments, the mirror copies can be dissociated from the primary application host and made available to a secondary host for backups and other off-host processing functions.

Point-in-time data images provided through database copies, file system snapshots, volume manager mirror copies, and disk device mirror copies enable quick application recovery from logical data corruption.

6.2.5 High Availability and Clustering

Application and data unavailability resulting from host failure can be addressed with database servers (in case of database host failure) and point-in-time mirror copies attached to secondary hosts. However, detecting server failure, activating secondary systems, and pointing users or applications to these secondary hosts requires manual intervention. In most cases these tasks can be performed by a few skilled individuals who may not be accessible at all times. High-availability and clustering solutions automate the detection of application service disruption due to host-related failures and their resumption on a designated secondary host. This failover process occurs transparently to the end user. Neither clustering nor high availability provide protection from logical data corruption.

Very often, the term clustering is used when referring to high-availability solutions. However, an important distinction between the two exists, especially from an applications and data perspective. High-performance clusters are used by applications that run on many independent servers with little or no sharing of data. In storage, clustering implies that instances of an application running on multiple hosts have simultaneous read and write access to the same data set. If a host fails, users or other applications connected to that host switch to a different cluster host, and application service resumes. Oracle Parallel Sever and its successor Real Application Clusters (RAC) are examples of clustered databases. With high availability, only one instance of an application accesses the data at any given time. When a host fails, another designated host takes control of the data resources and performs the necessary volume, file system, and application startup functions. As a result, a noticeable amount of time can elapse when the application service will be unavailable. Application downtime depends, to a large extent, on the amount of time required for application recovery. Applications such as Network File System (NFS) can be failed over in a relatively short period of time with minimal or no disruption to end users. However, recovery times of over 15 minutes are not uncommon for fairly active OLTP databases. Clustering solutions generally provide faster failover than do their high-availability counterparts, but they are usually more complex to implement and administer. Figure 6–6 shows examples of clustering and high-availability solutions.

Both high-availability and clustering solutions share similar hardware configuration requirements. Both have no single point of hardware failure. A typical hardware configuration for a given application consists of two host machines, mirrored data storage accessible to both hosts, a minimum of two redundant private heartbeat networks to monitor the health of application and hardware components, and at least one public network interface for user access per host. In the case of clustering, both hosts generally have active instances of an application, while under a high-availability scenario, the application could be active on one host while the other host "stands by," monitoring the active host and ready to take over in case of a failure. In an "active-active" high-availability configuration, individual hosts run different

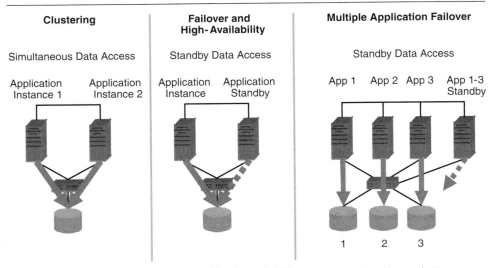

Figure 6–6 Examples of clustering and high-availability storage networking solutions.

applications and each host acts as a failover machine for the other's application. If a host fails, its application and data are taken over and services are resumed on the surviving host, and the application already running on that host continues without interruption. Hence, when implementing an active-active high-availability solution, adequate resources should be allocated on each machine to handle the additional load, or the expectation of degraded performance in case of a failover should be set.

Clustering and failover mechanisms can also be used for offensive storage strategies, such as scheduling hardware and software upgrades. During regularly scheduled maintenance, high-availability configurations and software facilitate simpler upgrades. While one host is acting as a standby, the other undergoes the upgrade, and vice versa.

SANs make it possible for multiple host systems and pools of storage to be interconnected. It is thus possible for a host to have access to the storage being used by other hosts in the SAN. In this environment, economies of scale can be leveraged when implementing high-availability solutions for multiple application hosts. A single, appropriately configured host could act as a standby machine for multiple application hosts, thus avoiding the need for a dedicated standby machine for each application host. Of course, the implicit assumptions are that not more than one host will fail at any given time, and if more than one host does fail, the standby host has adequate resources to handle the load.

Clustering and high-availability solutions reduce application downtime by providing automated and transparent application service resumption in the event of an outage of the underlying host machine. These solutions also enable offensive strategies such as reducing the cost of maintenance and upgrades.

6.3 Availability Across Geographies: Disaster Tolerance and Recovery

The location of a secondary data center merits concern when planning for business continuance in the event of a data center outage. To minimize the possibility of simultaneous outages of the primary and secondary data centers, location choices include factors such as not sharing a single power grid and not being in the same earthquake zone. This usually leads to primary and secondary data centers in geographic locations separated by hundreds, if not thousands, of miles. Solutions discussed in the previous sections—disk redundancy through RAID, clustering, and high availability—have inherent distance limitations and may not be suitable for business continuance of most applications across geographies. Latencies imposed by distance and bandwidth considerations play a major role in the choice of disaster tolerance and disaster recovery solutions, some of which are discussed in this section.

6.3.1 Offsite Media Vaulting and Recovery

Not only do backups provide a fundamental level of availability within the data center, they are also the last line of defense in case of a disaster. A vast majority of disaster recovery implementations for business applications today solely rely on recovery from media backups. Backup media designated for disaster recovery are usually stored in an offsite location that does not share risk factors with the primary data center location. Often, third-party vendors in offsite media storage contract for this purpose. Services include backup media pickup from the data center, storage of media in temperature- and humidity-controlled vaults, media inventory management, and return delivery of expired backup media. See Figure 6–7.

The offsite vaulting process starts with the formulation of backup and offsite retention policies. A sample backup policy could require full backups once a week and incremental backups once a day. In addition, the policy could require full backups on month-ends and year-end. The offsite retention policy could be retention of the daily incremental backups for two weeks, the weekly full backups for two months, the month-end backups for two years,

Offsite Vaulting

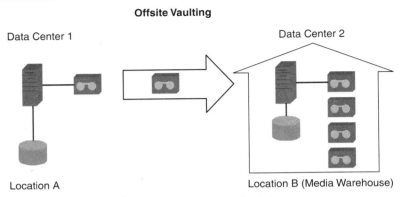

Figure 6–7 Offsite vaulting delivers geographic disaster tolerance.

and the year-end backups for 10 years. The backup and offsite retention policies should be based on the recovery point and recovery time objectives.

In addition to storing backup media offsite, keeping extra copies of backup media in the data center avoids time and management overhead to recall media for simple day-to-day data restore events. This requires creating duplicate copies before shipping out the backup media to an offsite vault. Duplicate media copies can be created in parallel during the backup process using parallel backup streams, or they can be created at a later time from the primary backup set. The choice often depends on factors such as available backup hardware and duplication features provided by the backup software. Creating backup copies in parallel allows the media to be sent offsite upon backup completion. Running a duplication process after the first set of backups delays sending the media offsite. If a disaster were to occur during this process, causing both sets of copies to be destroyed, the most recent backup media available for recovery could be at least a day older.

Before sending the backup media offsite, pick lists containing information on the media, contents, vault site slot locations, retention periods, and recall dates must be recorded. This information is usually shared between the data center customer and the offsite vault vendor. The process of duplicating media, ejecting the appropriate media from libraries, and creating pick lists can be automated either through the vaulting features available in certain backup software or through customized scripts, reducing the possibility of human error. Simple mistakes like ejecting the wrong media or setting incorrect retention can cause the disaster recovery efforts to fail.

To ensure successful recovery in the event of a data center outage, detailed recovery procedures must be documented and the procedures periodically and comprehensively tested at secondary sites. In addition to fine-tuning and debugging the recovery procedures and validating the integrity of backups, frequent recovery tests also enable the responsible recovery personnel to attain a level of comfort and a degree of familiarity with the necessary steps for successful execution when it really matters.

Depending on the amount of data to be restored, complete system recovery from backup media at a secondary site could take considerable time, and a large portion of data may need reentering or regenerating. In general, applications with RPOs and RTOs of a few days can employ offsite media vaulting and recovery as the primary means of business continuance. Even though applications with more stringent RPOs and RTOs have to look to other continuity methods, offsite vaulting provides added insurance.

6.3.2 Remote Mirroring and Failover

In campus environments, buildings just a few kilometers away are often chosen as secondary disaster recovery data center sites. In most cases, these are chosen to supplement another disaster recovery site much farther away or as an initial phase in the implementation of a strategy that ultimately involves a site at a greater distance. The proximity of a secondary campus site makes issues of bandwidth and latency relatively insignificant and enables easy access to the primary data center personnel for maintenance and recovery. The proximity also makes it possible to explore the use of availability technologies used within a data center for cross-campus availability.

Disk mirroring and failover technologies, discussed earlier for application availability inside a data center, generally require the host machine to be connected to the data storage devices through parallel SCSI cables or through a Fibre Channel-based network. Both interconnects impose distance limitations—a few meters in the case of parallel SCSI and a few kilometers for Fibre Channel. Hence, Fibre Channel is better suited than SCSI for cross-campus availability. Providing disk redundancy between campus buildings typically involves a host machine at the primary data center connected to two storage arrays via Fibre Channel—one in the primary data center building and the other in the secondary building. Volume management software on the host mirrors the two arrays. Adding a host at the secondary site, connecting it to the two arrays, and adding redundant heartbeat links provides key components for implementing automated failover between buildings using high-availability software.

Fibre Channel extenders and other devices based on FCIP, iFCP, and iSCSI technologies make it possible for a host at the primary data center to be connected to storage at a secondary data center located hundreds or even thousands of kilometers away. Extending disk mirroring, high-availability, and clustering solutions beyond the campus environment using these devices is impacted by latency, but often less than expected, as outlined in Chapter 10, "Long-Distance Storage networking Applications." For certain applications using mostly read-only and performing fewer write operations, these solutions are worth exploring. The latency issues can be addressed by volume managers with a preferred mirror read feature that enables all reads to be performed using the mirror at the primary site while still completing writes at both sites. Remote mirroring and failover solutions, when used in a campus environment, provide application and data availability if the primary data center building suffers an outage.

6.3.3 Data Replication

As discussed earlier, most disaster recovery implementations require the separation of primary and secondary data centers at reasonably large distances. In addition, most business-critical applications perform a significant number of write operations. As a result, solutions using local mirroring and failover techniques across remote distances require exploration. Technologies based on replicating data between hosts over WANs, which provide various methods of addressing latency and bandwidth issues, are generally better suited for disaster tolerance and availability of business applications.

6.3.3.1 MODES OF REPLICATION   Data replication can be categorized into three modes: synchronous, asynchronous, and periodic. In all three modes, the application's read operations operate on the primary storage. While write operations have to be written at both the primary and secondary sites for all three modes, they differ in terms of when and how the write operations are performed.

A write operation, in synchronous replication, is performed on the primary storage and simultaneously sent over a WAN to the secondary site. A successful write operation completes when both the primary and secondary storage acknowledge successful commits. As a result, the secondary site data always remains up to date with the data at the primary site. Activating the secondary site in the event of a primary site outage ensures that no data has been lost. However, the round-trip latency involved in committing the write at the secondary site can potentially impact application performance. Also, a network outage or hardware failure on the secondary site can cause write operations for the application at the primary site to be suspended when replicating in a synchronous mode.

Writes, under asynchronous replication, operate on primary storage and are also queued at the primary site for transmission. Once these operations are complete, the application receives acknowledgment of a successful write. Depending on the available bandwidth, outstanding writes are then sent asynchronously to the secondary site. This eliminates the performance impact due to round-trip network latency. Also, a temporary network outage or hardware failure at the secondary site does not impact application writes at the primary site. Most applications stagger write activity. In other words, the write activity has peaks and valleys, without a steady stream of data blocks at a uniform rate. For example, an ERP application can write several megabytes per second during year-end processing, whereas it may write only a few kilobytes per second during nonpeak hours. With asynchronous replication, depending on the activity levels and available network bandwidth, both sites can be up to date or the primary site could have a number of outstanding writes not yet committed at the secondary site. As a result, in the event of a primary data center outage, activating the secondary site could result in lost data. The basic principles of asynchronous replication are shown in Figure 6–8.

In periodic replication, data at the secondary site is updated at periodic intervals using data from the primary site. Just as in the case of asynchronous replication, application writes complete after acknowledgment from primary storage. Assuming local connection to the primary storage, no network round-trip latency is introduced. Periodic replication has the same exposure

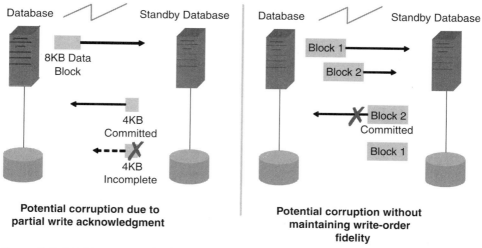

Figure 6–8 Intelligence required to avoid corruption during asynchronous replication.

as asynchronous replication in terms of data loss at the secondary site. The main difference between the two modes lies in the usage of network bandwidth. The asynchronous mode attempts to replicate data continuously, using the available network bandwidth, while periodic mode starts the data replication at defined intervals. Asynchronous mode generally provides better data currency at the secondary site when compared to periodic replication.

In order to ensure data integrity at the secondary site, especially for databases, logical application writes should be committed in their entirety, and write-order fidelity must be maintained within the application data set. Committing partial application data blocks or committing data blocks out of order in an application data set can result in data corruption. This rarely occurs in synchronous replication, since most implementations ensure primary and secondary site write completion before successful acknowledgment. However, implementations of asynchronous and periodic modes vary. Some implementations faithfully queue and replicate every logical write in its entirety and also maintain write ordering at the secondary, while other implementations may not be able to guarantee these attributes. Products in the latter category typically provide ways to periodically create and maintain consistent point-in-time copies of the data at the secondary. In the event of a primary site outage, recovery at the secondary site uses these point-in-time copies. Implementations that preserve write sizes and ordering at the secondary tend to provide better RPOs, since the more current replicated data set can be used for recovery instead of relying on an older point-in-time copy.

The data consistency chart in Figure 6–9 helps put the replication modes in perspective.

6.3.3.2 METHODS OF REPLICATION   A significant number of business applications reside on databases. Data writes for such applications generally pass through various layers before being physically written to a storage device. Some of the typical layers are shown in the "stack" in Figure 6–10.

As data can be replicated at any layer in the stack, we explore each of these possibilities in more detail.

- *Application Layer.* Application layer replication is accomplished by coding applications that perform writes to separate databases at the primary and secondary sites. For several applications this may not be feasible due to complexity. Although all of the application data writes initiated can be replicated using this method, it does not account for several other components, such as changes to the application or database

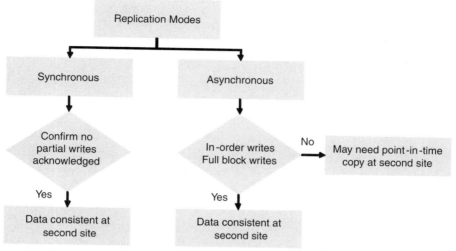

Figure 6–9 Data consistency chart.

binaries, parameter files, and structural database changes. Other methods of replication need to be considered for a complete solution. In addition, every application needs its own set of code to accomplish application-layer replication, even with the same underlying database product across all applications.

	Replication Layer Stack	Sample Application	Pros	Cons
Host	Application	Custom applications	Data integrity easily maintained at second site	Application-specific
	Database	Oracle Dataguard, Sybase replication, Quest Shareplex	Database administrator friendly	Does not replicate binaries or application components
	File System	NetApp SnapMirror, VERITAS Storage Replicator, NSI Doubletake	Active-active mode accessible during replication (non database)	Not available for raw-access database applications
	Logical Volumes	VERITAS Volume Replicator, Sun SNDR	Replicates all elements	Host support limitations
Storage Array	LUNs	EMC SRDF, HDS TrueCopy, XIOtech REDI SAN Links	Replicates all elements Multihost support	Storage device compatibility issues; may not operate across more than two arrays

Figure 6–10 Stack layers for various replication technologies.

■ *Database Layer.* Numerous products from database vendors and other third-party vendors address database-layer replication. Apart from integrated replication engines provided by the database vendors, more popular approaches involve using database transaction logs where database change information resides. Some log-based methods physically copy the transaction logs at periodic intervals from the primary database to a secondary, remote, standby database. Applying these transaction logs at the secondary site to the standby database makes it more current. Other methods send Data Manipulation Language (DML) commands, most likely SQL, derived from transaction logs, from the primary database to an active secondary-site database. These DML commands re-create the original database transactions in the secondary database. Regardless of the products and methods employed, replication at the database layer does not address replication of components potentially required for complete recovery, such as changes to application and database binaries, and other non-database-related data. See Figure 6–11.

■ *File System Layer.* Several factors must be considered before deploying file system-based replication. For performance reasons, databases or certain components of databases may be configured to bypass the file system and run on "raw" volumes. Obviously, replication at the file system layer will not be an option in such instances. When running on file systems, database files typically spread across multiple file systems. In order to ensure data consistency at the secondary site, especially in

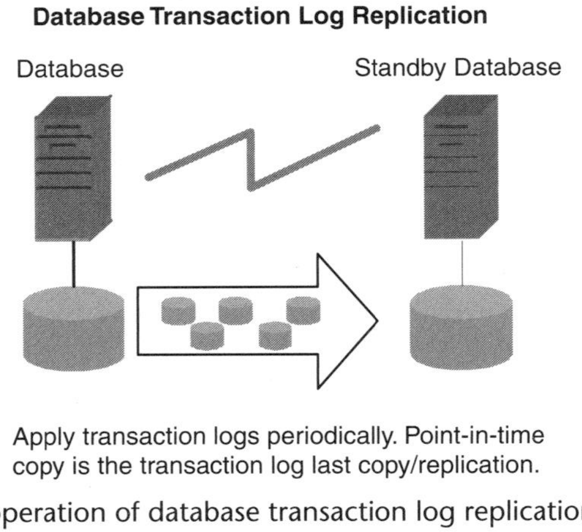

Apply transaction logs periodically. Point-in-time
copy is the transaction log last copy/replication.

Figure 6–11 Sample operation of database transaction log replication.

asynchronous mode, write ordering must be maintained not only within individual file systems, but also among file systems. This requires logical file system grouping within which to maintain write ordering. While replication products layered on top of file systems may enable this, most file systems have no such constructs. Hence, some replication solutions at the file system layer require containing the entire database to a single file system. Other solutions involve quiescing the database periodically for consistent point-in-time images. Replicating and maintaining these images at the secondary site serves recovery purposes.

■ *Logical Volume Manager Layer.* Host-based volume managers generally provide constructs for the grouping of logical volumes. Databases, whether running on file systems or on raw volumes, can be, and often are, configured within a logical volume group. This enables replication solutions at the logical volume manager layer to provide write ordering of data at the secondary site even in an asynchronous mode. Application binaries, database binaries, parameter files, and other nondatabase components can all be configured to reside within the same logical volume group as well. Hence, replication of all components in the system can potentially be addressed by a single replication technology at the logical volume manager level. However, host-based volume managers generally support a limited number of operating systems and therefore a particular volume-based replication technology may not be a viable option for all operating system platforms. Also, host-level volume management is not always used, and in these instances it becomes necessary to introduce the additional layer to enable volume-based replication.

■ *Storage Array Layer.* As is the case with volume-based replication, a majority, if not all, of application and database components can be replicated at the storage array layer. Storage array-based replication also provides the flexibility of not requiring a volume manager layer. Based on the design and implementation, some storage array-layer solutions ensure that write sizes and write ordering within the data set are maintained at the secondary site in an asynchronous mode. Others do not guarantee these attributes. Once again, in the case of the latter, point-in-time copy replication may be required for recovery. Storage array-based replication generally requires compatible (e.g., same vendor) storage hardware at the primary and secondary sites, limiting hardware choices. Most solutions also need additional channel extenders with geographically separated sites. Since most array-based replication products do not use the host's CPU cycles, it seems that applications would perform better than with replication at other layers. However, this may or may not be the case, depending on whether the application is CPU or I/O bound, since most array-based replication products tend to affect I/O performance.

6.3.4 Secondary Site: Recovery and Other Considerations

Beyond the geographic location, several other factors require consideration for secondary sites. Some organizations have fully functional data centers located in different geographies, each potentially providing services for different applications. In such cases, each data center, while being the primary for its own applications, can also act as a secondary site for applications housed at another data center. For organizations with a single data center, the first step in disaster recovery planning starts with selection of a suitable secondary site. Apart from building and maintaining a secondary site with the required infrastructure, a hot-site can be leased from third-party vendors who also typically provide equipment and related site services for disaster recovery.

Regardless of the ownership decision, periodic testing to ensure disaster tolerance and recoverability at the secondary site should be an integral part of the business-continuance plan. The testing process has to be as comprehensive as possible. It is not uncommon for some organizations to fail over application services on a regular basis and run them from secondary sites for an extended period. An additional benefit of being able to fail over to a secondary site is the flexibility to perform potentially disruptive maintenance tasks like hardware, software, and other infrastructure upgrades with minimal application downtime. When using data replication for disaster tolerance, hosts at the secondary site don't always need to be passive. For example, when replicating databases at the volume or storage array levels, second-site point-in-time copies can be activated for backup and reporting functions. This not only alleviates load on the primary system but also provides a mechanism for offsite tape storage without requiring physical transport.

Activating application and data services from a secondary site in the event of a primary data center outage involves several steps. One of the first steps triggers an outage notification alert to one or more responsible personnel. The outage itself could range from an application service being unavailable for an extended period to complete inaccessibility of the entire data center. Since migrating applications and activating them from remote data centers is complex, a decision has to be made on the switchover. If the decision is to migrate, the process could involve promoting the secondary hosts to primary status and performing all the necessary tasks of activating volumes, mounting file systems, starting up the database, and activating applications. These tasks can be performed manually using written policies and procedures, or they can be automated using scripts or through commercially deployed software enabling wide-area failover. Automation is generally preferred, since it makes regular testing and the occasional migration for maintenance easier. More importantly, it provides a measure of predictability for disaster recovery and tolerance.

6.4 Corporate Systems

This section discusses availability for a few applications common to most organizations. The discussion and the list serve as examples of a significantly larger applications and solution set.

Most business applications today provide connectivity over the Internet and an intranet through a Web interface. The architecture for these applications typically involves one or more of the following layers.

- *Load Balancer.* Users connecting over the Internet or an intranet are usually routed through load balancers to one of a set of servers at the next layer—probably Web servers. Redundancy at this layer is usually provided by duplicate hardware with failover. Single box failure is typically transparent to the end user.

- *Web Servers.* Web servers mainly serve either static Web pages or dynamically generated content. Usually, two or more Web servers with identical content are deployed for redundancy and load-handling purposes. Identical data on multiple servers can be maintained by the use of NAS, synchronous file replication, or a clustered read/write file system. Failure of a given server will not affect availability of the entire layer.

- *Application Server.* In terms of redundancy and availability, the application server layer is similar to the Web server layer. Redundancy features are usually provided by application software, and hence additional clustering or high-availability software will not be required at this layer.

- *Database Servers.* Most architectures employ database servers in the back end. Availability considerations for these back-end servers include all the tools, technologies, and methods discussed in the earlier sections. ranging from disk redundancy to wide-area failover.

- *Storage Area Network.* Redundancy at the SAN layer can be provided by the implementation of redundant SAN fabrics using redundant switches. In addition, some switches also provide complete redundancy within a single box. Software available from volume manager and array vendors enables multiple data paths between hosts and storage to be used for load balancing and transparent data-path failover.

- *Storage Subsystems.* Redundancy at the storage subsystem is provided by RAID implemented in hardware and software. Some high-end storage arrays also provide component redundancy within the array.

Various enterprise applications fit across redundancy layers for the larger storage infrastructure, as shown in Figure 6–12. Each application has its own specific requirements that merit attention.

6.4.1 External Web Sites

External Web sites typically serve static Web pages, which are periodically refreshed with updated content. These Web sites typically include the load balancer layer and the Web server layer. With mostly static content, the avail-

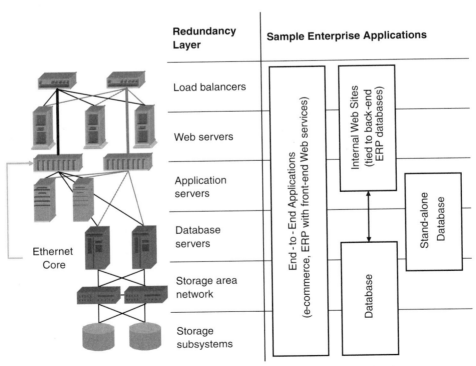

Figure 6–12 Layers of storage redundancy and sample enterprise applications.

ability requirements from a storage perspective are not incredibly strict assuming content can be easily reconstructed through backups. Real-time availability is provided by redundancy across load balancers and Web servers. Storage administrators would be wasting money to deploy real-time replication on Web sites serving mostly static content.

6.4.2 Internal Web Sites

Internal Web sites are more frequently tied to back-end applications, such as employee expense report tools tied to ERP systems. In this case, as internal Web applications become more integrated with the enterprise infrastructure, outages affect more people. These applications serve employees rather than customers, and extended outages wouldn't necessarily garner coverage on CNN. A balance needs to be reached between reasonable availability levels without incurring excessive costs.

6.4.3 E-Commerce

For most e-commerce applications, organizations pull out all the stops to guarantee that revenue-generating systems remain online 24/7/365. E-commerce applications typically have the most customer impact. More and more companies, even those not associated with e-commerce, sell products and services via external Web sites.

6.4.4 Email

Loss of email applications can dramatically impact company and employee productivity. However, email is generally an inwardly focused application and may not require the same availability as e-commerce. Legal issues often determine the type and duration of email retention. In the case of law firms, emails may require online access and retention on the order of years.

6.4.5 Enterprise Applications: ERP, CRM, Supply Chain

Traditional enterprise applications can easily affect all aspects of a business. Particularly in the case of large-scale business operations where the day-to-day movement of goods and services determines revenue streams, these applications fall into the mission-critical category and may be as important as e-commerce applications are to other businesses.

At the same time, some enterprise resource planning (ERP) applications—such as payroll, which could be easily reprocessed if necessary—might not require high-availability. If payroll were your core-competency, as is the case with companies like ADP, requirements would be different.

6.4.6 Call Centers

Call centers can be optimized for both high availability and optimized deployment using replication and wide-area failover technologies. In the case of customer service centers, databases could "follow the sun" around the globe. This allows the data to be closest to the call centers with the most activity. For example, a major U.S. customer service center may field calls domestically during U.S. business hours. However, at night, it may be more effective to move the call center overseas to India and have midnight calls attended to during Indian daytime business hours. In this case, having the database records in that location facilitates easier queries and request processing.

6.4.7 Making Use of Storage Redundancy Layers

Storage systems tailored to specific applications operate across a range of redundancy layers. To optimize storage deployments and availability requirements, storage administrators need to evaluate the architectural dependencies across redundancy layers. Using frameworks provided in this chapter, administrators can apply the right data protection and availability solutions for optimized deployment.

6.5 Chapter Summary

Business Continuity for Mission-Critical Applications

- Data protection and availability tools enable business continuity for mission-critical applications.

- A range of solutions grows in cost and complexity as availability requirements increase.

- Protection and availability options range from basic backup to wide area replication with failover.

6.1 Assessing Business Continuity Objectives

- Some of the steps to be taken in the assessment process include the following:

    - List all applications.

    - Identify dependencies between applications.

    - Create application groups based on dependencies.

- Prioritize application groups based on importance.

- Associate availability metrics for application groups and applications within groups.

- Recovery time objective (RTO) is a measure of the acceptable time allowed for recovery. RTO poses the question, How long can the application be down?

- Recovery point objective (RPO) measures the earliest point in time to which the application and data can be recovered. Simply put, how much data can be lost?

- Data protection and availability solutions can be mapped out by RTO and RPO and matched to appropriate application requirements.

- Factors affecting the choice of solution include

  - Appropriate level of availability

  - Total cost of ownership (TCO)

  - Complexity

  - Vendor viability in the long run

  - Performance impact

  - Security

  - Scalability

6.2 Availability within the Data Center

- Backup: Backing up the data on a regular schedule to a tape device provides a fundamental level of availability.

- Disk Redundancy—RAID: Since storage disks have some of the lowest mean time between failures (MTBF) in a computer system, mirroring the boot disk and using RAID storage provides resilience in case of disk failure.

- Quick Recovery File Systems: In the event of a system crash and reboot, using a quick recovery file system will speed up the reboot process, which in turn minimizes the amount of time the application remains unavailable.

- Point-in-Time Copies: RAID storage and high-availability software do not protect applications from logical data corruption. Online point-in-time copies of data ensure a more timely recovery.

- High Availability and Clustering: Deploying high-availability and clustering software with redundant server hardware enables automated detection of server failure and provides transparent failover of the application to a second server with minimal disruption to end users.

6.3 Availability Across Geographies: Disaster Tolerance and Recovery

- Offsite Media Vaulting and Recovery: Offsite tape backups provide regular archived copies for disaster recovery. Tape backup can take up to a week or more for full recovery.

- Remote Mirroring and Failover: In the event of a data center outage, replicating data over a WAN to a remote site server ensures application availability in a relatively short time period. Most methods of remote data replication provide a passive secondary standby system. In the event of a primary data center outage, the use of wide-area failover software, which provides failure notification and automated application recovery at the secondary site, ensures a relatively quick and error-free resumption of application service at the secondary site.

- Data Replication: Replication modes may be synchronous, asynchronous, or periodic.

- Methods of Replication: Redundancy layers exist across applications, databases, file systems, logical volumes, and storage devices or LUNs.

- Secondary sites require special consideration and may be used for protection and optimized deployments, such as failover and facilitating easier systems maintenance.

6.4 Corporate Systems

- Corporate systems span load balancers, Web servers, application servers, database servers, storage area networks, and storage subsystems.

- Applications include external Web sites, internal Web sites, e-commerce, email, enterprise applications (ERP, CRM, supply chain, etc.), and call centers.

- Each application has specific requirements that need to be mapped across redundancy layers to determine the optimal availability and protection measures.

7 Options for Operational Agility

As IT organizations strive to deliver networked storage solutions for their users, operational agility becomes increasingly difficult to achieve. With the efficiencies and increased possibilities of networked storage comes a wave of new architectures, new methods, and new rules that can leave any IT organization with expertise and functionality gaps. These voids in the knowledge base impact attempts to capture or retain organizational and operational agility related to networked storage.

The ability for organizations to react quickly to internal and external forces determines success or failure. Take, for example, the cost of downtime to Amazon.com or the need for remote backup applications at the NASDAQ clearinghouses. While these are obvious examples, the broader implication is that companies regularly need to roll out business-impacting applications or meet the growing storage demands of business units. The ability for any IT organization to react quickly and predictably to those requests varies depending on expertise and storage functionality.

In this chapter we discuss strategies for creating effective operational agility and provide specific examples as useful tools to understand when and how these solutions should be implemented. We discuss all facets of storage outsourcing and what costs and organizational impacts this may have. This leads to an exploration of the marriage between network service providers (NSPs) and storage with a specific focus on the need for remote storage services. Understanding alternative delivery methods, we examine all the ins and outs of effective service level agreements (SLAs) for internal storage provisioning and delivery. Finally, we cover the benefits of operational agility on streamlining application deployment. Streamlining is enabled with the ability to transition storage between systems and to effectively capitalize on incumbent corporate data assets.

7.1 Outsourced Storage

Cheaper, faster, better. This is the typical mantra of the general outsourcing market and represents the overall business solution and value proposition. In reality, there is nothing different when it comes down to storage outsourcing. However, outsourcing is not always a "one size fits all" solution. The most value created by storage outsourcing—or by outsourcing in general, for that matter—comes when the complexity of the solution outstrips the knowledge base of inhouse staff. Thus, as complexity increases, so does both the real and perceived value.

Figure 7–1 illustrates the relationship between complexity and value for storage functions within an organization. The functional specifics have been detailed in the previous chapters. Simply putting the pieces of the networked storage solution together, from a hardware perspective, is relatively straightforward and well documented throughout the industry. Administrators can choose either SAN or NAS, or can combine the two. Choosing RAID arrays is an age-old practice that does not create much strain on the average enterprise IT staff. Thus, the perceived value is quite low for the ability to accomplish those tasks. However, when bundled with the required software, networking, and infrastructure, the task becomes more complex. Here is a list of some of the questions that arise during this phase:

- How can I create a scalable network built for growth?

- How can I guarantee fabric and network interoperability?

- What is the best network design to achieve 99.999% availability?

- Which host adapters are best?

- Will my networked storage work correctly with my clustered servers?

- What levels of firmware are required?

- How can we use virtualization to our advantage? What is virtualization?

- How will SRM impact my deployment decision in the future?

Increasing the level of complexity to include people management adds additional challenges, compounding those already present. Enterprise networked storage teams grapple with the issue of hiring, training, and retaining storage talent. Additionally, the uniqueness of large-scale deployments creates a need to retain staff-centric intellectual assets. But, as the IT staff grows and gains incremental knowledge, its worth may exceed the firm's ability to

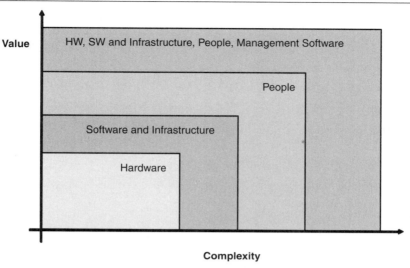

Figure 7–1 Increases in complexity of solution create value and need for outsourcing.

compensate and retain this talent. The "people" challenge is like fighting a two-front war for most CIOs. Putting the right pieces of the technology puzzle together is difficult enough, but also trying to juggle scarce human resources can drive IT managers to the brink.

Try putting it all together and also adding event and problem management. For large companies, this is the complexity peak of networked storage deployments. The introduction of event management has a ripple effect through all other areas: hardware, software, infrastructure, and people. More questions follow that the IT staff must answer:

- Do the right skill sets exist within the current operations center structure?

- Will my current ticketing system work with the storage environment?

- Does my hardware generate the right traps to achieve proactive management?

- Can I accomplish event correlation to filter out "noise"?

- Will my storage-event management system display other affected systems and users?

Compiling these pieces of the puzzle can easily lead to outsourcing. After all, outsourcing is a natural extension of corporate IT frustration and the inability to achieve defined goals and core business requirements from information systems. As we discuss the different flavors of storage outsourcing, we use these frameworks as a means to explore the pros and cons of each solution and where it may or may not fit within a particular organizational construct.

7.1.1 Storage Service Providers

Storage service providers (SSPs) offer a variety of outsourced storage services. These services have come in many different flavors and as many different forms over the past several years. However, at the core, these new entities sell and deliver very similar products and services. Examining what a full-service SSP offers and the operational agility value created, we will answer the following questions:

- What capabilities do SSPs offer?

- How is the service delivery accomplished?

- What components make up a managed service?

- What does the end user get as a part of the service?

- What service offerings and products are available today?

- Can the SSP maintain confidentiality and security of the data?

7.1.2 SSP Capabilities

The SSP business model is built on the premise that through scale and operational best practices, the service provider can offer a greater degree of service at a lower cost than a single enterprise could do independently. This section dissects the operational components of the SSP business model to provide insight into key considerations for a partnership with an SSP.

To serve the market, full-service SSPs must build a set of capabilities that mimic typical enterprise activities conducted with storage-focused IT staff. Figure 7–2 illustrates the specific capabilities required to offer a complete bundle of services. The key is that no SSP can offer any enterprise operational agility or flexibility within its storage-computing environment unless the SSP can offer exactly the same functionality within its service.

The need to replicate user environment services stems from the diversity of the following enterprise storage pieces:

- Applications

- Operating systems

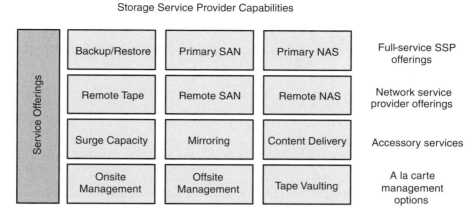

Figure 7–2 Service offerings for storage and network service providers.

- Business processes

- Incumbent host technology

Enterprise computing environments are largely unique, but most use similar technology to solve different business needs. For example, one company might use clustering software as a means to create availability, while another may use the same piece of software for load sharing. Thus, the storage environment must be configured differently in each scenario to account for the alternative architectures. In the first example, only one host is talking to storage at any single point in time, while in the second example both hosts are interacting with the storage and may require different volume creations and potentially different physical disk allocations.

The SLA is the heart and soul of any SSP. An entire set of practices and principles guides the service provider on a daily basis and drives value and agility back to customers and end users. The specifics of effective, ongoing SLA management are covered in Section 7.3. We begin here by defining the core components that make up the SLA and allow the service provider to successfully deploy various storage services and configurations while maintaining SLA adherence. These core components include the following considerations for SSPs:

- Instill and continually reinforce organizational discipline.

- Define business process.

- Make document procedures easily available and train delivery teams well.

- Include infrastructure certification for solutions.

- Maximize standardization at all times.

- Centralize operations as much as possible.

- Develop and implement storage management software to equalize the differences within the hardware infrastructure.

7.1.3 Closing the Normalized Infrastructure Gap

SSPs use value-added storage management software to differentiate their capabilities and provide a feature/function set at a lower cost point than companies could do independently. Normalizing the infrastructure of vendor equipment, specifically hardware, and bringing the end-service offering to an acceptable level of SLA readiness occurs by filling the normalization gap, as shown in Figure 7–3.

Closing the normalization gap applies to SSPs looking to provide customer SLAs and also enterprise customers creating internal SLAs for departments. Each vendor is ranked on attributes such as reliability, availability, and serviceability (RAS), software integration and reporting capabilities, and price. To go from a weighted average of these attributes to full SLA readiness, SSPs and enterprises must provide the appropriate storage management software and management oversight.

Having identified the base set of capabilities, we turn our attention to the various types of SSPs and focus on the services and offerings mentioned previously. The following section breaks apart the various offerings and unlocks the mysteries of the storage service delivery model.

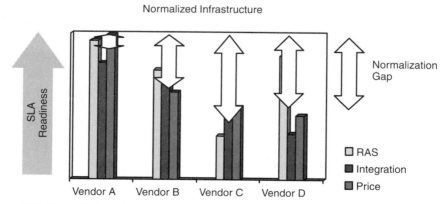

Figure 7–3 The effect of storage management software on the deployed infrastructure.

7.1.4 Complete Outsourcing

Fact: When most companies need electrical power, they do not go and build a generator plant. These companies buy electricity delivered over wires from a centralized facility that services many customers in the same region at the same point in time.

The fully outsourced IT delivery model is a tried and true practice. Companies such as EDS and IBM Global Services have delivered on thousands of contracts for outsourced IT services and will continue to do so for the foreseeable future. Companies like these have found the right place in the IT market, where scale, complexity, and value intersect. For some of the largest enterprise computing environments and for highly specialized applications, the fully outsourced contract provides the maximum degree of operational flexibility and organizational agility. Companies contracting EDS-like services long ago discovered that the ongoing cost of building the solution themselves was not a required core capability. The same reasoning applies to many companies outsourcing the operations of their data center or their call center. In their minds, the cost and complexity of achieving the required results creates a drag on the company from either an expense or a mindshare perspective. Because many IT shops often lack some key expertise, the contracting firm turns to outsourcing because it is the only way to get the job done right.

The same set of market conditions created the need for storage to be delivered as a service. More and more businesses conduct commerce electronically and rely heavily on Web-enabled applications, creating a surging demand for data storage capacity. As storage growth reached exponential levels, a cry could be heard from enterprise data centers for relief and the return to sanity. Thus, storage itself reached the intersection of complexity, scale, and value. The scale of the growth combined with compounding complexity matched the market-attributed value of storage services.

Another factor leading to the need to for fully outsourced solutions was a severe knowledge gap with the emerging networked storage solutions. Most IT organizations know about the efficiencies and ease of management of networked storage, but have no knowledge of how to implement these solutions. Common questions among an untrained IT staff might include these:

- Should I implement NAS or SAN, or both?

- Can multiple applications share the same physical disk?

- What is fabric?

■ How do I protect against single points of failure?

■ How do I bridge traffic to my installed IP network?

■ How do I leverage my current (IP–Ethernet) network?

■ How do backups get done with a networked infrastructure?

■ How do I maintain security?

■ What, exactly, is my total cost of operations today? What will they be in the future?

A question CIOs often ask when considering an outsourced storage model is, "So, what do I really get with this service, and what are my options?" Now that we understand the reason behind the fully outsourced storage model, let us turn our attention to dissecting the specific components of each offering.

7.1.5 Complete Outsourcing: Core Service Offerings

Primary Storage Area Network (SAN). The SAN service consists of the delivery of block-level storage access from a predefined set of hosts across a Fibre Channel fabric. Hosts are allocated storage volumes and capacity. Often, a minimum capacity amount is contracted from the provider and additional capacity added at the customer's request. The line of demarcation typically resides at the host connection to the Fibre Channel network access, but does not include the actual HBAs. The service provider monitors the environment for problems and reacts to events up to and including the HBA. Depending on the service provider or the specific contract, the storage array is a shared resource, and each customer has access rights to specific ports on the array (this mitigates much of the security risks associated with array sharing). Service metrics include

SLA: 98.5%–99.999% availability of storage access

Pricing example: Monthly charge for gigabytes under management (not just that which is used)

Primary Network-Attached Storage (NAS). The NAS service includes file-level access to a predefined storage capacity connected to specialized file servers. A customer connects with this service through a Gigabit Ethernet network delivered from the service provider. Typically, this consists of dual gigabit connections from the network delivered to a customer aggregation point. The aggregation point is where the customer has its hosts connected to an internally run network. The line of demarcation is the point at which the dual gigabit connections attach to the customer network. Dual paths and clustered file servers are used for increased service level availability. In most cases the file server and disk storage infrastructure are dedicated to each customer to mitigate security concerns and IP addressing conflicts. The service provider typically monitors the environment for network congestions, storage availability, and file server health. Service metrics include

SLA: 98.5%–99.999% availability of storage access

Pricing example: Monthly charge for gigabytes under management (not just that which is used)

Backup and Restore. The backup and restore service consists of the successful transfer of data from predefined host servers to a shared tape library infrastructure. The actual tape cartridges are dedicated to each customer, but the network, library, catalog disk, and backup servers are shared resources. A typical configuration for this service includes the creation of a dedicated Ethernet network (various speeds depending on throughput requirements) on the customer side and a set of Gigabit Ethernet connections to the shared backup network of the service provider. The service provider then passes that traffic along its shared Ethernet network through the backup server and writes the data to the tape within the library. Additionally, the service provider provides and configures all software required to initiate, schedule, complete, and report on the progress of backup jobs. This includes the configuration of database servers and file systems alike. Typically, the service provider commits to initiating and completing the backup job within a set time frame. The service provider is expected to monitor the status of all jobs to ensure proper completion within the window. Also, the service provider is expected to restart any failed or stalled job to comply with the backup window timeframe. Finally, the service provider delivers a success/failure report to the customer at the completion of all backup windows for all jobs, providing visibility into the health and welfare of the corporate assets. Service metrics include

SLA: Up to 95% success rate for all jobs within window during a month

Pricing example: Monthly charge for gigabytes transferred (backup or restore)

Remote SAN. The remote SAN service consists of the same components found in the primary SAN storage service with a couple of key additions. The service provider delivers wide-area or metro-area connections to the back-end storage infrastructure from the customer location, while also providing and configuring any software required to execute the remote read/write functions of the host disk interaction. Note that this service has been implemented primarily as a disaster protection solution for many companies but rarely used as a solution for primary storage access. High network costs and latency at distances greater than 10 km prevent anything but high-interval, asynchronous connections to the remote storage repository. Service metrics include

> **SLA:** 98.5%–99.999% storage availability and up to 99.999% network access availability

> **Pricing example:** Monthly charge for gigabytes under management and a separate charge for the network component

Remote NAS. The remote NAS service consists of all the same components found in the primary SAN storage service with a couple of key additions. The service provider also delivers wide-area or metro-area connections to the back-end storage infrastructure from the customer location, while also providing and configuring any software required to execute the remote read/write functions of the host disk interaction. Service metrics include

> **SLA:** 98.5%–99.999% storage availability and up to 99.999% network access availability

> **Pricing example:** Monthly charge for gigabytes under management and a separate charge for the network component

Remote Tape Backup and Restore. The remote tape service contains many components similar to the local backup and restore service, with a couple of key additions. Obviously, wide-area or metro-area network connections are required for this service. Also, the service includes the use of media servers to increase the data streaming rate and maximize the write speeds on drives, reducing overall system latency. The line of demarcation remains the same but includes the additional network component. Service metrics include

> **SLA:** Up to 95% success rate for all jobs within window during a month

> **Pricing example:** Monthly charge for gigabytes transferred (backup or restore) and the additional network component

Content Delivery. The content delivery service consists of the creation of read-only storage nodes that locate specific data in geographic proximity to potential end users. This is exclusively a file-level service, and the underlying infrastructure relies on standard file-serving NAS technology. This service is the most esoteric of all of the fully managed storage services and is usually implemented by large media outlets requiring massive amounts of continually replicated data. The read-only nature of the data source allows centralized data dispersal to remote geographies and guarantees uniform access by all end users. Service metrics include

SLA: 99.999% storage availability and access

Pricing example: Monthly charge for gigabytes under management and a separate charge for the network component required for content replication traffic

The complete SSP outsourcing option provides a turnkey solution for IT organizations struggling to create value through independent storage and infrastructure management. From an operational perspective, the SSP assesses the business requirements, architects a unique solution, creates the design specifications for the storage infrastructure, implements the prescribed solution, provides ongoing management, and delivers with service-level guarantees. This allows the IT staff to focus on more important projects core to the company's business, potentially with more direct revenue impact. Additionally, this preserves cash by deferring purchases of expensive storage and networking equipment. Finally, the solution meets requirements without extensive lab trials, technology research, vendor bake-offs, and risky decisions. All of these tasks and solutions provide a more flexible computing framework to drive value to the agile organization.

7.1.6 Terabyte Rental

IT organizations often need deep pools of storage capacity for a brief period of time. This need may be due to data migration requiring a staging area during the transfer or for surge capacity during a sales promotion for an online retailer. The typical response is to purchase and provision the excess capacity in advance of the need and allocate the space as required.

Obviously, the business's needs should be the first and foremost consideration. If the business unit needs the capacity, then the IT staff is compelled to make it available, assuming there is a supporting business case. However, this creates inefficiencies in capacity management and can cause the company to procure and deploy excess capacity that would not be needed in the normal growth of the core storage assets. Adding capacity uses valuable capital, may decrease future lease options, and creates an investment in dated technology. Since excess core capacity is deployed early to meet a short-term surge, using that capacity at a later date for core requirements makes it dated by default. With the pace of development and innovation in the storage sector, such a proposition sets any IT organization up for potentially incremental investments later on to adjust the match between core requirements and available assets. Figure 7–4 illustrates the overprovisioning of capacity to meet short-term surge requirements. In this case, incorporating terabyte rental allows Purchase 2 to meet current needs while avoiding the higher expense of Purchase 1.

Many SSPs offer an elegant solution to this problem that IT organizations face. Companies can rent capacity on a short-term basis to solve business needs while not interfering with normal deployment and growth of the core data center storage assets. This solution may require high-speed network connections or may depend on the nature of the applications slated for the collocation facility. However, this solution protects the company from vendor and technology lock-in while preserving cash and allowing the IT staff to focus on core business requirements.

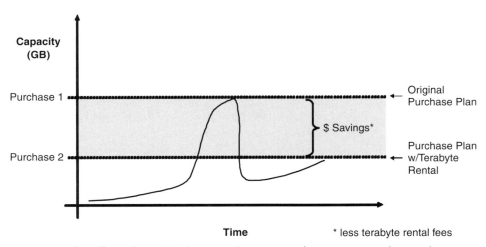

Figure 7–4 The effect of provisioning capacity to meet short-term capacity requirements.

7.1.7 Storage Management Offsite

Offsite storage management is a way for organizations to take advantage of the SSP's expertise and management capabilities while retaining control and decision making for hardware deployment and physical disk requirements.

SSPs offer best practices and remote monitoring capabilities to enable IT organizations to act like an internal service provider to their business units. The SSP provides the company with detailed configuration and design requirements along with a supporting bill of material (BOM). This creates an optimal infrastructure design for the IT organization and allows the SSP to effectively accomplish monitoring and event management tasks.

Internal IT teams create service levels around provisioned storage and implement effective charge-back scenarios, transforming the data center from a cost center to a value center. This service applies to SAN, NAS, and backup/restore configurations.

The key to this service is provision of configuration details and procurement requirements, which frees the IT staff to focus on the level-one management tasks and develop solutions to the more complex challenges. The remote monitoring, event management, and reporting capabilities are often too complex for most IT shops and require deep-seated knowledge along with extensive coding and scripting. For most companies, the scale of their storage assets does not warrant this level of initial investment and ongoing commitment. Thus, the SSP allows the company to deliver a solution internally while maintaining flexibility at a lower cost than it would if the company decided to do it on its own. Figure 7–5 creates a useful comparison between the offsite and onsite management solutions.

Typical service configurations include a series of monthly host connection fees as well as monthly capacity under management fees.

7.1.8 Storage Management Onsite

Onsite storage management is similar to the offsite service, but in this case the SSP also provides the people to perform the daily storage infrastructure management. While the company still procures and maintains ownership of the storage hardware and physical disk array systems, the SSP staff performs the day-in and day-out tasks of storage management. The customer still purchases and deploys storage based on the prescribed configurations set forth by the SSP and continues to use the SSP's expert design services and resident knowledge. This removes the need to invest deeply in internal subject matter expertise.

The most compelling reason to incorporate this service into data center designs is the reduction of the workforce-carrying costs. Storage expertise can be a significant human resource expenditure that can be dramatically reduced or eliminated. On the flip side, companies must be careful not to eliminate resident storage skills entirely. Without inhouse knowledge of storage, companies risk vendor lock-in, ultimately reducing their deployment options.

Figure 7–5 details the differences between the offsite and onsite management options offered by SSPs. The colored areas are where the SSP would perform the activities.

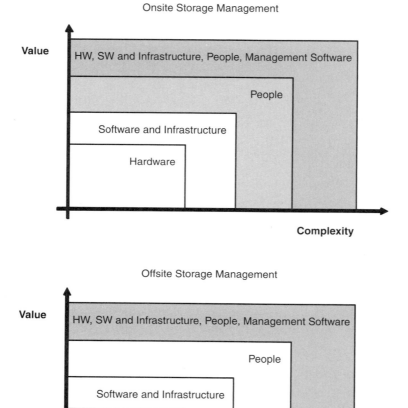

Figure 7–5 A comparison of the activities between onsite and offsite storage management.

7.2 Integrated Network Services

Network service providers (NSPs) have long pontificated about the need to build high-bandwidth, scalable networks delivering many classes of traffic. In fact, the concept of bundled services has fueled both vendor product development and current service provider growth and acquisition strategies over the last decade.

It is no wonder, then, that providing storage capacity as a service tied to service provider offerings is an important revenue stream for the current crop of local and national providers. More importantly, these providers are bundling together an assortment of services that add significant value to organizations. An IT organization can now turn to a single provider for geographically dispersed computing capabilities through collocation services, interconnect network solutions, inbound Internet access, voice services, and now storage services along with a multitude of ancillary offerings.

As we discuss the specific offerings, it is important to understand that the solutions are delivered exclusively as fully managed services. To this extent, the core value created for the IT organization will be similar to that of the complete outsourced model within the SSP framework. Thus, these services provide the most utility when the complexity outpaces the expertise of the staff or when the provider can offer the solution at a lower cost than the IT staff could deliver on its own. However, the integrated network solutions have some very specific and important nuances that create uniqueness in their application. Most notable are the possibilities present in the bundled strategy.

7.2.1 Storage and Networking Services

IP and storage convergence open opportunities and applications for delivering storage services via network connections. Once storage devices are freed from captive server connections, the networked storage infrastructure delivers greater flexibility and manageability. The ability for this traffic to flow across the ubiquitous IP networking infrastructure enables NSPs to offer storage services to their existing customers. The existing nature of these relationships and extensive reach of the service providers creates a win for the IT organization in the form of increased value creation, while the service provider increases utilization across the network, building incremental revenue streams.

Some of the services offered by NSPs include

- Remote SAN

- Remote NAS

- Remote tape backup and restore

- Combined collocation and storage

There is true value to the IT organization in this one-stop shop, which has the expertise necessary to design and deploy the appropriate solutions. All too often, overburdened IT professionals piece together a solution that could be effective, but the staff lacks the clarity to put together the right pieces of the puzzle. For example, an enterprise IT organization building a robust remote tape backup solution a few years ago had the right pieces at its disposal. The backup software was designed to be distance-independent, the hosts had Ethernet connections, the internal IP network connected the hosts together, many vendors offered wide-area interconnects, IP bandwidth was readily available, and the library infrastructure was in place. However, the cost and complexity of putting together the complete solution retarded deployment except for in the largest companies. Now, NSPs can bundle these solutions at an internal cost much lower than that of the single IT group, and these providers can offer a simple connection at an affordable rate to a multitude of end users.

7.2.2 Content Delivery, Capacity Distribution

The NSPs also possess the unique ability to offer a capacity distribution service that effectively creates storage solutions for IT organizations in need of boundaryless computing that spans the globe. The most prevalent instances of this need are Web-based applications for business, Web-based media outlets, and large enterprises with remote offices.

In this solution, the IT organization creates, owns, and manages the primary storage infrastructure. Then, the primary storage connects to the service provider network to take advantage of its national or global facilities' reach for distribution or replication closer to the end users. Companies are not forced to build the internal expertise, construct the remote facilities, or bundle the network services together, and therefore reduce complexity and cost. This heavily repeated theme of this chapter represents the critical decision point whether or not to contract these services and generate the requisite operational agility to win in today's hyper-competitive market.

7.3 Managing Service Level Agreements

Building a management strategy to deliver high-quality storage services is an increasingly strategic requirement for enterprises. In order to provide an effective and meaningful level of service, organizations need to set appropriate business objectives; design, test, and set standards for equipment; establish processes that support service levels; and build tools to automate, measure, and support the process.

Meaningful service delivery is now the mantra of today's IT organizations. To build crossfunctional agility up and down the organization, excuses are no longer acceptable regarding downtime, performance, and resource allocations. Many IT organizations want to offer SLAs to their end users as a way to illustrate service and commitment. In addition, the SLA measures the performance of the IT staff by how well it provides a valued service. This generates a risk/reward profile that fosters service development, predictable cost reductions, and an improved end-user experience. But an SLA is more than a piece of paper; it requires an organizational commitment wrapped in people, process, and systems that make the SLA tangible.

While it may be easy to understand the business value of service levels, supporting SLAs create operational challenges that need to be addressed. Several supporting management processes lie at the foundation of building SLA-ready storage environments. These management processes are designed and executed in an effort to build and deliver dependable storage environments and infrastructures that can have service levels written against them.

In this section we explore the details and fundamentals for delivering meaningful SLAs:

1 Disciplined adherence to business objectives

2 Process documentation

3 Infrastructure certification

4 Standardization and security

5 Centralization of key management tasks

6 Effective management software that normalizes the entire environment

7.3.1 Discipline and Business Objectives

One of the first activities associated with delivering an SLA-ready storage environment is defining measurable business objectives, measured through real-time metrics such as reliability and availability. The objectives are delivered through a combination of discipline and process that cuts across all organizational activities and constitutes an effective storage management foundation.

Organizational discipline is a difficult metric to track and measure. Discipline is one of those "soft" skills that can easily be lost if the day-to-day work of a company does not reinforce the activity's importance. The value of people following processes in a repetitive and predictable fashion (organizational discipline) creates significant efficiencies and reliability within the storage environment. Discipline consequently directly supports the SLA. Without a disciplined organization, the activities associated with engineering, command, and execution of the SLA become disjointed and less meaningful. For example, it is almost impossible to effectively monitor the storage infrastructure if the organization has not taken the time and effort to create and design centralized configurations. Thus, the discipline to create centralized designs enables effective monitoring.

Relationships exist between disciplined design and ongoing processes for superior management. For instance, to fully support the SLA business objectives, an enterprise must institute effective change management within its infrastructure. In fact, research by the Gartner Group states that enterprises can never achieve more than 99 percent system availability without effective change-control processes.[1] By combining optimal storage architecture design and effective ongoing management processes, organizations can potentially realize higher availability levels within their infrastructures.

The storage SLA process supports effective delivery and sets the tone for the entire chain of events revolving around storage management. As detailed in Figure 7–6, there are three phases in this process: plan, execute, and manage.

The plan phase determines the promised items and whether they can be supported by the infrastructure deployed. The planning phase creates the SLA, and the subsequent phases support and execute on the commitment. The execute phase comprises a series of checkpoints to ensure the right infrastructure is in place. It culminates in the activation of the service and represents the beginning of ongoing service delivery. The manage phase contains command and control activities and incorporates critical business processes such as billing and customer satisfaction and support.

Creating business objectives around the SLA creates an important link between business goals and the activities required to deliver highly available and scalable storage environments. It also reinforces the discipline required for flawless execution in support of the SLA.

7.3.2 Process Documentation

While we have already discussed the vital importance of effective processes, it is critical to ensure the documentation of the processes. Documented procedures remove ad-hoc reactions from the equation. Giving those responsible

---

[1]Donna Scott, *Surviving in a 24/7 World*, Gartner, October 2001, p. 16.

Storage SLA Process

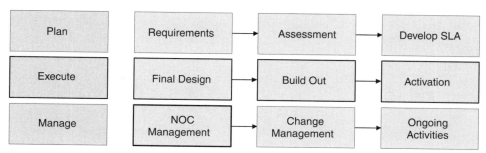

Figure 7–6 The storage SLA process.

for managing the data storage infrastructure access to the set of predefined problem-solving frameworks accomplishes this task. If these frameworks are followed according to their original intent, the operator can depend on predictable reactions from all parts of the infrastructure. Predictable reactions from the infrastructure allow the operator to manage contentions within the environment, aiding in maintaining the SLA. The documentation must be readily available and accessible by anyone who requires it. Without accessibility, the process and documentation are virtually worthless.

7.3.3 Certification

Certification provides organizations with a clear set of infrastructure choices to support various classes of SLAs. This requires filtering the vast stream of available vendor products and then funneling a select few into manageable, fully understood, carefully engineered designs that meet the storage needs of any application. Creating a lab environment and testing procedures to determine the suitability of available products accomplish this goal. Findings in the lab become blueprints for installing and operating proven storage solutions. This ensures that installations around the world in Tokyo, London, and New York are standard—giving all end users consistent, guaranteed service levels.

The certification process should review potential technology to see how it performs in each of the following 10 categories. It is important to note that this is not the testing phase, but rather an initial survey to see whether a component should be considered for implementation within the infrastructure.

Certification Performance Categories

1. Scalability

2. Manageability

3. Host support

4. Features

5. Cost

6. Reliability

7. Performance

8. Security

9. Vendor support

10. Rapid deployment

If the technology passes these steps and is deemed worthy of inclusion within the infrastructure, then the certification phase turns to the testing process. Lab testing should follow a process in which the end result is an SLA-supportable standard design.

A standard infrastructure testing process should include the following:

- Step 1: Review the target requirements and create test plan.

- Step 2: Run tests and publish results.

- Step 3: Create and define the standard implementation design.

- Step 4: Document design considerations.

- Step 5: Implement pilot deployments.

7.3.4 Standardization

Standardization helps support the management tasks of the SLA more efficiently, while minimizing risks. The effort to standardize has ripple effects across many components, including

- **Process documentation:** The cornerstone checkpoint to ensure that the infrastructure and operating procedures are standardized.

- **Certification:** The certification process researches and generates standard infrastructure configurations.

- **Management software:** Depends 100 percent on the standard deployment of the storage infrastructure to operate correctly.

- **Centralized operations:** Relies on a set of operating standards to ensure proper resolution to change, event, and problem management issues.

- **Security:** The assessment of all security considerations related to onsite and offsite data management.

- **Monitoring:** Dependent on standardized infrastructure deployment and operating standards that guarantee the health of the environment.

Standardization reinforces operational agility. Effective standardization compartmentalizes the infrastructure and associated tasks in an orderly way that allows the IT staff to divide the labor into segments. These segments contain critical path issues and promote problem-solving ownership from within the staff, creating a more agile and effective delivery team.

7.3.5 Centralization

Centralization for storage management provides superior command and control with the decision-making pieces in one place. In addition, centralization makes command and control highly scalable and flexible as the storage under management grows and changes over time.

Centralization also helps to reinforce installed processes and promote discipline. It is easier to train and buttress process skills and simpler to build accountability and incentive metrics within the operations staff. Figure 7–7 illustrates and identifies the interrelationships between the phases and roles within the centralized framework.

Quality Assurance: The initial configuration and service level should be checked for quality assurance during the activation process. This is where the end-user architecture is introduced into the infrastruc-

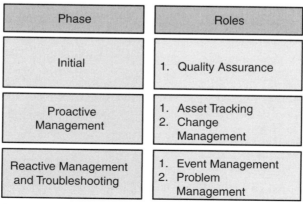

Figure 7–7 Description of the relationships between centralization phases and roles.

ture. The quality assurance role is a four-stage process, which ensures that

1. Appropriate contacts are known.

2. The network operation center (NOC) personnel can monitor and receive "traps" from the architecture.

3. The end-user network is redundant and secure.

4. The information is documented and understood.

Asset Tracking: An asset repository should track the physical configuration and topology information as well as contacts, documentation, and the history of changes made to an environment. Through software integration, this information should be automatically linked to the change and event management processes and software.

Change Management: Centralization allows changes to be documented, tracked, timed, and approved by a unified quality assurance team. Once changes are complete, the information can be captured and integrated into a central asset-tracking repository.

Event Management: The implementation of event management software should trigger "traps" for any event. Event management combined with the asset-tracking system and trained technicians enables the end user to intelligently react to any event detected within the environment. Through integration with the asset-tracking system, NOC operators will have immediate access to all troubleshooting documentation.

Problem Management: Once SLA-impacting events are detected, NOC operators should follow the escalation procedures outlined in the SLA, follow detailed processes to initiate event tickets, and own the problem until resolution. NOC operators should act as bandleaders to ensure all aspects of the SLA are well coordinated across the infrastructure and organization.

Centralization is the glue that holds all the moving pieces within the infrastructure together. Without a well-coordinated and centralized effort, the SLA and therefore the operational benefits are at risk.

7.3.6 **Normalizing Management Software**

As discussed earlier in this chapter, software that acts like an underlying operating system for the storage infrastructure helps deliver storage SLAs. This is the software layer that normalizes the storage infrastructure (see Figure 7–3) by bringing intelligence to the core of the network. Without this piece, intelligence will be confined to the individual parts that make up the edges of the network, preventing a full view across the multiple platforms and limiting the scalability and ultimately the manageability of the infrastructure.

Specific value created from implementing this type of management framework includes

- Accurate and consistent information across a multivendor, distributed infrastructure

- Seamless integration with storage and data management applications, as well as with end-user applications to form a scalable storage and data management environment

- Standardization and automation of best practices for supporting the SLA

- More cost-effective, SLA-ready storage environment

An operating system is the fundamental software that allows applications to run on specific hardware platforms. Programs, such as Microsoft Word and PowerPoint, communicate through an application programming interface (API), which precludes the need for users to even think about the existence of an operating system. These interfaces provide access to the operating system, which in turn controls the machine.

An effective storage management software package should be the interface that frees end users from having to focus on the hardware. The software should act as the operating system that makes this happen by providing services to the management applications with which it is integrated. Through a hardware integration layer similar to that of traditional operating systems, the storage operating system should manage the resources of, execute changes to, and track the status of the entire infrastructure.

Managing storage SLAs should be treated with the appropriate attention by any IT organization. The benefits clearly drive towards creating more businesswide agility by removing the downside risk and managing application expectations. But the cost and complexity of designing and implementing such a strategy should not be underestimated. As various vendors continue to develop storage management software, the task of creating SLA-ready storage infrastructures becomes more simple and straightforward to implement. But to date, no silver bullet exists. This leaves the burden of accomplishment squarely on the shoulders of the IT and development staff to build a framework that creates meaningful business benefit without constraining the core needs of the entire organization.

7.4 Application Deployment

The ability to efficiently and rapidly deploy business-critical applications can determine the difference between success and failure in many of today's markets and industries. Because many business units depend on certain applications to complete daily activities, the maintenance, upgrading, and deployment of these applications can have a significant impact on organizational operations. For many years, the storage infrastructure has been the long pole in the tent with regard to application deployment. The direct-attached nature of the storage capacity and often the internal server-based storage presented a costly and complicated data migration in order to accomplish even a simple server upgrade. However, the advent of network storage and the exponential cost reductions of the associated capacity have freed IT managers to dynamically allocate storage capacity and have created deep pools of space for incidental migrations and infrastructure upgrades.

In this section, we examine the transitioning of systems and also delve deeper into the ways companies create business value through the rapid response model of application deployments.

7.4.1 Transitioning Between Systems

As previously stated, the advent of networked storage has alleviated many constraints when transitioning systems and applications. In addition, the convergence of IP and data storage affords a greater degree of ubiquity in the access options to the storage capacity as well as easing its management.

Now that the storage infrastructure resides within the network construct, application servers need not be concerned with the physical location of the storage capacity. The servers must remain aware of the network access constraints and also the operating system rules. In order for the operating system to access the storage, volumes must be created or mapped to the system. This is a well-understood task, and most operating systems have

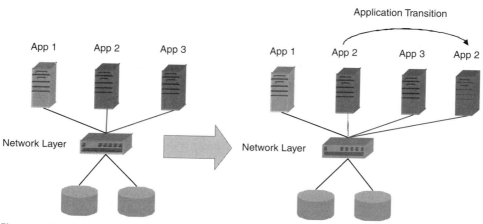

Figure 7–8 Lack of disruption when changing the application server.

built simplicity into the volume creation and mapping effort. Thus, the operational benefits of system transfer are easy to attain. Figure 7–8 illustrates the system transfer concept as it relates to the networked storage infrastructure.

When an exchange server becomes too slow for the number of users attached to the system, IT staff can schedule the required application downtime and focus on rebuilding the application on a faster system without being overly concerned with the underlying data. The data physically resides within the network infrastructure. This significantly lowers the burden for system transfer and allows the organization to more easily adopt new technologies that increase productivity while leveraging the ease of management associated with networked storage.

With the network infrastructure in place, the location of the new application server could be internal or located at a service provider data center. The fluid nature of the infrastructure allows easy migration to a complete or partially outsourced storage infrastructure. The same techniques could be used for companies completing post merger-and-acquisition integration of systems.

One issue to consider is the complexity surrounding data protection. Whenever systems are changed or applications are moved, there is a need to reconfigure the backup and recovery software resident on the target hosts. This is not a difficult task, but must be conducted to ensure proper protection across the entire system.

7.4.2 The Rapid Response Model

The rapid response model can demonstrate an IT organization's ability to provision systems and applications on a just-in-time basis. Additionally, it provides the IT staff with the capability to deploy applications rapidly without dreadful lead times. Organizations need to invest in application, system, and people inventory to accommodate such requests. The investment need not be heavy, as the appropriate match of storage networking infrastructure with outsourced capabilities could deliver the requisite arsenal for rapid response. This is akin to the flexible production system employed by the likes of Toyota and other large-scale manufacturing operations.

7.5 Corporate Asset Management

Increasing numbers of companies have become reliant on the data residing within their storage infrastructure. Applications rely on it, and key transactions depend on the ability to store and retrieve critical pieces of data throughout the business life cycle. Thus, organizations must begin to treat their storage capacity in the same way they would analyze, protect, and manage other corporate assets, such as a factory or real estate. After all, the data that resides on the physical disks and tape within the storage infrastructure represents the collective intellectual input and output of the entire company. In today's information-driven economy, these assets are too valuable to leave unprotected or poorly managed.

7.5.1 Capitalizing Corporate Data

Organizations must be compelled to keep the storage infrastructure well organized as well as protected in order to take advantage of the information that it contains. A company gains tremendous operational agility when it creates a system that is easy to mine for key data and information. This ability can create exceptionally high levels of knowledge sharing and transfer across all segments of the company and will enable the firm to be stronger than the simple sum of its parts. A company in a competitive market will recognize a clear operational and competitive advantage over the rest of the market if its IT staff can focus on mining the key data sets instead of simply minding the health and welfare of the subsystems. This represents the concept of capitalizing on those unique corporate assets.

7.6 Chapter Summary

Options for Operational Agility

- Create organizational options to be agile.

- Use outsourcing and service providers when it makes sense.

- Become well educated about your true capabilities and costs.

- Formulate the right decision framework.

- IT data centers should strive to be value centers and not cost centers; the company wins when you think this way.

- Take advantage of external expertise when required.

- Commit to flexibility.

- Treat your data like true assets and continue to act accordingly.

7.1 Outsourced Storage

- Managing the complexity of complete storage architectures can easily outstrip the skills of inhouse staff.

- Complexity increases from hardware, to software and networking infrastructure, to people, to complete integration with management software.

- As complexity increases, so does perceived value to the organization.

- Outsourcing (in full or in part) allows companies to accomplish best-of-breed solutions economically.

- Storage service providers (SSPs) offer a wide array of services requiring close examination.

- SSP capabilities span virtually all storage-related functions from SAN and NAS, to backup and recovery, to remote connectivity, to specific management options.

- SSPs employ service level agreements (SLAs) to benchmark offerings.

- SSPs close the gap between vendor equipment and stringent SLAs by deploying software and organizational management.

- IT outsourcing has been practiced for years by IBM Global Services, EDS, and others.

- Storage outsourcing is just a more specific tactic targeted to today's infrastructure needs.

- SSPs deliver services based on the premise that through scale and knowledge they can provide greater cost advantages than companies could do internally.

7.2 Integrated Network Services

- Network service providers (NSPs) embrace storage solutions due to the amount of billable traffic placed on their network.

- With IP as a viable storage delivery mechanism, both for NAS, IP SANs, and Fibre Channel across IP, NSPs can offer integrated storage and network services.

- Primary NSP storage offerings include remote SAN/NAS, remote tape backup and restore, and collocation for storage.

- NSPs, with an available network and geographically dispersed data centers, offer content delivery for companies requiring replication to numerous locations.

7.3 Managing Service Level Agreements

- SLAs illustrate and document the commitment of the offering between provider and consumer.

- SLAs may exist between SSPs and companies or even within companies between the IT department and business units.

- Measurable objectives such as reliability and availability define SLAs.

- Organizational discipline can be more important than underlying technology in SLA delivery.

- SLAs are delivered in phases: plan, execute, and manage.

- Process documentation guarantees administrators have clear procedures to follow.

■ Certification allows IT groups a chance to evaluate if a set solution will meet their enterprise needs.

■ Standardization aims to create as many "template" solutions as possible for the IT group, minimizing management overhead.

■ Centralization keeps storage operations in an accountable, manageable framework.

■ Normalizing the infrastructure helps meet SLA-readiness criteria for reliability and availability.

7.4 Application Deployment

■ Network infrastructures facilitate rapid application deployment or transition.

■ Applications can be relocated within data centers or across data centers, including service provider locations.

7.5 Corporate Asset Management

■ Data as a corporate asset requires the oversight, protection, and policies provided by networked and outsourced storage configurations.

8

Initiating Deployment

Through this point in *IP Storage Networking—Straight to the Core,* the topics primarily covered provide an explanatory approach to storage networking with a focus on IP-oriented solutions. In the following three chapters, we delve deeper into deployment scenarios that combine traditional SAN concepts with nontraditional models for new storage platforms. Those nontraditional models involve both network shifts and intelligence shifts.

On the infrastructure side, the storage industry is witnessing a rapid commoditization of components. It seems that just about any storage-related problem can be tackled with one or more servers with specialized software. While these products and solutions might not solve all enterprise needs immediately, keeping a close eye on the progress of general-purpose products offers flexibility and options for IT professionals.

Meanwhile, the network build-out for storage solutions offers location choice for storage services. Coupled with the migration to open-systems platforms and Ethernet and IP networks, product consolidation opportunities and cost savings arise.

While IT professionals can reap savings from IP storage network deployments such as SAN extension, storage consolidation, and service provider SANs, there are added benefits to leveraging an IP storage network model in nontraditional applications.

Chapter 8 includes two specific examples around fixed content, email, and images, and how customers used storage configurations that exploited IP and Ethernet infrastructure in conjunction with distributed services to maximize operational efficiency.

8.1 Infrastructure Design Shifts

When evaluating new infrastructure deployments, IT managers need to consider key themes that shape current and future storage architectures. Two primary themes are the fluidity of end-to-end storage communications and the ability to shift storage services across various architectural components. While the first theme essentially leads to the second, taking each individually clarifies cause and effect.

8.1.1 Fluidity of End-to-End Storage Infrastructure

Through the history of technology, less-expensive and seemingly "less functional" components have evolved to suit applications previously unrealized by both users and vendors. A well-documented example of this phenomenon is Clayton Christensen's *The Innovator's Dilemma: When New Technologies Cause Great Firms to Fail.* In his work, Christensen outlines how smaller form-factor disk drives drove new market opportunities unrecognized by incumbent vendors and customers. For example, few predicted that the 5.25-inch disk drive would suit needs previously served by 9-inch platters. This resulted in a tumultuous cycle among disk drive vendors listening (and not listening) to customer input, with similar effects taking place with the introduction of 3.5-inch and 2.5-inch drives. In the end, smaller form factors prevailed.

The pace of technical development within the storage networking industry is creating a new-found fluidity across the infrastructure. Specifically, the commoditization of components across disk drives, storage nodes, server I/O interconnects, and networks is driving a price decline while enabling greater features and functionality. While these changes may not lead to immediate enterprise deployment, both storage networking vendors and customers should keep an eye on the ability to build an end-to-end storage infrastructure with increasingly commoditized technology.

- **Disk drives.** New drive types, such as serial ATA, and increasingly smaller and denser form factors enable more storage per rack with lighter power requirements along with reduced costs.

- **Intelligent storage nodes.** Ranging in functionality from basic NAS filers, to protocol conversion routers, to virtualization engines, intelligent storage nodes are increasingly appearing as Intel x86 rack-mounted servers with a variety of storage controllers, such as iSCSI, Fibre Channel, and parallel SCSI. These servers may run a version of Windows, Linux, or any other operating system, for that matter. While these servers may not offer the speed of specialized hardware or application-specific integrated circuits (ASICs), they present a fundamental shift in the placement of storage services and platform delivery.

- **I/O interconnects.** Developments such as PCI-X and PCI-Express promise to simplify the input and output mechanisms of servers. Creating high-speed, general-purpose, serial I/O interconnects allows for greater server-to-peripheral speed, functionality, and scalability. More sophisticated I/O interconnects further enhance intelligent storage nodes.

- **Device interconnects.** Similar to I/O interconnects, device interconnects are one step further removed from the CPU. Parallel SCSI, Fibre Channel, and Ethernet are examples of device I/O interconnects. Typically, an HBA will provide one of those interfaces externally and connect to the CPU via a PCI-based I/O interconnect. Some device I/O interconnects may be embedded directly on server motherboards.

- **Network.** Chapter 4, "Storage System Control Points," covered the introduction of network control points and the migration of IP and Ethernet technologies into the storage market. There is no more dramatic way to increase the fluidity of the infrastructure than to provide an open-systems network technology used throughout the world today. By allowing storage traffic to move across IP and Ethernet networks, with or without the presence of other types of storage subsystems, the overall storage network becomes more transparent and fully integrated with overall corporate networking services.

The end-to-end storage chain from a hardware deployment perspective is outlined in Figure 8–1. For example, *blade servers* are chassis-based units with hot-swappable modules. These modules may or may not have embedded disk drives. Almost all have embedded Ethernet on the motherboard, and some may have other device I/O interconnects such as Fibre Channel or InfiniBand. Blade servers allow for high rack density and the ability to allocate distributed resources across a lower cost point.

In each segment of the chain thereafter, we see that enabling technologies continue to drive down cost while providing additional functionality. For example, iSCSI as a device I/O interconnect commoditizes that portion of the chain by directly linking to Ethernet. Intelligent storage nodes, leveraging the cost and performance of Intel x86 platforms, dramatically drive down the entry price point of sophisticated storage devices. In this category the ecosys-

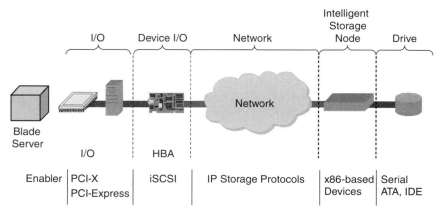

Figure 8–1 Commoditization and open-systems drive fluidity of the end-to-end storage chain.

tem of the x86 chip (operating systems, developers, tools, volumes) provides momentum to capture new market opportunities.

While the example of an intelligent storage node in Figure 8–1 is essentially an in-band device, such as an IP-to-Fibre Channel protocol converter, intelligent storage nodes can reside anywhere in the system. For example, SAN appliances that manage capacity services using virtualization could reside as out-of-band devices anywhere in the network.

Particularly when looking at new, distributed NAS applications and object-oriented approaches such as EMC's Centera line, the form factor of the one-rack unit-mounted server continues to appear. Coupling Ethernet-focused NAS and object-oriented storage platforms with block-oriented storage technologies delivers a powerful flexibility mechanism for consolidation. Most importantly, this open-systems, commodity-oriented hardware approach enables IT managers to build robust, enterprise class solutions. While perhaps not capable of serving all enterprise requirements, storage networks using x86 intelligent storage nodes are likely to gain from x86 ecosystem benefits and will increasingly capture a larger percentage of the overall functionality.

Benefits of the x86 ecosystem include

- *Size reduction:* smaller sizes provide more form-factor flexibility.

- *Power reduction:* lighter power requirements increase operating range.

- *Development scope:* large number of developers and software tools.

- *Industry volumes:* high volumes drive lower cost.

- *Scalability:* increases in performance provide built-in scalability.

8.1.2 Migrating Storage Functions in a Fluid Environment

With a centralization on lower cost, commodity-oriented hardware for end-to-end storage functions, the migration of storage functions increases. The proliferation of storage appliances means that storage functions can easily move out of traditional host-based or target-based implementations and into network implementations. This trend was covered in more detail in Chapter 4. The increasing availability of lower cost platforms within the storage distribution layer means that this trend will only continue.

If we combine the core, distribution, and access layers of the storage models covered in Chapter 2, "The Storage Architectural Landscape," and Chapter 5, "Reaping Value from Storage Networks," along with the adoption of intelligent storage nodes, we get the model shown in Figure 8–2.

The layered architecture of the IP storage model allows maximum flexibility by removing dedicated requirements between storage platforms (NAS, SAN, and object) and the underlying infrastructure. The same flexibility occurred when removing the direct-attached link between servers and storage. Now customers have widespread choices when locating storage services and storage platforms. For example, NAS servers can be easily set up and configured using Microsoft's Server Appliance Kit (SAK). An x86 PC running the SAK could also have a small back-end SAN, allowing a portion of a storage pool to be allocated to NAS platforms. The SAK would represent an intelligent storage node in Figure 8–2.

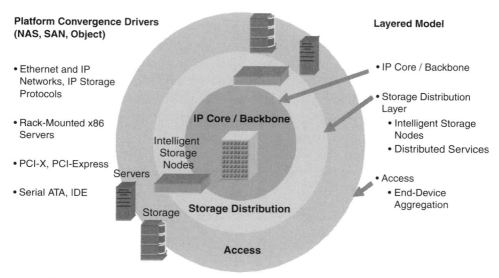

Figure 8–2 Applying fluidity to the IP storage model.

Common SAN-oriented solutions that fit the IP storage model include protocol conversion and volume functions. For example, a customer might want to provide remote office access to Fibre Channel storage. In that case, a server could be deployed with both iSCSI and Fibre Channel PCI adapters. The Fibre Channel adapter connects to the storage, and the iSCSI adapter connects to the IP network used for remote access. This intelligent storage node may also provide basic volume aggregation features to the remote servers for storage allocation.

Object-oriented storage platforms separate metadata about the storage object from the actual user data in the storage object and provide an easy, indexable, referenceable means to access and retrieve that information. For data types where the indexing information can add up to a significant portion of the data storage, separation of the metadata provides scaling and performance advantages. Consider email as an example. In the case of a short, two- or three-line email, the metadata about an email (to, from, date, subject, size, etc.) can add up to as much as the data itself (i.e., the actual message text). Many object-oriented platforms run on rack-mounted x86 servers, using IP and Ethernet as the primary communications means and storage access.

8.1.3 Retention of Specialized Storage Equipment

The use of x86 platforms as intelligent storage nodes is not meant to imply the replacement of other specialized storage equipment. We are likely to see the continued deployment of enterprise-class storage functions on specialized hardware platforms for storage. These were outlined in a figure from Chapter 4, repeated here as Figure 8–3. Within the network fabric or SAN core, hardware-enabled appliances, switches, and directors will continue to be deployed for the most demanding applications. There is simply no way that a multipurpose server platform could reach the same performance levels as custom hardware and ASICs. Yet even today these custom hardware products are gravitating towards more modular, flexible design. In the director category, vendors have introduced multiprotocol and application-specific blades, providing significant robustness to migrate additional storage functions into these devices.

On the target side, RAID systems with intelligent controllers are likely to outperform more generic platforms. The caching functions of large storage systems provide significant throughput advantages for high-transaction applications. Given the design integration benefits of having the cache closely integrated with the drive controllers, this element of storage functionality

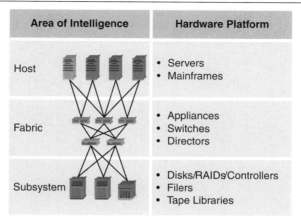

Area of Intelligence	Hardware Platform
Host	• Servers • Mainframes
Fabric	• Appliances • Switches • Directors
Subsystem	• Disks/RAIDs/Controllers • Filers • Tape Libraries

Figure 8–3 Locations for storage intelligence.

will likely remain subsystem-focused and part of hardware-specific platforms such as the multi-terabyte disk arrays from Hitachi, EMC, and IBM.

Areas of intelligence in Figure 8–3 can be viewed as an overlay on the IP storage model in Figure 8–2. The host and subsystem intelligence layers fit in the access layer of the IP storage model. The fabric intelligence translates to the storage distribution layer and the IP core.

8.2 Qualifying and Quantifying IT Deployment

Faced with the requirement to keep storage up and available all the time, IT professionals need to continually qualify and quantify new deployments. Earlier in the book, we covered the trend towards defensive storage purchases, particularly the focus on disaster recovery solutions. In this section, we cover offensive approaches to evaluating storage projects and focus on measurement techniques that take a more strategic view of the overall enterprise infrastructure.

8.2.1 Minimizing Improvement Costs

To measure and minimize improvement costs, the IP storage model can be used to categorize the role of the IP core across storage deployments. Overlaying the intelligence areas of host, fabric, and subsystem with the access, distribution, and core layers allows IT planners to map solutions that can best take advantage of IP storage networking in the larger enterprise context. As shown in Figure 8–4, a variety of current and planned storage platforms can be mapped to the IP storage model. For NAS, servers directly access NAS

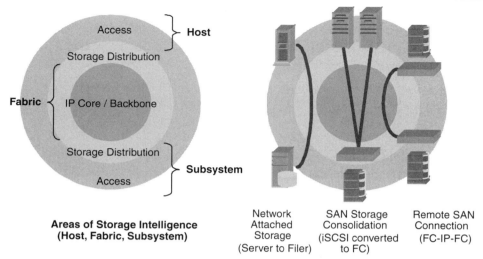

Figure 8–4 Overlaying host, fabric, and subsystem intelligence with the IP storage model.

filers across an IP and Ethernet core. For storage consolidation applications, iSCSI servers might connect to an IP-to-Fibre Channel router to consolidate on enterprise storage. In the remote replication case, Fibre Channel disk systems are linked to each other across an IP and Ethernet network.

Looking at the broader enterprise storage landscape, we see the emergence of product categories across the primary storage platforms of SANs, NAS, and object-oriented storage. As shown in Figure 8–5, each storage platform has a variety of products that make up the complete solution. These products fit across access, distribution, and core layers. Let's take the example of a conventional Fibre Channel SAN. In a typical scenario, a customer might have Fibre Channel servers and disk arrays. These products would fit into the access layer. A SAN appliance, such as an intelligent storage node for virtualization, would fit in the distribution layer. Fibre Channel switches would fit into the core. Note, however, that the core of this product suite, being Fibre Channel–centric, cannot be consolidated with other product cores from NAS- or object-based storage, as those cores are built with IP and Ethernet networks.

This kind of infrastructure outline can help when planning platform consolidation (through product consolidation) and also in balancing storage intelligence across various layers. Let's dig deeper into the example of remote replication for a SAN. A current solution might include two Fibre Channel disk arrays with subsystem intelligence for mirroring and replication. These intelligent arrays include all of the required software to make use of trans-

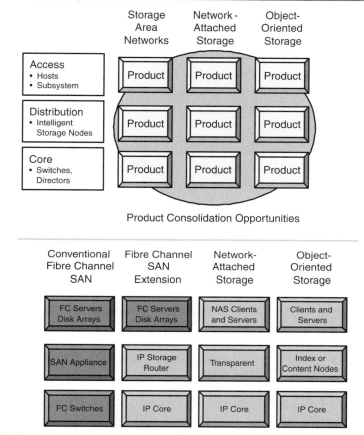

Figure 8–5 Minimizing improvement costs through product consolidation.

parent distribution and core layers. A new solution might migrate some of the remote replication functionality from the disk subsystem into an intelligent storage node within the distribution layer, such as a storage router, which is also capable of replication functions. This disintermediation of storage functions provides customers additional choices of subsystems and could also facilitate easier integration or use of the IP core.

8.2.2 Designing an Effective Migration

An effective migration combines the maximum use of existing resources and personnel with the most easily implemented additions. IT professionals must consider a range of hard and soft costs associated with storage deployments that include the choice of devices, network fabrics, storage software, and personnel.

The flexibility of commoditized elements in the storage chain allows storage architects to combine the performance of specialized hardware platforms with the low-cost flexibility and functionality of intelligent storage nodes. In many cases, both types of platforms can be combined for an optimal solution.

One example of combining custom storage hardware with modular intelligent storage nodes is storage reclamation. This cost-effective, low-impact, high-return solution showcases the best of conventional and nonconventional approaches. Frequently, enterprise customers will need to complete major overhauls of their storage infrastructure at the expense of retiring older equipment. Consider, as one customer did, a forklift storage upgrade from SCSI-attached to Fibre Channel-attached disk arrays. The capacity and performance of the new Fibre Channel arrays significantly simplified the group's storage operations—so much so that they found themselves unable to find a use for the SCSI-attached arrays. The SCSI-attached storage could no longer fill enterprise needs in the data center. While it may have been able to suit less intensive departmental needs, the SCSI interface prevented easy access across a wide variety of departmental users.

Enter the intelligent storage node. Based on an x86 server platform, the customer made use of an iSCSI-to-parallel SCSI router with volume aggregation functions. This device "front-ended" the SCSI arrays and presented iSCSI-accessible volumes to departmental users over existing IP and Ethernet networks. The customer was able to effectively migrate this SCSI storage into a broader enterprise context, making use of an existing IP and Ethernet core with minimal additional investment in IP storage routers.

8.2.3 Calculating Total Cost of Ownership and Return on Investment

For years, total cost of ownership (TCO) and return on investment (ROI) have been used as measures for justifying IT investments. These quantitative measures attempt to boil down the myriad tangible and intangible costs into a simple, easy-to-understand "go" or "no go" decision on the IT project at hand.

The typical TCO calculation accounts for a range of cost factors, including the capital acquisition, installation and training, support, maintenance, and ongoing administration. The complementary ROI calculation measures the savings from completing the project and the payback on the initial investment over a period of one or more years.

Typical TCO and ROI analyses are project-centric and often do not incorporate synergies across enterprise IT expenditures. When planning for major IT investments, companies should consider the investment beyond the scope of the IT department. Treating IT as a corporate investment broadens the implications for business success or failure, and more accurately reflects the fit with company strategy.

Treating IT as corporate investment requires

- Demonstrated ROI path

- Short-, mid-, long-term company gain

- Ongoing match with business growth outlets

The corporate planning process requires

- Consistency with company strategy

- Manageable cost

- Acceptable technical and commercial risk

- Competitive differentiation and sustainability

8.2.4 Managing an IT Portfolio

Beyond single IT projects, the true value of IT investments is realized through portfolio management. When considered in this framework, companies can take advantage of high-risk and low-risk projects with a variety of paybacks. Since many new technology initiatives fail, spreading investment dollars across numerous projects helps reap overall returns. The same principle has been applied with financial diversification for years.

Portfolio management is often confused with project management. The distinctions are outlined in Figure 8–6.

In the same manner that investment portfolio managers balance risk and returns, senior IT professionals must balance a variety of projects across the business criticality and innovation axis. A properly managed portfolio will invest in projects that fit within each of the sectors, as shown in Figure 8–7.

8.3 IP Storage Network Scenarios

The IP storage model can be applied to a wide range of scenarios. In this section, we explore some typical SAN applications. In the following section, we explore actual case studies that carry the IP storage model further with distributed storage intelligence and functions.

The three IP storage network scenarios covered, SAN extension, storage consolidation, and service provider SANs, all overlay onto the concentric

STRATEGIC	TACTICAL
Portfolio Management	**Project Management**

- Are we doing the **RIGHT** projects?
  - Visibility, Alignment, Risk, Priorities, Balance, Value

- Are we spending in the **RIGHT** areas?
  - Investment Types, Strategic Objectives, Estimated Cost, Budget

- Do we have the **RIGHT** resources?
  - Primary Skill, Resource Type, Allocation, Capacity

- Are we doing projects well?
  - Scope, Budget, Schedule, Resources, Deliverables, etc.

- Are projects on time and budget?
  - Schedule, Status, Forecast Cost, Budget, Actuals

- Do resources know what they are doing?
  - Task Assignments, Schedules, Timesheets

Figure 8–6 Separating portfolio management from project management. *(Source: Mainstay Partners)*

circles of the IP storage model. In each case the IP core represents a different element of the universal IP network. For SAN extension, the IP core is the metro-area or wide-area IP link connecting the remote sites. For storage consolidation, the IP core might be redundant enterprise Gigabit Ethernet switches. For service provider SANs, the IP core is the high availability metro Ethernet

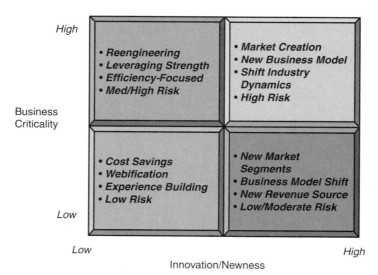

Figure 8–7 A technology investment portfolio. *(Source: Mainstay Partners)*

network. The multidimensional approach and broad applicability of the IP storage model presents strategic cost savings across a portfolio of IT projects.

IP storage networking, particularly in the context of metro- and wide-area networking options, is covered more thoroughly in Chapter 9, "Assessing Network Connectivity."

8.3.1 SAN Extension

SAN extension fits most corporations' needs for remote mirroring, backup, and recovery. Typically, to guarantee availability in the event of a site disaster, the remote location is several kilometers away at a minimum, though up to hundreds and thousands of kilometers is not uncommon. A conventional approach of connecting two Fibre Channel SANs natively has limitations in that the link must be dedicated fiber-optic cabling and cannot take advantage of the IP core.

Implementing an IP storage connection using intelligent storage nodes such as IP storage switches or gateways allows customers to leverage existing IP cores for remote connectivity. The IP core may be in the form of a dedicated or provisioned metro- or wide-area IP network. Figure 8–8 depicts an IP core for remote mirroring applications.

Use of an IP core for remote mirroring benefits TCO and ROI in the following ways:

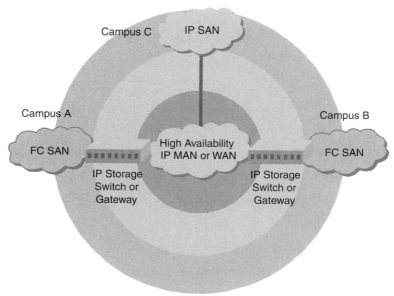

Figure 8–8 Using IP networking for SAN-to-SAN remote mirroring.

- Familiar IP and Ethernet management tools for IP networks lead to lower training costs.

- More IP and Ethernet components lowers hardware costs for end users.

- Centralization on IP core enables migration path to new IP storage deployments.

- Robust IP security and encryption tools protect mission-critical data.

8.3.2 Storage Consolidation

Another common SAN application is storage consolidation, which provides the benefits of pooling storage resources together for sharing, centralized management and administration, and addition and removal of resources. With isolated storage islands, each server group has dedicated storage resources. Dedicated resources lead to high management costs and poor scalability and availability of storage and servers. This type of configuration can easily lead to server and LAN bottlenecks, and single points of failure.

Storage consolidation using an IP storage model allows companies without extensive Fibre Channel resources to make maximum use of their IP infrastructure. In this case, as shown in Figure 8–9, a customer could deploy

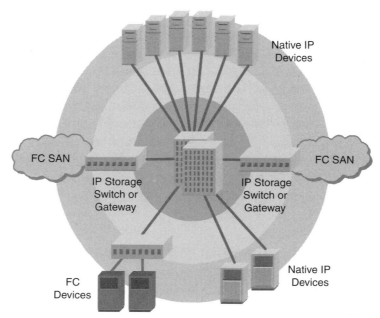

Figure 8–9 Using an IP core for storage consolidation.

Gigabit Ethernet switches as an IP core, surrounded by iSCSI and Fibre Channel storage access nodes. Protocol conversion can easily be provided by IP storage switches or gateways. This scenario provides massive consolidation on an IP storage fabric.

Use of an IP core for storage consolidation benefits TCO and ROI in the following ways:

- Single enterprise focus simplifies management and administration costs.

- Network consolidation leverages existing IP and Ethernet resources and staff.

- Consolidation reduces overall storage amount and perhaps some servers.

- Use of additional IP and Ethernet components lowers TCO in hardware and software.

8.3.3 Service Provider SANs

Chapter 7, "Options for Operational Agility," covered the benefits of using storage service providers to maximize operational efficiency. In many cases, companies create the services and offerings of a professional provider at a similar cost. It therefore frequently pays to outsource some portion of the storage infrastructure.

Before block-based IP storage networks emerged, most service providers were restricted to parceling out customer storage on a SAN-by-SAN basis. This could involve dedicated links between each customer and the service provider. Since the availability and cost of dedicated fiber-optic cabling makes this difficult in metropolitan areas, most SSPs offered services within collocation facilities.

Using widely available IP networks, SSPs can take advantage of relatively inexpensive bandwidth to offer a variety of storage services. The multiple customer configuration is shown in Figure 8–10.

Use of an IP core for service provider SANs benefits TCO and ROI in the following ways:

- Readily available IP bandwidth saves provider and end-user costs.

- IP infrastructure can be easily partitioned, allowing multiple customers to be segmented within one network.

- The IP network makes use of Open Shortest Path First (OSPF), Border Gateway Protocol (BGP), and autonomous regions for maximum scalability.

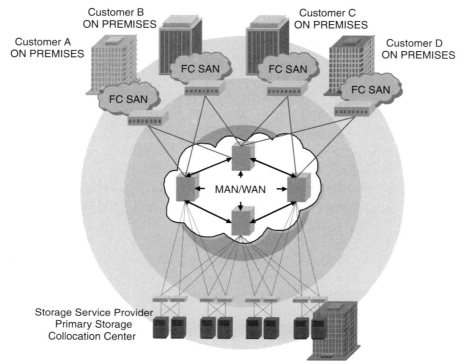

Figure 8–10 Metropolitan area IP connectivity for outsourced storage services.

8.4 Maximizing Operational Efficiency

The examples in the previous section present several compelling reasons to deploy an IP core as part of a storage network deployment. Though the examples span a range of conventional SAN applications, the inclusion of the IP core delivers cost savings and functionality not available in traditional implementations. But the reach and potential for storage applications that make use of a robust, high-speed IP core go well beyond the types of examples described so far.

With the increasing fluidity of the end-to-end storage chain, as evidenced by the introduction of commoditized networks, interfaces, and hardware platforms, and the ability to distribute storage functions across these components, several new storage applications emerge. These applications take advantage of available infrastructure beyond conventional means and deliver powerful opportunities to tailor storage infrastructure to particular needs.

In this section, we take a specific look at two implementations for dealing with fixed content and the solutions that were applied. These customer scenarios complement other types of IP storage network examples in the book by maintaining the IP core as a central deployment theme. When storage strategies are combined, companies can develop synergistic technology opportunities that favor lower TOC and increased returns.

8.4.1 Fixed-Content Storage Networking Impact

The type of mission-critical information enterprises store is shifting from traditional database and transaction information to fixed-content information such as email, business documents, medical images, check or invoice images, log files, and other static, flat-file information. Mission-critical fixed content does not change after creation, but it contains important information that must be stored and accessed over a long period of time. Fixed content is growing so rapidly that it is overtaking the amount of database and transactional information stored in corporate networks. According to a study by the Enterprise Storage Group, fixed-content information is growing at a compound annual growth rate (CAGR) of 92 percent, while database and transactional information is growing at a CAGR of 61 percent. As a percent of overall storage within the enterprise, fixed-content information will overtake database and transactional information by the end of 2004, as shown in Figure 8–11.

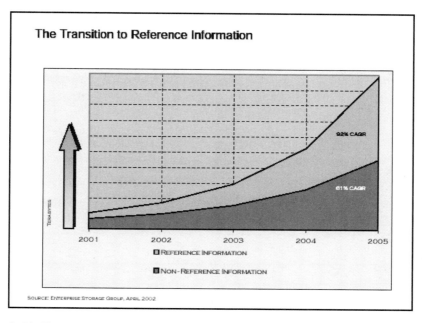

Figure 8–11 The transition to reference information. *(Source: The Enterprise Storage Group, April 2002)*

Today's storage solutions are built for high-availability enterprise applications such as online transaction processing (OLTP), enterprise resource planning (ERP), and data warehousing, with fixed content a relatively small part of the enterprise storage need. As such, the bulk of today's systems cater to the needs of dynamic data and applications. In this dynamic data world, data is stored in volumes and files, and performance is focused on block and file I/O and system availability. In the fixed-content world, data is stored in objects with metadata and "content address" tags, and performance is focused on metadata query processing, real-time indexing, and retrieval. Fixed content drives two changes in today's storage paradigm, the focus on vertical performance intelligence and the necessity for a networked system.

Storage network performance has moved from historical measures of disk density, fault tolerance, and input-output speed to new measures based on application performance. Similar to how databases have been tuned to perform on specific storage platforms, so must other performance-intensive applications be tuned. In order for a fixed-content system to perform well, applications, database, content search, and storage management must act in concert with hardware components. As such, a vertical performance intelligence emerges in which the link between applications and storage become as important to performance as the individual components themselves. The entire vertical software stack, from application to storage management, must be tuned to address the needs of fixed-content storage. This is different from legacy storage systems, which predominantly focus on component or horizontal intelligence.

One way the storage infrastructure performs in such an environment is to physically separate the data from the metadata. Separating data from metadata implies the necessity for a networked infrastructure that can scale the two components independent from each other. Figure 8–12 outlines a comparison between the needs of fixed content and dynamic data storage.

Dynamic: OLTP, ERP, Data Warehousing ...	Fixed Content: Email, Images, Documents ...
Throughput Block and file I/O	Retrieval Speed Metadata query processing
Availability 99.9999% uptime	Availability 99% uptime
Total Cost of Ownership Component versus component cost	Total Cost of Ownership Greater upstream and downstream cost implications (e.g., more exchange servers required to point to data)

Figure 8–12 Comparing dynamic and fixed-content characteristics.

8.4.2 An Email Storage Case Study

Email has been singled out as a runaway train driving many storage and storage-related expenditures. The requirement, real or perceived, to store and access this information over time poses a serious problem for IT departments and budgets. Not only must IT departments store this information, but users must also have ready access to it to conduct business effectively. In many corporate enterprises, email and office documents are the primary source of the company's corporate history, knowledge, and intellectual property. Therefore, protection of and timely access to this information is as mission-critical as an online transaction database. Due to SEC regulations, many financial services companies must store email for at least three years. In 2002 the SEC planned to levy over $10 million in penalties to financial services companies for noncompliance to these regulations. In other regulated vertical industries, such as pharmaceuticals, transportation, energy, and government, similar regulatory trends mandate saving email and other fixed content (e.g., customer records, voice recordings) for long periods of time. The proliferation of corporate scandals in 2002 will push this trend out into other vertical industries. Email has become the de facto audit tool for all mission-critical areas of a business.

According to the Radicati Group, average email storage per user per day will grow from 5 MB in 2002 to 8.6 MB by 2006. See Figure 8–13.

To explore the impact of fixed-content email storage on storage network design, let's consider a financial services company that charges its user departments approximately $0.25 per MB per month to store email and email attachments. With a current email box limit of 50 MB, this company spends approximately $150 per user per year. With raw storage hardware at approximately $0.05 per MB, this means that other hard and soft costs of

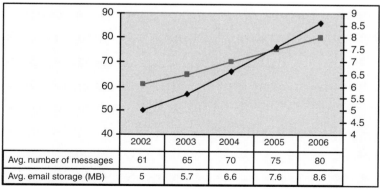

	2002	2003	2004	2005	2006
Avg. number of messages	61	65	70	75	80
Avg. email storage (MB)	5	5.7	6.6	7.6	8.6

Figure 8–13 Increase in email use per user per day. *(Source: The Radicati Group, Inc.)*

storing email are over 50 times the cost of the raw storage media alone. Industry benchmarks indicate that the costs of managing storage are normally 7 to 10 times the cost of storage, but email presents some extraordinary demands on the system.

The problem arises from storing email over a long period of time. The first component of the storage architecture is storing the email online, where users have a capacity limit for their mailbox, perhaps 50 MB as in the example above. The second component of the architecture is more problematic, as it archives the email when it has dropped off the mailbox infrastructure but still needs to be accessed. Archives are valuable only if a user can access information within a minute or two to solve a business need. For example, quality control managers, audit teams, and compliance officers must be able query and retrieve email over multiyear periods to conduct their everyday business processes.

To illustrate the magnitude of archiving email, consider the following example from another financial services company. This company archives 1.5 TB of email per month, with an average size of 33 kilobytes (no attachments). To meet regulatory requirements, email must be stored and must be accessible for a minimum of three years. With 54 TB and 1.64 billion objects to store, the demands and costs explode:

- 54 TB of storage for the data in its native form.

- 18 TB of storage for the database index that points to structured information (e.g., to, from, date, reference).

- 9 TB of storage for the content search engine that points to the unstructured information in the text of the email (e.g., company and topic names.) This can be stored as record fields or via binary scan that is used to create a unique content tag for the entire message.

In this case, the storage and management of the metadata becomes a bigger problem than the storage of the data itself. The costs of the storage real estate are only the beginning as you consider the CPUs and backup infrastructure necessary to support these systems. The staffing costs are also significant if you consider what DBA resources are needed to manage an index with 1.64 million entries.

To solve email storage management, customers have deployed solutions that separate the metadata from the actual data to provide highly scalable indexing solutions, as shown in Figure 8–14.

The separation of index information from content allows allocation of independent resources. In Figure 8–14, the intelligent storage node represents

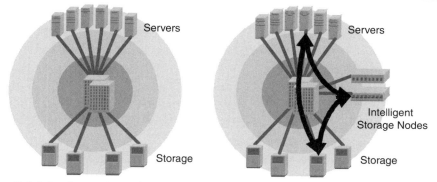

Figure 8–14 Implementing a distributed system for email storage.

an indexing node, and additional nodes can be added as needed. If the querying time needs acceleration, but the total amount of data hasn't changed, adding additional indexing nodes can help. Similarly, if more storage is required for content yet there is flexibility on query and access times, only storage needs to be added. Of course, the flexibility is derived from the separation of resources on a network, typically by using IP and Ethernet.

While this type of storage solution varies significantly from the IP storage network configurations described earlier in this chapter, it highlights the breadth of solutions that make use of the IP core.

8.4.3 Imaging Fixed Content

Fixed content comes in a variety of types, each requiring a specific optimized storage solution. Email indexing data is relatively easy to manipulate. Consider the simplicity of sorting by standard email fields such as to, from, date, subject, and so on. Even without indexing data, the ability to take a binary scan of an email message is quite simple. Standard images, specifically digital photographs, are not easily indexed via metadata or binary scan and therefore cannot universally benefit from the same solutions. Anyone with a digital camera knows the trials and tribulations of keeping track of digital pictures and how complicated the filing of that data can get.

Yet digital images are rapidly consuming storage, both individually and for companies that specialize in processing, printing, and storing digital media. Every boost in the megapixel capabilities of a new camera directly impacts the amount of storage required for the photographs.

In 1999 several companies jumped into the online photo business, offering digital photograph storage as a way for consumers to share and print photographs over the Internet. Many of these companies did not survive the dotcom meltdown and were out of business within a couple of years. However, several survived and continued to prosper. In the race to stay in business, managing storage played an increasingly competitive role in these businesses. Without a cost-effective means to handle the influx of terabytes of customer photographs, these companies could not survive.

One promising company that recognized this challenge early on and took an aggressive approach to managing storage costs is Snapfish. In January 2000, during the initial build-out of its storage infrastructure, the company spent just shy of $200,000 per terabyte for roughly 8 terabytes of usable storage. By late 2002, that figure dropped to roughly $10,000 per terabyte. While some of that price decline can be attributed to macroeconomic factors and the pricing power transfer from vendors to customers, it is also a direct result of an aggressive company campaign to drive storage costs down through adaptive infrastructure and shift in the architectural model for storage.

8.4.4 Achieving the Ten-Thousand-Dollar Terabyte

In January 2000 Snapfish executives selected a complete storage solution from a prominent enterprise storage vendor. The package included a single tower with just over 8 usable terabytes for $1.6 million, or roughly $200,000 per terabyte, and a three-year support and maintenance agreement. To facilitate the image storage, Snapfish selected a NAS approach and front-ended the storage with a vendor-provided NAS head. Both the database files of customer data and the images were housed on the same storage. However, this particular solution lacked flexibility in that the vendor controlled all maintenance and configuration changes. In the rapid development of Snapfish's business and infrastructure, this relationship proved inefficient in handling the customer's needs.

By the end of 2000, the company knew it had to make adjustments to fuel the dramatic growth in its business. One of the unique aspects of Snapfish's business model is that it develops print film for customers, yet also provides a wide range of digital photography services. But with a roll of film using about 10 megabytes of storage, and over 100,000 rolls coming in every month, Snapfish was expanding by over 1 terabyte a month. A lower cost solution for image storage was needed.

Since the transactional nature of the Web site required more rapid response than the high-volume nature of the image storage, the company split its storage requirements. It moved the customer database information to storage provided by its primary server vendor, facilitating tighter integration and minimizing support concerns. At the same time, it moved the high-capacity image storage to specialized NAS filers. The new NAS storage included just over 6 terabytes at an approximate cost of $120,000 per terabyte. This cut storage costs by over 40 percent, but more importantly, placed the company in an advantageous position. By going through the process of selecting and migrating to a new vendor, it developed the technical expertise to handle a shift in the storage infrastructure and gained negotiating leverage in vendor selection.

Another unique aspect Snapfish's business is high-resolution image retention. The company stores high-resolution images of customer photographs for up to 12 months based on a single print purchase. This leads to enormous requirements for high-resolution storage. Only 10 percent of the overall storage requirements serve low-resolution images, such as those that are used for display on the Web site. Therefore, the company has two distinct classes of image storage. Low-resolution images are frequently accessed, require rapid response times, but do not consume excessive storage space. High-resolution images have medium access requirements, require moderate response times, and consume approximately 90 percent of the total storage. Of course, in both cases, reliability and high availability are paramount.

The quest to find low-cost storage for high-resolution images led Snapfish to place a bet on a low-cost NAS provider using a commodity NAS head with less expensive IDE drives on the back end. Towards the end of 2001, it took a chance with a moderate storage expense of $18,000 for 1.6 terabytes for a cost of $11,250 per terabyte—a startling drop to just over 5 percent of the cost per terabyte only two years prior! Unfortunately, that purchase came with a price of excessive downtime that ultimately became untenable. Yet the aggressive nature of Snapfish's storage purchasing, including what could be called experimentation, continued to add migration expertise and negotiating leverage to the organization.

Ultimately, the company went back to specialized NAS filers, though this time it selected a product line that included IDE drives. By returning to the brand-name vendor it had used previously, it did pay a slight premium, purchasing over 8 terabytes at a cost of approximately $25,000 per terabyte. This provided the required reliability and availability but kept the cost of the high-resolution image storage low.

At the time of this book's printing, Snapfish was in the middle of its next storage purchasing decision as the direction of the overall industry moves towards distributed intelligence throughout the network with a focus on the IP storage model. The continued addition of individual NAS filers left the IT department with a less than optimal method of expanding storage. With

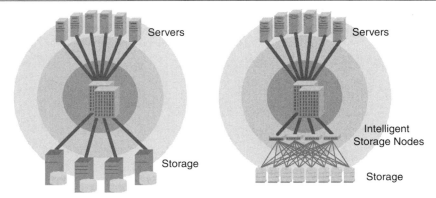

Figure 8–15 Distributed intelligent storage nodes for NAS scalability.

each filer having a usable capacity of under 10 terabytes, the configuration fostered "pockets" of storage. Also, having to add a filer to increase the number of spindles in the configuration (or the total number of disk drives) meant adding overhead simply to expand capacity.

Snapfish looked to a distributed NAS solution. Instead of the traditional filer-based approach, this new solution incorporated a set of distributed NAS heads, each connecting to a common disk space. Server requests can access any available NAS head that in turn queries the appropriate disk drives to retrieve the files. The solution provides significant scalability and requires only additional disk drives, not additional filers, to expand capacity.

This distributed NAS solution builds upon a Gigabit Ethernet core for the storage infrastructure and fits into the overall IP storage model. In this case, the access layer holds the disk drives, which are IDE-based to provide a low-cost solution. The distributed NAS heads fit in the IP storage distribution layer, providing file access between servers and disk drives. By maintaining an IP core, the IT department has tremendous flexibility to add other storage platforms to the overall infrastructure as needed. Simplified diagrams of the initial and future configurations are shown in Figure 8–15.

8.5 Chapter Summary

Initiating Deployment

- Effective deployment couples traditional SAN concepts with nontraditional models for new storage platforms.

- Nontraditional models involved both network and intelligence shifts.

8.1 Infrastructure Design Shifts

- The storage infrastructure chain is undergoing rapid commoditization of hardware platforms.

- Disk drives such as serial ATA provide more density with lower power requirements and at lower cost than other drive types.

- x86 server platforms are now used to build NAS servers, multiprotocol routers, and storage subsystems.

- New I/O interconnects such as PCI-X and PCI-Express provide higher throughput and smaller form factors, eliminating previous systems design constraints.

- Device interconnects such as Fibre Channel, parallel SCSI, and Ethernet are increasing in speed, becoming more functional.

- Networking and I/O spaces are converging.

- Including x86-based systems in the storage hardware food chain dramatically affects the overall cost structure due to benefits of the x86 ecosystem, such as size reduction, power reduction, development reach, and industry shipment volumes.

- The migration to a more open-systems and commoditized infrastructure means that storage services can more easily move throughout the system.

- Specialized storage hardware based on proprietary ASICs and accompanying software will continue to dominate the high-end enterprise markets.

8.2 Qualifying and Quantifying IT Deployment

- The IP storage model maps network utilization across storage platforms to key storage services locations.

- IT professionals need to balance products in access, distribution, and core layers across storage platforms.

- Product consolidation opportunities exist across categories to deliver cost savings.

- Effective migrations couple existing environments with open-systems deployment.

- Use of the IP storage model leads to product lifecycle extension through applications such as storage replication.

- Realizing financial gains from technology requires treating IT as a corporate investment.

- Coupling IT investment with corporate planning processes ensures financial fits with business goals.

- IT professionals must manage both strategic and tactical goals of project management.

- Use of portfolio management for technology guarantees long-term sustainability.

8.3 IP Storage Network Scenarios

- SAN extension, storage consolidation, and service provider IP storage scenarios make use of core IP networking infrastructure for cost savings and return on investment.

- Use of an IP core for remote mirroring benefits TCO and ROI.

  - Familiar IP and Ethernet management tools for IP network lead to lower training costs.

  - More IP and Ethernet components lowers hardware costs for end users.

  - Centralization on IP core enables migration path to new IP storage deployments.

  - Robust IP security and encryption tools protect mission-critical data.

- Use of an IP core for storage consolidation benefits TCO and ROI.

  - Single enterprise focus simplifies management and administration costs.

  - Network consolidation leverages existing IP and Ethernet resources and staff.

  - Consolidation reduces overall storage amount and perhaps the number of servers.

  - Use of additional IP and Ethernet components lowers TCO in hardware and software.

- Use of an IP core for service provider SANs benefits TCO and ROI.

  - Readily available IP bandwidth saves provider and end-user costs.

  - IP infrastructure can be easily partitioned, allowing multiple customers to be segmented within one network.

  - The IP network makes use of OSPF, BGP, and autonomous regions for maximum scalability.

8.4 Maximizing Operational Efficiency

- Maximizing operational efficiency requires merging common IP storage networking applications with new storage applications, such as those dealing with fixed content.

- Fixed content, or reference information, is growing at a faster rate than other types of data storage.

- Fixed-content storage characteristics differ from dynamic content in performance characteristics, availability requirements, and TCO.

- Email is one of the largest consumers of corporate data storage and falls into the fixed-content category.

- The cost of managing email typically exceeds the cost of email storage by a factor of as much as 50 times.

- Since indexing information is so critical to email, separating the index information (or metadata) from the email itself helps build more scalable systems.

- Intelligent storage nodes can be used as indexing nodes to allocate resources to speed query and retrieval times.

- IP storage networks deliver a highly scalable, flexible platform for distributed content-addressed storage.

- Imaging fixed content has different indexing requirements than imaging text-based information.

- As a vital part of business costs, one online photography company, Snapfish, learned how to manage its storage costs effectively through aggressive networked storage strategies.

■ Initial costs per terabyte for Snapfish were close to $200,000.

■ Two years later, the company was assessing storage configurations at less than 10 percent of that cost.

■ Snapfish built core competencies in migrating between vendors.

■ Snapfish took risks on new technologies.

■ Snapfish is currently evaluating a distributed NAS model that would include NAS heads and scalable back-end storage.

■ The distributed NAS platform moves NAS functions into the IP storage distribution layer and retains inexpensive disk space in the access layer.

■ All of Snapfish's configurations have built upon a core IP and Ethernet network.

9 Assessing Network Connectivity

Looking at the complete picture of local and remote storage solutions, network connectivity continues to play an increasingly larger role in the overall deployment. Resources are distributed—requiring a network. Solutions must accommodate enormous scalability—requiring a network. Also, business continuity mandates remote sites for backup and availability—requiring a network. Fortunately, with IP and Ethernet–focused storage communication, both in data center installations and across MANs and WANs, much of the existing infrastructure can be used.

Network storage deployments combine both defensive and offensive thinking. On the defensive side, companies can protect data repositories using as much of the existing network infrastructure as possible, providing business continuity and higher asset utilization. On the offensive side, companies can focus future storage networking investments in line with other corporate data networking initiatives, realizing greater economies of scale with high-ticket items like bandwidth. Network consolidation also contributes significantly to reduced management cost by centralizing on common platforms.

Understanding the makeup of existing corporate data networking infrastructure allows storage architects to properly design systems involving local and remote network connectivity. Chapter 9 begins with an explanation of layered protocols and how those translate to use in storage networks. An outline of metropolitan- and wide-area storage networks follows to provide an understanding of the basic deployment models.

Since traditional storage networking products were separate from mainstream data networking products, a new category of products has emerged. These products bridge data center storage networking with metropolitan- and wide-area connectivity. However, as those lines blur, so do the products, and a number of separate platforms provide conversion features.

Chapter 9 also includes a description of bandwidth services offered by telecom providers. The last mile of connectivity has always been a challenge. However, there have been many recent advances to increase that segment of the network. Consumers have witnessed the change from dial-up modems to high-speed cable and DSL connections. Today, thousandfold bandwidth increases are available to companies for remote storage network bandwidth. Bottlenecks are shifting, and the resulting change in products and services requires that storage administrators take a closer look at new networking options.

9.1 Modern Networks Use Layered Protocols

Over the past few centuries, the transportation of physical goods has evolved from using specialized railcars, wagons, and ships that were loaded manually to using universal cargo containers that can be moved over railroads, highways, and oceans without repacking. Likewise, over the past few decades, the transportation of electronic information has evolved from proprietary systems to systems that use standard protocol layers so data now can travel around the globe over various types of networks in a common IP packet.

Layer one, the *physical layer*, can be likened to a railroad. As long as the wheels fit the rail width, it doesn't really matter what type of railcars are used. It could be boxcars, hopper cars, or flatcars—the railroad moves them all. Twisted-pair and fiber-optic cables, including their carrier signals, are examples of physical-layer networks, as are wave division multiplexers *(muxes)*. Since they also provide rudimentary framing, Synchronous Optical Network (SONET) and Synchronous Digital Hierarchy (SDH) do not fit the exact definition of a physical-layer network, but often get listed as such anyway. Perhaps they could be likened to railcars, which generally are considered to be part of the rail service. Here, too, they will be called physical-layer protocols. SONET and SDH offer only fixed-bandwidth service and connection-oriented addressing, whereas most *layer two* protocols offer variable bandwidth service and the more flexible connectionless addressing, so the characteristics of SONET and SDH are a bit more like layer one than layer two.

Layer two, the *link layer*, is analogous to big-rig truck trailers. They can be pulled on most streets and highways, moved on flatbed railcars, and even can be driven onto a ferryboat for short trips across water without unloading the contents. Ethernet, Token Ring, and Fibre Channel are examples of link-layer network protocols and can be transmitted over almost any type of physical layer network.

Layer three, the *network layer*, would correspond in this example to universal cargo containers. There are only subtle differences between shipping systems based on truck trailers and those based on modular cargo containers. For long-haul shipments by rail or sea, it is more efficient not to ship the wheeled trailer, so it is common to ship only the containers and place them on another wheeled trailer at the destination for local distribution. Compared to trucking systems, perhaps today's global containerized cargo-routing systems are a bit more sophisticated and universal.

That may be a good representation of the subtle differences between layer-two and layer-three networking. For long-haul data transmission, it's a bit more efficient to strip off the Ethernet frames and send only the network-layer packets, reframing them with Ethernet again at the destination for local distribution. Likewise, the layer-three network-routing algorithms are more sophisticated and universal. IP, DECnet, and AppleTalk are examples of network-layer protocols. Over the past few years, IP has become the de facto standard.

These analogies are shown in Figure 9–1. Just as cargo containers can be placed on big-rig truck trailers and driven onto flatbed railcars for long-haul transportation, IP packets can be encapsulated in Ethernet frames and transported over SONET multiplexer networks (SDH outside North America).

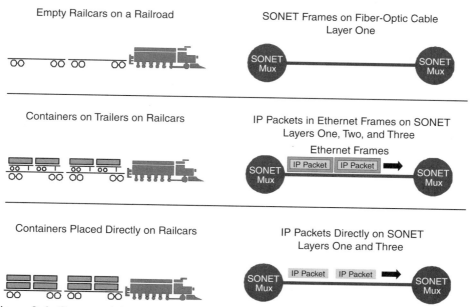

Figure 9–1 Cargo and data transport analogies.

Most SONET (and SDH) muxes now have Ethernet interface cards, so Ethernet LAN switches can be connected directly to the muxes. Extending the railroad comparison, for somewhat better efficiency, cargo containers can be placed directly on the railcars, just as IP packets can be sent directly over SONET multiplexer networks using packet-over-SONET routers.

Packet-over-SONET routers strip off the Ethernet frames as they are received from the LAN switches and forward only the IP packets to the multiplexers, using the SONET format. The process is reversed at the destination so that Ethernet LAN switches can be used for local distribution of the IP packets. In this case, using the designation that the SONET muxes are layer-one devices, the long-haul portion of the network does not use layer two, as the layer-three packets are sent directly over the layer-one network.

Figure 9–2 shows a comparison of the protocols that are used to transport the data end to end, along with the transmission rates commonly used today. Note that the networking industry generally expresses rates in *bits per*

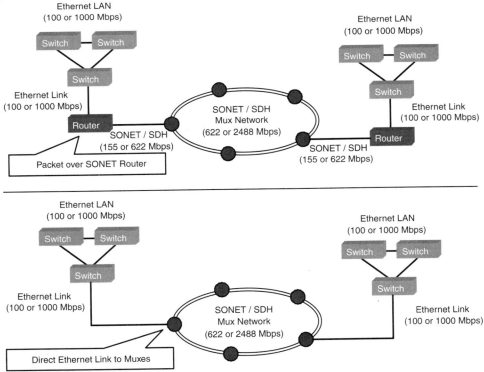

Figure 9–2 Ethernet interfaces on multiplexers enable direct link from LAN switches.

second (bps), rather than in *bytes per second (Bps)*, as is common in the storage and computing industries.

Now that SONET muxes have Ethernet interface cards, routers no longer are needed at each site to convert Ethernet into the SONET format. That has given rise to a new type of metro-area service, from a new category of service providers, sometimes called *Ethernet Local Exchange Carriers (ELECs)*. The ELEC's *subscribers* (customers) see only Ethernet—most likely Fast Ethernet (100 Mbps) or Gigabit Ethernet (1000 Mbps)—rather than SONET or SDH, at each end of their connection.

For reference, here is some additional service provider lingo: The equipment provided by the subscriber is called *customer premises equipment (CPE)*. The interface between the subscriber and the service provider is the *demarcation point*. In this case, the ELEC's demarcation point is Fast Ethernet or Gigabit Ethernet, thereby reducing the CPE cost, as no router is needed to convert from Ethernet to SONET.

It also is possible to interconnect the Ethernet switches directly with dedicated fiber-optic cable—especially within an office complex or a campus, where it may be somewhat easier to trench new cable or route it through underground steam tunnels. Metropolitan- and wide-area dedicated fiber is more difficult to get, since it must cross public and perhaps private property. Still, some service providers may lease unused *(dark)* fiber to end users or trench new fiber under city streets for a large one-time charge or a long-term lease agreement.

Even where it's available, the cost of dedicated fiber in the metropolitan and wide areas generally has remained quite high, and the installation times are excessive. Consequently, most organizations use public networks with customer interfaces provided at layer one (typically SONET or SDH), layer two (Fast Ethernet and Gigabit Ethernet, now available in many metropolitan areas), or layer three (IP). The Internet is the largest public IP network, and its performance and reliability have become quite good. In fact, virtually all organizations now use it for transmitting email messages, and small ones typically use the Internet for all applications. For critical data transmissions, however, most midsize and large organizations also build their own private IP router network, overlaid on a public SONET/SDH backbone network.

There are additional upper layers in the networking stack, such as TCP (Transmission Control Protocol) at layer four, and other actions such as load balancing. The common models extend through layer seven. However, since most MANs and WANs are generally limited to layers one through three, and layer four typically applies to end systems, the discussion in this chapter is focused on the lower layers.

9.2 Options for Metropolitan- and Wide-Area Storage Networking

Although the proportion of data centers using SANs is growing, most mass storage devices are attached directly to servers or NAS filers via SCSI cables. Some direct-attached storage (DAS) has been converted from SCSI to Fibre Channel, even though SANs have not yet been deployed. Direct-attached disk arrays can be backed up to other arrays and tape libraries by sending the data back through the attached server, across the LAN, to the target storage device through its attached server.

DAS has the advantage of being simple, but it places an added load on the servers and the LAN, as they handle the same data twice (once to write it and again to replicate it). The performance may not meet the requirements of the application, since the servers must convert the more efficient *block-mode* data into file format for transmission across the LAN, then back again to block mode for storing on the target array or tape. Still, if the applications can tolerate the reduced performance, this approach also enables simple remote backups, as the data that is converted into a file format uses Ethernet and IP as its network protocols. In most cases, as shown in Figure 9–3, file-

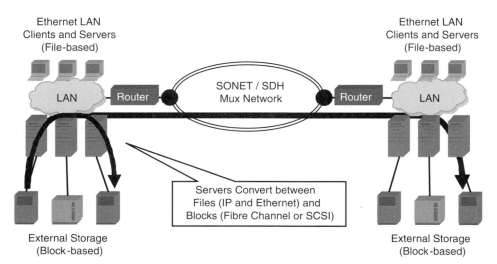

Figure 9–3 File-based backup locally, via the LAN, and remotely, via the existing data network.

based storage data simply can share the organization's existing data network facilities for transmission to other data centers in the metropolitan and wide areas.

Data centers outfitted with SANs not only enjoy the benefits of any-to-any connectivity among the servers and storage devices, but also have better options for local and remote backup. *LAN-free* and *serverless* backups are enabled by the addition of a SAN, and those functions can be extended within the metropolitan area via dedicated fiber, as shown in Figure 9–4.

As outlined in the previous section, dedicated fiber is generally costly, requires a lengthy installation process, and is not available at all locations. In those cases, it may be possible to run fiber a much shorter distance to the multiplexer that is nearest to each data center and send the storage data over an existing SONET/SDH backbone network.

This approach became possible with the advent of Fibre Channel interface cards for the multiplexers. These cards are similar to those developed for Gigabit Ethernet and, as with the Ethernet cards, encapsulate the Fibre Channel frames to make them compatible with the SONET or SDH format for transmission between locations. In this case, the network demarcation point would be Fibre Channel, so subscribers simply can connect their Fibre Channel SANs to each end of the network, with no need for protocol conversion, as shown in Figure 9–4 by the dashed lines.

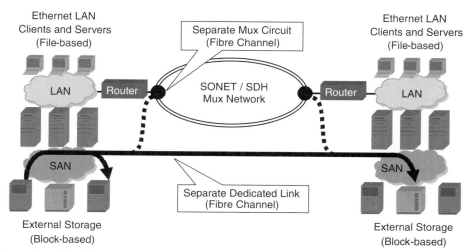

Figure 9–4 Block-based backup locally, via the SAN, and remotely, via dedicated fiber or over the existing SONET network, using a separate circuit and Fibre Channel interface cards in the muxes.

There are, however, some drawbacks to this approach. As the transmission distance is increased, it takes more time to move control messages and data between locations, as dictated by the laws of physics. Fibre Channel switches originally were designed for use within data centers, where transmission delays can be measured in microseconds rather than milliseconds, and the rate at which they transmit data is approximately inversely proportional to the distance between switches.

Performing operations in parallel can overcome some the performance impact of long transmission delays. It is possible to have other data on the fly while waiting for the acknowledgments from earlier transmissions, but that requires large data buffers, and most Fibre Channel switches have relatively small ones. Consequently, the buffers fill quickly in long-distance applications, and the switches then stop transmitting while they wait for replies from the distant devices. Once a *write-complete* acknowledgment and additional flow control credits are received, the switches can clear the successfully transmitted data and fill their buffers again, but the overall performance drops off dramatically over distances of 20 to 30 miles, as the buffers are not large enough to keep the links full.

Inefficiency is another drawback. The channels or logical circuits used by SONET and SDH multiplexers have fixed bandwidth, so what's not used is wasted. Gigabit Ethernet and Fibre Channel circuits on these multiplexers have similar characteristics, but there are dozens of applications that use Ethernet, and only storage uses Fibre Channel. This means that the cost of the Fibre Channel backbone circuit cannot be shared among applications, as is the case with Ethernet.

Besides sharing a circuit, efficiency also can be improved by subdividing a large circuit into multiple smaller ones. For example, a service provider's multiplexer with a single OC-48c backbone link can support, say, three OC-12c subscribers and four OC-3c subscribers. That would limit the subscribers' peak transmission rates to 622 Mbps or 155 Mbps, in return for significant cost savings, as the service provider can support many subscribers with a single mux and pass some of the savings on to subscribers.

For smaller data centers that don't require full Gigabit peak rates, IP storage networks work fine at sub-Gigabit data rates. All standard routers and switches have buffers that are large enough for speed-matching between Gigabit Ethernet and other rates. In contrast, the minimum rate for Fibre Channel is approximately one Gigabit per second.

Figure 9–5 shows the standard transmission rates for SONET and SDH. The small letter *c* suffix indicates that the *OC-1* channels are concatenated to

SONET (North America)	SDH (Rest of World)	Rate
OC-3c	STM-1	155 Mbps
OC-12c	STM-4	622 Mbps
OC-48c	STM-16	2488 Mbps (2.5 Gbps)
OC-192c	STM-64	9953 Mbps (10 Gbps)

Figure 9–5 Rates for SONET and SDH transmissions.

form a single, higher speed channel. For example, *OC-3c* service provides a single circuit at 155 Mbps, not three logical circuits at 52 Mbps.

Today, most midsize and high-end data subscribers use 155 Mbps or 622 Mbps services. The higher rates are very costly and generally are used only by service providers for their backbone circuits. In those applications, OC-192 is more common than OC-192c, probably because the clear-channel 10 Gbps OC-192c router interface cards only became commonly available in 2001, just as the frenzied demand for broadband services started its decline and service providers dramatically scaled back their expansion plans. OC-192 cards, which support four OC-48c logical circuits, already had been installed, and most service providers have continued to use them rather than upgrading.

However, as the demand for broadband network capacity eventually resumes its upward march, and as 10 Gbps Ethernet becomes more common in LAN and IP storage network backbones, high-end subscribers will ask their service providers for clear-channel 10 Gbps metropolitan- and wide-area connections. At that time, routers and Windows Driver Model (WDM) products will be outfitted with more OC-192c interfaces. Meanwhile, the equipment vendors are developing even faster OC-768 interface cards, which support four 10 Gbps OC-192c circuits, so the service providers may wait until they become readily available to upgrade to those products.

Other types of multiplexers are used to deliver services at rates below 155 Mbps. In North America, 45 Mbps *(DS3 or T3)* is popular, and the equivalent international service is 34 Mbps *(E3)*. The bandwidth ultimately can be subdivided into hundreds of circuits at 64 Kbps, which is the amount traditionally used to carry a single, digitized voice call.

Note that in all cases, the services operate at the same speed in both directions. This is called *full-duplex* operation. For storage networking applications, it means that the remote reads and writes can be performed concurrently.

Because Fibre Channel requires at least one or two Gigabits per second of backbone bandwidth, the Fibre Channel interface cards are designed to consume half or all of an OC-48c multiplexer circuit. Many potential subscribers to metropolitan-area Fibre Channel services currently may have only a single OC-3c connection to handle all of their nonstorage data services for those sites, so adding Fibre Channel would increase their monthly telecom fees by a large factor.

At least one mux vendor has tried to overcome this Fibre Channel bandwidth granularity problem by adding buffers and a speed step-down capability to its Fibre Channel interface cards. That may allow Fibre Channel to run over a less costly OC-3c circuit. There are, however, some practical limitations to this approach. Since there are no standards for this technology, these solutions are proprietary, and the speed step-down cards on each end of the circuit must be the same brand. That makes it difficult to find a global solution or change service providers once it has been deployed.

Fortunately, all of the problems with long-distance Fibre Channel performance and efficiency have been solved, within the laws of physics, by IP storage switches. Because they can convert Fibre Channel to IP and Ethernet, the switches can be used to connect Fibre Channel SANs to the standard IP network access router, as shown in Figure 9–6.

By connecting to the service provider network via the router rather than directly, users may be able to get by with the existing network bandwidth—

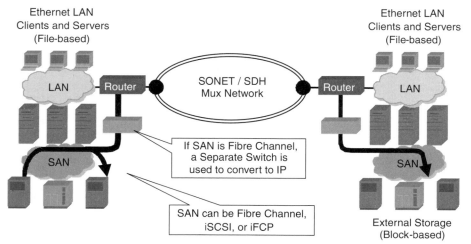

Figure 9–6 Block-based backup locally, via the SAN, and remotely, via the existing SONET network, using IP storage protocols.

especially if they already have 622 Mbps or Gigabit Ethernet service. The resulting cost savings can be significant, and the storage network performance can be installed and tuned easily, using familiar network design practices. This approach also uses standards-based interfaces and protocols end to end, so there's no risk of obsolescence or compatibility problems.

IP storage also has the flexibility to be used with the new ELEC services. Subscribers may elect to use the same network topology—that is, a router at each network access point—as shown in Figure 9–6. In that case, the link between the router and the network would be Fast Ethernet or Gigabit Ethernet rather than SONET or SDH, but all other connections, including the storage links, would remain unchanged.

Should subscribers elect instead to eliminate the routers, as shown previously in Figure 9–2, the IP storage link would be connected to a Gigabit Ethernet LAN switch or directly to a Gigabit Ethernet port on the ELEC's access mux. Connecting to a LAN switch has the economic advantage of sharing the existing backbone connections (assuming there is ample bandwidth to do that), while the direct ELEC link would provide a second, dedicated circuit for higher volume applications.

9.3 Metropolitan- and Wide-Area Storage Network Products

As shown in the previous section, IP storage can be used for metropolitan- and wide-area networking, regardless of the type of SAN used. Fibre Channel currently is, by far, the most common SAN protocol, but the IP storage protocols, iSCSI and iFCP, now have begun to move into the SAN itself.

Ultimately, pure IP storage networks will use iSCSI in every end system, but with several million Fibre Channel end systems already in use and iSCSI end systems just emerging, the conversion to pure IP could take many years. Meanwhile, two transition protocols have been developed (FCIP and iFCP) to enable Fibre Channel SANs and end systems to communicate over standard IP networks.

FCIP (Fibre Channel over Internetworking Protocol) was developed as a simple tunneling protocol for interconnecting Fibre Channel SANs over IP networks. iFCP (Internet Fibre Channel Protocol) also was designed for linking Fibre Channel SANs over IP, but has advanced features that offer better scalability and manageability, and it can be used for building IP SANs within the data center. Figure 9–7 shows a summary of the IP storage protocol recommendations.

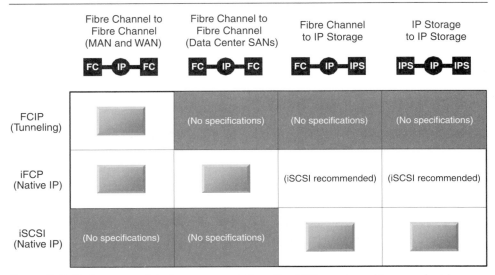

Figure 9–7 IP storage protocol recommendations for SANs, metropolitan-, and wide-area connections.

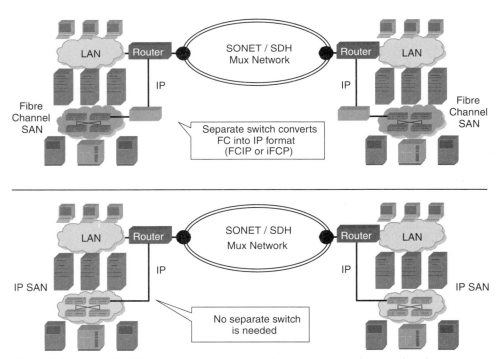

Figure 9–8 Native IP SANs can be interconnected across metropolitan and wide areas with no additional conversion equipment.

The iSCSI and iFCP protocols support data center SANs as well as metropolitan- and wide-area IP storage networking. In IP SAN applications, the core of the SAN is native IP and Ethernet—the same protocols used in MANs and WANs—so no additional conversion is needed to connect an IP SAN to the backbone network. A single iSCSI or iFCP product can be used for both the SAN and the MAN and WAN access, as shown in Figure 9–8.

Within the data center, IP SANs can be expanded easily, using off-the-shelf Gigabit Ethernet switches, which now support well over 200 wire-speed ports. As shown in Figure 9–9, native IP (iSCSI) end systems can be connected directly to the Gigabit Ethernet core switches, and Fibre Channel end systems can be linked to the core switches using standard multiprotocol storage switches that support IP, iSCSI, and iFCP.

It seems likely that at least a one-port FCIP or iFCP gateway could be built into an interface card for a Fibre Channel switch, and some Fibre Channel switch vendors have announced that they are working on that capability. That would offer the advantage of eliminating the external Fibre Channel-to-IP conversion switch. However, the SAN itself then would remain as a conventional Fibre Channel switch fabric rather than being a native IP SAN, so another (iSCSI) interface card would have to be developed for the Fibre Channel switch to support native iSCSI end systems.

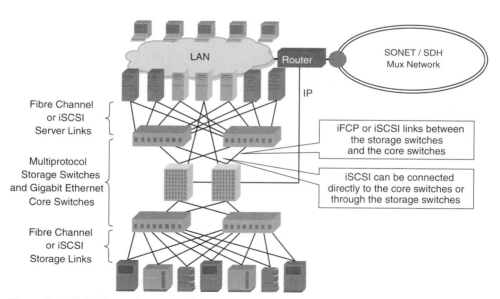

Figure 9–9 IP SANs can be expanded easily, using standard Gigabit Ethernet core switches.

With IP end systems, a Fibre Channel core, and an IP MAN or WAN, it would be necessary to convert iSCSI into Fibre Channel and then back again to IP (FCIP or iFCP) for connecting to MANs and WANs. Managing such a network could be a challenge, and there may be some danger that the iSCSI control frames would be lost during the multiple protocol conversions as they travel from end to end. Therefore, it's probably simpler and safer to use an IP core if the SAN contains iSCSI end systems.

9.4 MAN and WAN Services

Over the past few years, the network services industry has undergone a boom and bust cycle. As a result, many new service providers entered the market, but some already have gone out of business. What's left behind, though, in the United States and other parts of the world, is a glut of installed but unused fiber-optic cable. At the same time, wave division multiplexer vendors continue to improve their products to support more and more logical circuits on the cable that's already in use, further expanding the supply of circuits.

While this boom-and-bust cycle has thrown the networking industry into a state of confusion, the resulting fiber-optic cable surplus has helped to drive down the monthly lease prices paid by subscribers—especially in unregulated areas. In regulated areas, the service provider simply maintains prices and leaves the unused fiber unlit. But even in those areas, new technologies, such as fixed wireless and line-of-sight optical, now offer cost-effective alternatives.

The *last mile* and *local loop* are terms sometimes used in reference to the local connection between the customer premises and the serving *central office (CO)*. For residential dial services, the local loop almost exclusively is metallic twisted-pair cables. With DSL technology, it is possible to transmit a few megabits per second of data over a two- or three-mile long metallic circuit.

Nonresidential subscribers typically have more options for the local network connection. In densely populated urban areas, there could be many potential subscribers in a single building, so service providers may install fiber-optic cable to the building before they have an order, speculating that they can recover their installation costs by landing multiple customers later.

Those installations typically include a SONET or SDH multiplexer that serves as the network access point for all of the subscribers. The mux may be located within the building, but usually not on any customer's premises, since around-the-clock access is required by the service provider and because subscribers don't want their data passing through a potential competitor's facilities. Service providers sometimes refer to this as *customer located equipment (CLE)* to distinguish it from CPE or CO equipment.

In a high-rise office building, the CLE is linked to the subscriber's offices with a cable that passes through a *riser* conduit or elevator shaft. The demarcation point is the end of the cable that terminates on the customer's premises. Today, the riser cable typically is fiber optic, but it also may be coaxial cable for DS3 and E3 services, or twisted-pair metallic cable for voice and lower speed data services.

In some instances, the service provider may install the multiplexer in a *street cabinet* or an underground *telecommunications vault,* which can serve as the network access point for subscribers in many adjacent office buildings. If an existing cabinet or vault has room and a suitable environment for the mux, the service provider can use it as a quicker and cheaper alternative to leasing CLE facilities inside the building.

Office buildings in suburban areas generally have no fiber-optic cable installed unless the previous tenant paid for its installation. Still, it may be only a few blocks away or even passing in front of the building, which would reduce the cost and time required to extend it to a new subscriber. Figure 9–10 shows some of the various methods used by service providers for connecting to their data networking subscribers.

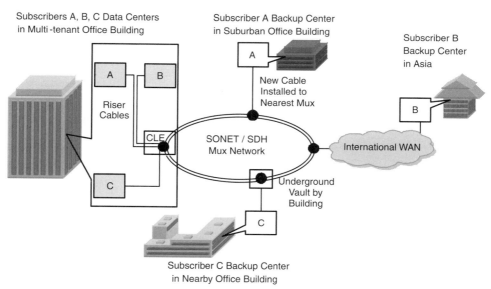

Figure 9–10 Service provider connections vary by subscriber density and location.

With telecom deregulation and reforms in the 1980s and 1990s, the distinctions among categories of service providers have blurred. In simple terms, *local exchange carriers (LECs)* handle metropolitan and regional services, and *interexchange carriers (IXCs)* handle long-distance services. But now it's possible for the LECs and IXCs to get into each other's businesses. *Competitive local exchange carriers (CLECs)* and ELECs generally compete only with the LECs, but some of them have national links between metropolitan areas.

Any of these service providers also could be an *Internet service provider (ISP)*. There are many independent ISPs as well. While the traditional service providers generally specialize in layer-one services, such as dial-up and high-speed data connections, ISPs handle layer-three (IP) data. As previously defined, layer-three packets are sent over layer one facilities or, as in the case of Ethernet services, over layers one and two. If there are multiple service providers involved, the ISPs typically split off their Internet-bound data at the COs, send it to their own backbone facilities or an *ISP peering point,* and leave the remaining network traffic (such as voice and non-Internet data) for the other service provider to handle.

As described previously in this chapter, shared SONET and SDH network subscribers each are assigned fixed-bandwidth point-to-point channels that are logically separated from all other subscribers' data. By comparison, in layer-two or layer-three networks, such as the Internet, subscribers share a multipoint network, each using a variable portion of a large pool of bandwidth as needed, typically making its bandwidth utilization much greater.

This inherent ability to pool bandwidth among layer-three network subscribers enables ISPs to offer a range of prices, according to the amount of *oversubscription* used and the resulting service quality. Residential Internet services may be economical, but most of them include no commitments by the ISPs to limit the network latency or deliver a specified minimum amount of bandwidth. At the other end of the range, ISPs may offer more costly premium services, including *service level agreements (SLAs),* which are aimed at business customers.

Virtual private networks (VPNs) can be used to prevent eavesdropping by other subscribers in a shared public network, such as the Internet. VPN software or dedicated VPN switches encrypt the IP packet and wrap it in another unencrypted IP packet whose address, but not its payload, can be read by the Internet routers. The process then is reversed at the destination and the original packet is delivered intact. VPNs also can be used in private

IP networks to isolate and protect the data from eavesdropping by other users within the organization. VPN technology is explained in greater detail in the following section of this chapter.

The more costly premium Internet services are used for most storage networking data, since its volume and criticality typically surpass that of any other type of data. Or more likely, the storage networking data is sent instead over private shared IP networks. In either case, *data compression* can be used between sites to reduce the bandwidth required, thereby cutting the bandwidth cost or improving the performance of the applications.

Some IP storage switches and most IP routers now offer data compression, so the storage data can be compressed before it's sent to the router, or it can be compressed along with all other data by the router itself. Depending on the repetitiveness of the data, the compression ratios can be as great as 5:1 or better. For backup applications that span long distances or require large volumes of data to be transmitted, data compression can substantially reduce one of the biggest budget items—the cost of bandwidth.

Another possible source of cost savings—especially for relatively short distances—is some form of local loop bypass. Dedicated fiber was mentioned as an alternative previously in this chapter, but its installation cost may be prohibitively high. However, less conventional alternatives recently have become available and probably merit investigation for use where fiber-optic service is costly or not readily available.

Fixed-wireless devices now support data rates of tens of megabits per second over distances of a few miles. Radio-frequency interference and the requirement for rooftop installation sometimes can present insurmountable challenges, but the signal quality is getting better and the size of the equipment is being reduced, which makes it suitable for more applications.

Free-space optical systems also may be a workable alternative for local bypass. They do not suffer from radio interference, but the signal can be affected by physical interference, such as buildings, birds, or fog. Assuming that other buildings can be avoided and a line-of-sight link can be established, the impact of some of the other hazards can be reduced by installing backup links so the signal may be able to find a better alternative path.

Performances of hundreds of megabits per second over distances of a mile or so now are possible for some of these optical systems. Another advantage is that the transceivers can be installed indoors, behind many types of office windows, so it may be possible to avoid the hassle of installing the units on rooftops.

9.5 Security for Storage Networking

The emergence of IP as a network transport for storage has initiated discussions about why IP is not secure for storage. While there are some valid security concerns for the merging of traditional storage and networking topologies, the vast majority of them have already been solved within the data networking community. Many storage pundits who claim IP cannot be secure seem to forget that companies have been running high-speed, secure connections for just about every other enterprise application under the sun. It is highly likely that the robust, enterprise-class security solutions companies rely on today will also work for their IP storage configurations.

That said, security is a multifaceted issue that can easily conjure up fear in the mind of the consumer, which stalls adoption. On the contrary, customers should embrace the entry of IP networking to storage as a means to use the plethora of existing security solutions on the market, ranging from inexpensive, easily implemented, software-based firewalls and encryption tools to gigabit-speed, hardware-assisted 3DES encryption, the most secure commercially available encryption mechanisms.

While Chapter 3, "The Software Spectrum," covered a few lower level security basics, this section clarifies the product implementations required for secure storage networking, particularly those that make use of IP storage and involve shared metropolitan- and wide-area transports. The intricacies of storage security within local environments could fill several chapters, and that discussion is intentionally left out of this section.

9.5.1 Areas of Storage Security

The first task in understanding IP storage security is to break down deployment areas. We can simplify these areas into device I/O, data center SANs, and the SAN interconnect. Device I/O represents the server HBAs or subsystem controllers. These could be either Fibre Channel, IP, or other interface technology. Data center SANs are generally made up of Fibre Channel switches, IP storage switches, or regular IP and Ethernet switches. The third area, SAN Extension, is typically IP- and Ethernet-focused using a layer one optical transport.

Each area mandates the appropriate level of security. For the data center SAN, numerous security solutions exist within Fibre Channel fabrics and new IP storage fabrics. Features like zoning and authentication ensure that only the right users have access to the right storage at any given time. Implemented through a variety of hardware and software features, existing data center SAN security provides a high degree of protection.

Often, security threats focus on mixing traditional SAN topologies with other data center networking topologies. IP storage configurations do not mandate a mix of these networks, and it is perfectly legitimate for customers to have a completely separate IP and Ethernet infrastructure for storage traffic. In fact, many customers do this today to keep heavy-load NAS traffic apart from day-to-day LAN messaging traffic.

Also within the data center SAN, the device I/O components can assist in security features. Fibre Channel HBAs are recognized by Fibre Channel switches and incorporated into standard zoning features. Fibre Channel HBAs can also be recognized by IP storage switches that convert the Fibre Channel traffic to an IP core. In both cases, SAN fabric management provides for security features of zoning, authentication, and access.

For IP end systems, such as iSCSI HBAs, some industry debate has taken place as to whether those devices should build in IP encryption. While some customers may want to have every IP end node encrypt traffic, the performance penalty for such security can be high. Further, it is unlikely that in a small, data center IP SAN, IP storage traffic between a server and a storage subsystem is vulnerable to attack—at least, it is no more vulnerable than any other type of IP traffic within the company's network.

Most frequently, companies protect their LANs and similarly can protect their IP storage networks with IP security protection that resides at the egress point of the data center. In networking terms, the demarcation point is often referred to as the *firewall* between the internal corporate systems and external Web-focused systems. This demarcation point can be effectively used for IP security solutions as well.

Figure 9–11 shows the different areas of storage security and where VPN equipment comes into play for protecting data center SANs. VPNs allow customers to create secure, encrypted connections between two identified end points. This is an economical security solution when combined with shared metropolitan- and wide-area IP transport.

Other security solutions can be implemented across local-, metropolitan-, and wide-area topologies. In layer one networks the security is physical—different links or optical wavelengths keep data paths separate.

In layer two networks the security may use the Media Access Control (MAC) layer. Each end device has a unique MAC address, such as Ethernet MAC or Fibre Channel MAC, that can be used to assist with authentication.

Fibre Channel encryption and IP encryption (IPSec) are possible within data center SANs and can be implemented either on the end-node device or within the switching network.

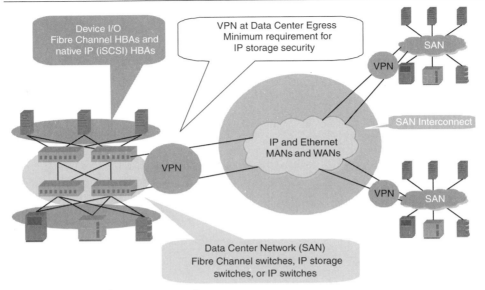

Figure 9–11 Areas for storage security.

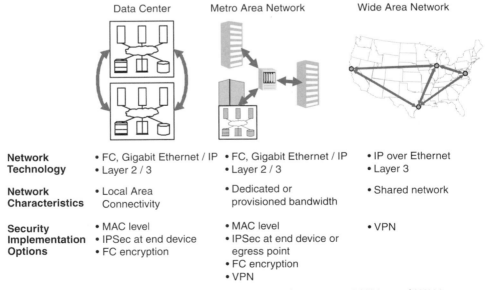

	Data Center	Metro Area Network	Wide Area Network
Network Technology	• FC, Gigabit Ethernet / IP • Layer 2 / 3	• FC, Gigabit Ethernet / IP • Layer 2 / 3	• IP over Ethernet • Layer 3
Network Characteristics	• Local Area Connectivity	• Dedicated or provisioned bandwidth	• Shared network
Security Implementation Options	• MAC level • IPSec at end device • FC encryption	• MAC level • IPSec at end device or egress point • FC encryption • VPN	• VPN

Figure 9–12 Sample security implementation across data center, MANs, and WANs.

For layer three transports, often used in the wide area, VPNs are the most common form of security.

These implementations are outlined in Figure 9–12.

9.6 Chapter Summary

Assessing Network Connectivity

- Networks play a role in all storage configurations, both locally within the data center and across metropolitan- and wide-area topologies.

- Effective deployment requires offensive and defensive thinking for networking.

- Defensive strategies aim to protect existing data using as much of the existing network infrastructure as possible.

- Offensive strategies aim to consolidate current and future investments in line with corporate data networking initiatives for greater economies of scale.

- New product categories bridge traditional storage networking with mainstream data networking.

- Last-mile connectivity continues to rapidly improve, presenting companies with radically different cost and bandwidth models that can influence metropolitan and remote storage networking options.

9.1 Modern Networks Use Layered Protocols

- Data networking is analogous to modern shipping systems and operates with a layered architecture.

- Layer one is the physical layer and can be likened to a railroad.

- SONET (Synchronous Optical Network) and SDH (Synchronous Digital Hierarchy) are layer-one networks.

- Layer two is the link layer and is analogous to big-rig truck trailers.

- Ethernet, Token Ring, and Fibre Channel are layer-two network protocols and can be transmitted across almost any layer-one network.

- Layer three is the network layer and can be compared to containerized freight containers.

- The advantage of a standard container size is the flexibility to move across layer-two and layer-one topologies with virtually no modification.

- IP is the de facto network-layer protocol and can be transported across Ethernet (layer two) or directly on layer one (packet-over-SONET).

9.2 Options for Metropolitan- and Wide-Area Storage Networking

- DAS can use file-based backup over the LAN, with remote connections using existing wide-area transports for other data networking traffic.

- While simple to configure, DAS places added loads on the servers and the LAN bandwidth.

- Some applications can tolerate block-to-file conversions for LAN-based backup; others cannot.

- SANs allow direct network connectivity for backup and other storage operations both locally and across MANs.

- For metropolitan distances, Fibre Channel SANs can use a dedicated link or operate within the existing SONET or SDH network (layer one).

- Fibre Channel SANs operating at 1 or 2 Gbps require the entire optical link be dedicated to SAN traffic.

- Optical links are frequently a high-ticket item and should be provisioned and shared across the entire company.

- Converting Fibre Channel to IP and Ethernet for metropolitan- and wide-area networking allows shared use of expensive optical circuits.

- Ethernet frames can be multiplexed by a layer-three switch or router with SONET or SDH links to the metropolitan optical network.

9.3 Metropolitan- and Wide-Area Storage Network Products

- Metropolitan- and wide-area storage products employ a variety of IP storage protocols for optimized deployment.

- Each protocol implementation is specifically suited to a combination of Fibre Channel and IP SANs and devices.

- IP storage products such as IP storage switches, routers, gateways, and HBAs often make use of multiple protocols, depending on application and topology requirements.

- Conventional storage networking products such as Fibre Channel switches and directors may also implement specific IP storage protocols to accomplish required conversions.

- IP storage switches, routers, and gateways can be deployed to connect two Fibre Channel SANs across MANs and WANs.

- IP storage switches can also be deployed within data center configurations to establish an IP core for the SAN.

- A SAN already using an IP core (such as iSCSI or iFCP) will have IP access built in and not require additional conversion equipment for metropolitan- or wide-area connectivity.

9.4 MAN and WAN Services

- The network services industry has undergone a boom-and-bust cycle.

- A glut of fiber-optic cable has been left behind in the wake of bankruptcies and other debacles, leaving ample supply of unused bandwidth available for corporations.

- The last mile or local loop has traditionally been the biggest bottleneck for companies to get high-speed access to optical networking services.

- Commercial areas frequently have access to optical bandwidth, particularly in downtown business districts.

- Local exchange carriers (LECs) handle metropolitan and regional networking services.

- Interexchange carriers (IXCs) handle long-distance services.

- Competitive local exchange carriers (CLECs) and Ethernet local exchange carriers (ELECs) compete with LECs by offering new services and may also have links between metropolitan and regional areas.

- LECs, IXCs, CLECs and ELECs generally provision layer-one and layer-two networks.

- Internet service providers (ISPs) generally provision layer-three networks.

- ISPs can pool bandwidth among layer-three network subscribers, enabling a range of prices and services.

- Virtual private networks (VPNs) allow secure connections on layer-three networks.

- Data compression helps reduce the need for bandwidth—critical for more expensive layer-one or layer-two networks.

- New options in fixed-wireless and free-space optical systems present attractive last-mile bandwidth access.

9.5 Security for Storage Networking

- The introduction of IP networking to storage has brought with it numerous questions about security.

- Most data center SAN security has been solved using comprehensive zoning mechanisms for fabric configuration, device access, and management.

- Metropolitan- and wide-area networking have been secured using encryption and VPNs—solutions that have served the mainstream data communications market for years.

- Security areas can be broken down to device I/O, data center SANs, and metropolitan- and wide-area SAN interconnect.

- Each area mandates its own security considerations.

- The minimum requirements for IP storage security is a VPN at the data center egress point to a shared or provisioned network.

- Additional security options are available within data center SANs and at the device I/O level.

- Implementing end-to-end encryption for IP storage security may have performance impacts.

10
Long-Distance Storage Networking Applications

Impressive forces of nature continually shape our planet. Over the ages, earthquakes have formed mountain ranges and floods have carved huge canyons that today attract tourists and sports enthusiasts. However, when people and buildings—and data centers—are in their path, these forces can be devastating.

In the early 1990s, Hurricane Andrew flooded more than three dozen major data centers. Since that time, we have become even more dependent on quick access to stored data. Most IT managers now have remote data replication systems for disaster recovery, but those systems can be costly and cumbersome to manage.

Remote data replication consists of archiving or mirroring. Archiving is a commonly used process in which data is written to portable media, such as optical disks or magnetic tapes. For disaster recovery purposes, the disks or tapes are physically transported to an offsite location and stored. Depending on the regulatory or self-imposed replication requirements, the data may be transported across town or hundreds of miles away.

Data mirroring operates over a metropolitan- or wide-area storage network and can be fairly bandwidth-intensive, as it requires either continuous replication using synchronous mirroring of disk arrays or batch processing for asynchronous mirroring. Mirroring enables two sites to share the same set of data so that either can continue to operate on that data in the case of a site outage. Due to the distance and performance limitations of the conventional Fibre Channel switch technology, mirroring had, until the advent of IP storage networking, been used mainly for critical applications and had been limited to relatively short distances.

10.1 IP Storage Networking Expands Remote Data Replication

The distance and performance limitations of Fibre Channel switches primarily are the result of practical rather than technological barriers. As mentioned in Chapter 9, "Assessing Network Connectivity," virtually all of the world's private and public networks now use IP as their communications protocol, so all other protocols, including Fibre Channel, must be converted to or encapsulated in IP packets for transmission across standard IP networks. Beyond that, conventional Fibre Channel switches typically have none of the wide-area networking facilities that are common in IP switches, such as large data transmission buffers, intelligent credit spoofing, and data compression, which collectively improve long-distance network performance.

Some of the new multiprotocol storage switches include all of those wide-area IP networking facilities and provide wire-speed protocol conversion between Fibre Channel and IP. Therefore, they can be used to front-end existing Fibre Channel switches or Fibre Channel end systems and link them via standard IP networks to remote locations that can be hundreds or even thousands of miles away.

With large data transmission buffers and intelligent credit spoofing, the multiprotocol switches can convince the Fibre Channel switches or end systems to forward chunks of data much larger than the amount that could be stored in their own buffers. The multiprotocol switches continue to issue credits until their own buffers are full, while the originating Fibre Channel devices suppose that the credits arrived from the remote site. Credit spoofing affects only the flow rate of the data and not the data itself or its end-to-end write-complete acknowledgments, so the integrity of the data never is compromised.

The added reach and performance of IP storage networking gives IT professionals more options for backup and consolidation. Data centers can back up each other, or a centralized backup data center can be established and shared among the primary data centers, as shown in Figure 10–1.

Since storage data can be moved faster and farther over economical high-speed networks, it now is possible to back up more applications at greater distances from the areas that might be impacted by an earthquake or hurricane. During off-peak periods, the storage network can be used to transfer data to archival sites, where it can be copied to optical disks or tapes. Compared to physically transporting the media, storage networking offers a less labor-intensive, more secure, and more reliable approach. Centralizing the

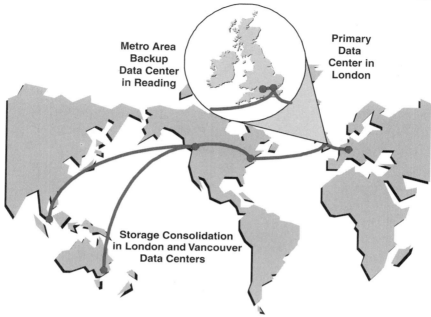

Figure 10–1 Remote data replication and centralized backup with IP storage switches.

media transfer also may be more economical, as many sites can share the backup equipment and staff.

10.2 The Technology Behind IP Storage Data Replication

Today, virtually all high-speed networks use fiber-optic cables to transmit digital voice and data. While the speed of light in a vacuum is about 186,000 miles per second (300,000 Km/s), the index of refraction of the typical *single-mode* fiber-optic cable reduces that to about 100,000 miles per second, or 100 miles per millisecond.

In other words, if the distance between the primary and backup data centers within a metropolitan area were 50 miles, then the 100-mile round-trip delay would be about a millisecond. Conventional Fibre Channel switches can tolerate a millisecond of delay without much performance degradation, but the locations that can be reached within a millisecond may not be sufficiently far from the primary data center to escape the same disaster, defeating the purpose of the backup data center.

Consequently, many IT professionals want to transfer block-mode storage data beyond the metropolitan area to other cities. The backup center may also serve as a centralized data replication site for data centers in other cities that are much farther away. Taken to the extreme, that could be thousands of miles, resulting in tens of milliseconds of round-trip latency. For example, it would take about 50 ms for data to be transmitted over fiber-optic cable on a 5,000-mile round trip across the United States or Europe. For reference, this transmission latency also is called *propagation delay*.

Added to that delay is the latency of the switches, routers, or multiplexers that are in the transmission path. Today's optical multiplexers add very little latency, and Gigabit Ethernet switches also add only tens of microseconds (a small fraction of a millisecond), but some routers can add a few milliseconds of latency to the data path. Modern routers, however, are much faster than their earlier counterparts. For example, in a test conducted by the Web site *Light Reading,* the maximum latency of a Juniper M160 router with OC-48c links was about 170 microseconds. In a typical network, data would pass through two or three of these routers in each direction, adding only about a millisecond to the round trip. This form of latency typically is called *switching delay, store-and-forward delay, insertion delay,* or *node delay.*

The third type of latency is *congestion delay* or *queuing delay.* As in highway design, shared network design primarily is a tradeoff between cost and performance. Highways that have more lanes can carry more vehicles at full speed, but also are more costly to build and are underutilized except during peak commuting periods. So, taxpayers are willing to put up with a few extra minutes of driving time during peak periods to avoid the large tax increases that would be needed to fund larger capacity roads. Likewise, shared networks can be designed to handle peak data traffic without congestion delays, but their cost is much greater and the utilization much lower, so most organizations are willing to tolerate occasional minor delays.

Within a building or campus network, where 100 Mbps or 1 Gbps of LAN traffic can be carried over relatively inexpensive twisted-pair cables and Gigabit Ethernet switches, the average network utilization may be only a few percent—even during peak hours. But MAN and WAN facilities are much more costly to lease or build, so network engineers typically acquire only enough capacity to keep the average MAN or WAN utilization below 25 to 50 percent. That amount of bandwidth provides a peak-to-average ratio of 2:1 or 4:1, which generally is sufficient to handle the peak periods without adding unacceptable queuing delays.

As mentioned in the previous chapter, most service providers have installed much more capacity over the past few years by upgrading their routers and transmission links to multi-gigabit speeds. Those upgrades have resulted in dramatic improvements in the overall performance of their networks while reducing all types of latency and error rates.

For example, the AT&T IP network consistently provides end-to-end data transmission at close to light speed with near-zero packet loss rates. The network's current performance can be monitored via the AT&T Web site: *http://ipnetwork.bgtmo.ip.att.net/current_network_performance.shtml.*

Figure 10–2 shows the results of a query made at 1:30 p.m. Pacific Time on a typical Tuesday afternoon, which would be near the nationwide peak U.S. network loading period.

As shown, most of the latency figures are quite impressive. Assuming a nominal propagation delay of one millisecond per hundred miles, the round-trip latency between New York and San Francisco would be about 59 ms (5,900 miles) plus the delays attributable to the routers and some congestion queuing, which one would expect during this peak period. In this case, however, the round-trip latency was measured to be only 61 ms, which means that the sum of the delays caused by the routers and the congestion queuing

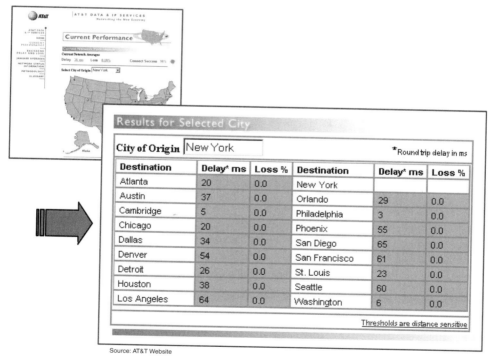

Source: AT&T Website

Figure 10–2 IP network performance is close to light speed and packet loss is near zero. *(Source: AT&T Web site)*

was two milliseconds. With at least two routers (most likely more) in the data path adding latency in each direction, the network congestion delay must be negligible for this link and many of the others measured.

Not all IP networks perform this well, but IP can handle far worse conditions, as it originally was designed to tolerate the latencies of congested global networks that, in the early days, could be hundreds of milliseconds. TCP/IP, which runs on top of IP, also withstands packet loss with no loss of data and is resilient enough to provide a highly reliable transfer of information. With the advent of the IP storage protocols, which adapt block-mode storage data to the standard TCP/IP stack, mass storage data now can be transmitted over hundreds or thousands of miles on IP networks.

This new IP storage capability lets IT professionals make their data more accessible in three important ways:

- Mirroring, rather than just archiving data, for instant access to the backup data.

- Using new high-speed IP networks with backbone links up to 10 Gbps for faster transfers.

- Moving the backup data center beyond the metropolitan area for greater survivability.

10.3 Sizing the Link Bandwidth for Long-Distance Storage Networking Applications

As described previously in this chapter, there are two primary types of data mirroring: *synchronous* and *asynchronous*. In determining which to choose, IT managers first must answer the question, Should the storage in our primary data center become completely inaccessible, how much data can we afford to lose? If the answer is none, then synchronous mirroring must be used; otherwise, either asynchronous or synchronous mirroring can be used.

Synchronous mirroring requires that each write must be completed successfully on both the primary and the secondary disk array before the servers or initiators can write more data. That ensures that both sets of data are identical at all times. In general, increasing the network bandwidth available to synchronous mirroring applications increases the write performance of both the primary and the secondary disk arrays, as the pacing factor is the time it takes to transmit the backup data across the network and receive a response from the secondary array. But even with ample network bandwidth, other factors may come into play, which limit the performance. Those factors are explained in the next section of this chapter.

Given enough network bandwidth, disk arrays that are mirrored asynchronously also can be kept in lockstep, but the asynchronous mirroring application provides no guarantee of that. Instead, only a best effort is made to keep the secondary disk array updated by the primary array. Some IT managers may elect to perform batch updates only periodically—say, once per hour or once per day—rather than allow continuous updates.

For continuous updates, increasing the network bandwidth available to asynchronous mirroring applications reduces the amount of lag between the updates to the primary and the secondary arrays, so less data is lost should the primary array go off line. For periodic updates, an increase in the amount of bandwidth available simply shortens the backup time. That has become increasingly important as overnight backup *time windows* shrink due to globalization of commerce and the resulting need for around-the-clock access to data.

There are many ways to estimate the amount of bandwidth needed for metropolitan- and wide-area asynchronous mirroring, but a fairly good starting point is to size the network links for the *peak hour*. At times within that hour, there may be insufficient bandwidth to handle sporadic bursts of data, but for most applications, the bursts last only a few seconds, after which there is ample bandwidth again and the secondary array can catch up.

Assuming that the bursts are not sustained, the peak hour estimate can be used. This approach also can be used for applications in which there are sustained bursts, but which can tolerate the loss of a few minutes of data. In this case, it is okay for the secondary array to fall behind for extended periods of time.

If historical traffic patterns are not available for the primary array, then the activity rate for the peak hour can be estimated by using the procedure shown in Figure 10–3.

Figure 10–4 shows a numerical example of an estimate of the activity rate for the peak hour.

Once the data rate for the peak hour has been measured or estimated, the network bandwidth requirements can be calculated. As mentioned in the

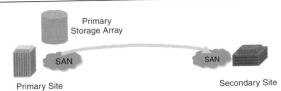

- Determine the amount of data stored on the primary storage array.

Primary Storage Array

SAN   SAN

Primary Site   Secondary Site

- Estimate the portion of the primary storage that is changed on a peak day. For example, the peak day might be a certain day of the week or the last day of each fiscal quarter.

- If the activity on that day is concentrated mainly into, say, eight or ten hours, then an average hourly data rate for the peak day should be calculated over that amount of time rather than over 24 hours.

- If there is a peak hour during the peak business day, it should be used for the estimate rather than simply taking the average rate. For example, if from 1:00 to 2:00 p.m. the data rate is two or three times the average, the circuit should be sized for that rate.

Figure 10–3 Estimating the amount of data to be mirrored during the peak hour.

- The usable capacity of the primary storage array is 12 TB (terabytes). However, the array only is about one-third full, so assume that 4 TB (4000 GB) of actual data is stored.

- On the peak day, approximately 15 percent of the data is changed:

  $$4000\ GB \times 0.15 = 600\ GB$$

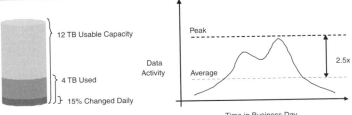

12 TB Usable Capacity

Data Activity

Peak

Average

2.5x

4 TB Used

15% Changed Daily

Time in Business Day

- During the day, most of the activity occurs between 9:00 a.m. and 7:00 p.m. (ten hours), so the average amount of data written per hour during that period is approximately

  $$600\ GB\ /\ 10\ hours = 60\ GB/hour$$

- The amount of increase over the average for the peak hour of the day is not known, so a peak-to-average ratio of 2.5 is used:

  $$60\ GB/hour \times 2.5 = 150\ GB/hour$$

Figure 10–4 Numerical example of a peak hour data activity estimate.

- Convert the peak hour data estimate from gigabytes per hour to megabytes per second.

- Add approximately 10 percent for network protocol framing overhead.

- Convert from megabytes (*MB*) to megabits (*Mb*). There are about 1.049 million (2^{20}) bytes in a megabyte of data and there are eight bits in a byte of data, so the conversion factor is 8.39.

Figure 10–5 Estimating the amount of traffic on the network links.

previous chapter, network bandwidth is measured not in bytes, but in bits, per second, so care is needed to insure the correct units are used. Also, some framing overhead is required to transport the data over the network, and that must be added to the bandwidth calculation, as shown in Figure 10–5.

Extending the results of the numerical example for calculating the peak hour, the network bandwidth estimate is shown in Figure 10–6.

Some of the new multiprotocol storage switches and IP routers have a data compression facility, which reduces the amount of network bandwidth needed. For highly repetitive data, the compression ratio can be better than

- The amount of data written to the primary storage array during the peak hour is 150 GB. That can be converted to megabytes per second *(MBps)* as follows:

  150 GB/hour x 1000 MB/GB = 150,000 MB/hour
  150,000 MB/hour x 1 hour/3600 seconds = 41.6 MBps

- Including the additional framing overhead, the amount of WAN traffic generated per second during the peak hour is

  41.6 MBps x 1.1 = 45.8 MBps

- In bits per second (bps), the estimated WAN bandwidth required for this application is

  45.8 MBps x 8.39 Mb/MB = 384 Mbps

Figure 10–6 Numerical example of a network link traffic estimate.

10:1. Ratios for mixed storage data typically range from about 2:1 to 5:1, so an estimate of 3:1 is fairly conservative.

For the example shown in Figure 10–6, the assumption of a 3:1 data compression capability would reduce the bandwidth requirement from 384 Mbps to 128 Mbps, which could be handled safely by a standard OC-3c (155 Mbps) network link. Without data compression, a much more costly OC-12c (622 Mbps) network link would have been required for this application.

If, during the peak hour, there are sustained bursts of data, and the loss of a few minutes of data is unacceptable, then a better network bandwidth estimate may be needed. Fortunately, in situations where network designers know that there are sustained bursts, the knowledge most likely was derived from historical traffic patterns on the primary disk array, so that same traffic pattern information also can be manipulated to produce a better bandwidth requirement estimate.

For example, if the goal were to limit the data loss to no more than 10 seconds, the historical traffic pattern observations could be sliced into 10-second samples and the network link could be sized to handle the largest observed value. That may call for a link that has much more bandwidth and costs much more than the one that was derived from the peak hour calculations.

If the cost of the faster link is too great, a calculated risk can be taken as a compromise. More sophisticated statistical analysis could be used to determine, say, the 95th percentile value of the peak 10-second observations, and the necessary network bandwidth could be derived from that. In that case, the link would be expected to handle all but 5 percent of the peak data rates for any 10-second interval. Depending on the variability of the data rate, it's possible that the 95th percentile of the 10-second interval data rates could be covered by the bandwidth needed for the peak hour.

Other analysis tools can be used to produce bandwidth requirements estimates. For example, if the raw traffic data is available for the primary array, it can be relatively easy to use time series analysis to produce an estimate of the peak loading for various intervals of time. A basic *moving average* model can be used, adjusting the averaging period to correspond to the maximum amount of data loss that can be tolerated and taking the peak values produced by the model.

In general, as the sample intervals become smaller—one second or subsecond—bandwidth models for asynchronous mirroring become virtually identical to bandwidth models for synchronous mirroring. However, since there is no possibility of data loss for synchronous mirroring, the amount of bandwidth allocated to those applications affects instead the amount of time that the servers have to wait for the data to be written remotely before they can proceed to the next write operation. That waiting time also is affected by the latency of the network, which is examined in the next section.

10.4 Estimating the Effects of Network Latency on Applications Performance

Providing the storage network with sufficient bandwidth is a necessary, but not sufficient, step to ensuring good performance of a storage networking application. If excessive network latency is causing the application to spend a large amount of time waiting for responses from a distant data center, then the bandwidth may not be fully utilized, and performance will suffer.

As mentioned previously, network latency is comprised of propagation delay, node delay, and congestion delay. The end systems themselves also add *processing delay,* which is covered later in this section.

Good network design can minimize node delay and congestion delay, but a law of physics governs propagation delay: the speed of light. Still, there are ways to seemingly violate this physical law and decrease the overall amount of time that applications spend waiting to receive responses from remote sites.

The first is credit spoofing. As described previously, credit spoofing switches can convince Fibre Channel switches or end systems to forward chunks of data much larger than the amount that could be stored in their own buffers. The multiprotocol switches continue to issue credits until their own buffers are full, while the originating Fibre Channel devices suppose that the credits arrived from the remote site.

Since the far-end switches also have large buffers, they can handle large amounts of data as it arrives across the network from the sending switch. As a result, fewer control messages need to be sent for each transaction and less time is spent waiting for the flow control credits to travel end to end across the high-latency network. That, in turn, increases the portion of time spent sending actual data and boosts the performance of the application.

Another way to get around the performance limitations caused by network latency is to use parallel sessions or flows. Virtually all storage networks operate with multiple sessions, so the aggregate performance can be improved simply by sending more data while the applications are waiting for the responses from earlier write operations. Of course, this has no effect on the performance of each individual session, but it can improve the overall performance substantially.

- Determine the actual route distance between the endpoints of the network link. The service provider usually can furnish that information. Assume a propagation delay of one millisecond per hundred miles (round trip).

- Determine the number of switches and routers in the data path. The service provider also can furnish that information or at least estimate it. Assume a relatively conservative estimate of two milliseconds per switch or router. Be sure to include the number of nodes in both directions for the round trip delay.

Figure 10–7 Estimating the propagation and node delays.

Some guidelines for estimating propagation delay and node delay are shown in Figure 10–7.

Network congestion delay is more difficult to estimate. In a well-designed network—one that has ample bandwidth for each application—it simply may be possible to ignore the effects of congestion, as it would be a relatively small portion of the overall network latency. Even in congested networks, the latency can be minimized for high-priority applications, such as storage networking, through the use of the traffic prioritization or bandwidth reservation facilities now available in some network equipment.

Congestion queuing models are very complex, but a method for calculating a very rough approximation of the network congestion delay is shown in Figure 10–8.

Figure 10–9 shows a numerical example of estimates for the total network latency.

- Determine the current average utilization of the network link without the storage application (0–100 percent).

- Subtract that value from 100 percent to derive the proportion of bandwidth that is available for the new storage networking application.

- Divide the total node delay by the proportion of bandwidth available for the new storage networking application. For example, if all of the bandwidth is available for storage networking, the divisor will be 1.0, and there will be no additional congestion queuing. On the other hand, if only half of the bandwidth is available, the divisor will be 0.5, which would predict that the node delay would be doubled by the congestion queuing.

Figure 10–8 Estimating the congestion queuing delay.

- The distance between the endpoints of the network link, which connects the primary and secondary data centers, is 200 miles. Therefore, the round-trip propagation delay is:

  200 miles x 2 = 400 miles

  400 miles x 1 ms/100 miles = 4 ms

- There are four routers in the path taken by the data, so the estimated round trip node delay is:

  4 nodes x 2 x (2 ms/node) = 16 ms

- The current average network link utilization without the storage application is 15 percent, so the amount of bandwidth available for the new storage networking application is:

  100% − 15% = 85%

- With congestion processing delay, the round trip node delay is increased to:

  16 ms / 0.85 = 19 ms (in this case, the congestion delay adds 3 ms)

- The total network latency (propagation delay + node delay + congestion delay) is:

  4 ms + 16 ms + 3 ms = 23 ms

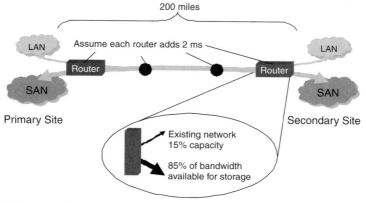

Figure 10–9 Numerical example of total network latency estimate.

In simplest terms, the maximum rate at which write operations can be completed is the inverse of the network latency. In other words, if the data can be sent to the secondary array, written, and acknowledged in 23 ms, as in the numerical example, then in one second, about 43 operations can be completed for a single active session, as shown below:

$$1s / 0.023s = 43.5$$

The rate of remote write operations can be increased linearly, up to a point, by increasing the number of active sessions used. So, if four sessions were used in the example, the performance would increase to 174 write operations per second:

$$43.5 \times 4 = 174$$

As mentioned, there is a point at which other factors may limit the performance of the remote write operations. For example, transactions with large block sizes may be limited by the amount of network bandwidth allocated. Or, in applications that have plenty of bandwidth, the performance of the serverless backup software used to mirror the disk arrays may have an upper limit of, say, 40 to 50 MBps.

10.5 The Effects of TCP on Application Performance

In Chapter 9, Ethernet and Fibre Channel were cited as examples of layer-two protocols, and IP was cited as an example of a layer-three protocol. Where end systems are involved, additional networking layers may be used to provide important facilities, such as data integrity. IP uses TCP to guarantee end-to-end data integrity and automatic flow control. The term *TCP/IP* is used to indicate that both protocols are employed.

Initially, it was thought that TCP/IP could not be used for storage networking applications, as it would place an excessive load on the end systems—the servers, disk arrays, and tape libraries. TCP requires a large amount of processing power and, until recently, had been handled by the server CPU, limiting the amount of TCP a box can run and still have useful cycles left over.

However, early in 2002, TCP offload adapters became commercially available and changed this workload balance. These specialized adapter cards include a hardware-based TCP offload engine that handles IP storage protocols at full wire speed over a Gigabit Ethernet interface. The loading on the server CPU is no greater than that of a Fibre Channel HBA, so TCP/IP has become a viable storage networking protocol. Vendors now are sampling 10 Gbps TCP offload engines and have promised to deliver IP storage adapter cards that have 10 Gbps Ethernet interfaces during 2003.

Although the limitations of the TCP computational intensity have been overcome, another limitation—flow control—still can cause network performance problems. TCP was designed for use in very large networks and, indeed, it is used today by hundreds of millions of users of the world's largest network, the Internet. To ensure fairness and accessibility by millions of simultaneous users, TCP uses a fairly conservative flow-control algorithm.

In effect, each user is granted a modest initial data flow rate that increases as acknowledgments are returned from the destination end system when the IP packets are received without errors. If packets are dropped or contain errors, the sending system must fall back to a much lower flow rate and start once again to ramp its rate. In a well-designed network, TCP has little impact on performance, but in a congested or error-prone network, the overall performance can be cut by more than half.

To improve the operation of TCP/IP, a specification is being developed for a more aggressive version of TCP. It sometimes is called *fast-start TCP,* as its initial flow rate will be greater, and it will recover more quickly from lost packets. Fast-start TCP is expected to reach volume production by about 2005.

10.6 Chapter Summary

Long-Distance Storage Networking Applications

- Natural and unnatural disasters can have devastating effects on data centers and the loss of critical data.

- Most companies have remote replication technologies that are costly and cumbersome to manage.

- Remote data replication consists primarily of archiving and mirroring.

- Archiving typically uses removable media and is transported offsite.

- Mirroring operates over metropolitan- or wide-area distances and allows a second site to take over if the first site becomes unavailable.

- Most mirroring technologies have been based on Fibre Channel that, due to performance limitations, could be implemented only over relatively short distances.

10.1 IP Storage Networking Expands Remote Data Replication

■ Limitations of Fibre Channel switches are practical as much as technological.

■ Virtually all private and public networks use IP as their communications protocol, so any other protocol must be converted to access these networks.

■ New multiprotocol storage networking switches can convert Fibre Channel to IP, eliminating previous limitations and restrictions.

■ Multiprotocol switches have large buffers that augment Fibre Channel switch buffers to allow for long-distance transmissions.

■ Storage networking applications, including replication, can now traverse greater distances than before.

10.2 The Technology Behind IP Storage Data Replication

■ While the speed of light is 186,000 miles per second (300,000 Km/s), the refraction index for a typical single-mode fiber-optic cable reduces that speed to approximately 100,000 miles per second, or 100 miles per millisecond.

■ A typical 50-mile trip, 100 miles round way, incurs roughly one millisecond of "speed-of-light" or propagation delay.

■ Native Fibre Channel operates well within one millisecond of delay (100 miles), but many companies want the remote replication site located at farther distances.

■ Switches and routers that sit within the long-distance networking chain typically add anywhere from microseconds to milliseconds of delay, called switching or node delay.

■ Congestion delay occurs when network traffic must wait for a clear path during peak traffic times.

■ In LANs or MANs, capacity is easier and cheaper to install than in WANs, resulting in much fewer congestion delays.

■ Well-architected WANs can reach speeds close to the speed of light with very low packet loss.

- IP networks also can handle a variety of network types including higher latency, congested networks.

10.3 Sizing the Link Bandwidth for Long-Distance Storage Networking Applications

- Synchronous mirroring requires that each write be completed on both the primary and secondary arrays before the application continues.

- Asynchronous mirroring separates the two arrays by an identified number of writes, allowing the application to continue without waiting for the second write.

- Synchronous mirroring typically requires more bandwidth and lower latency.

- To estimate link requirements, the peak hour changes in the data set must be quantified.

- Approximately 10 percent is added for network protocol framing overhead.

- Converting this estimate to Megabits per second delivers the simplest estimate of network bandwidth required.

- Compression reduces the overall bandwidth requirements, allowing a smaller sized link to be used safely.

- Statistical analysis of traffic patterns allows IT managers to assess cost and risk tradeoffs regarding the size of the link required.

10.4 Estimating the Effects of Network Latency on Applications Performance

- Network latency is a combination of propagation delay, node delay, and congestion delay.

- End systems can also add processing delay depending on the amount of time required to process the operation.

- Good network design can minimize congestion and node delay, but laws of physics still govern propagation delay.

- Credit spoofing and large buffers can offset latency effects by placing more data in the pipeline at any given moment.

- Multiple, parallel sessions offset latency effects by reducing overall time for the transaction.

- Propagation delay can be estimated at one millisecond per hundred miles. The mileage used should be the round-trip distance.

- Node delay can be estimated based on the number of nodes and a conservative estimate of two milliseconds per node.

- Congestion delay can be roughly estimated by dividing total node delay by the portion of the link available for storage traffic.

10.5 The Effects of TCP on Application Performance

- IP is a layer-three protocol used for network transmissions.

- TCP is used in conjunction with IP to guarantee end-to-end data integrity and automatic flow control.

- TCP offload solutions remove previous limitations caused by TCP CPU consumption on end systems such as servers, arrays, and tape libraries.

- TCP was designed for congested networks and therefore has conservative flow-control algorithms.

- TCP flow control grants each user a modest initial rate that increases as acknowledgments are received from the destination system.

- If a packet is dropped or contains errors, the sending system readjusts to a lower rate and starts again to modestly increase the flow.

- In well-designed networks, TCP has little effect on performance.

- In congested networks, TCP can cause overall performance to decrease by more than half.

- The fast-start TCP specification aims to develop a more aggressive version of TCP.

11 Managing the Storage Domain

11.1 Incrementing to Simplicity

The high technology industry rides a nonstop wave of innovation. For those who work with information technology products and services, the promise of simpler, easier, faster, and more elegant solutions instills a mission of improvement. Feeding that appetite with a continuous rollout of inventions creates a continuous cycle of exposing shortcomings and identifying resolution. From any viewpoint, it is at once both an inspiring and daunting process.

Shifts across the storage networking landscape, from its inception through commoditization, indicate that this continuous improvement cycle is likely to maintain an accelerated pace. The introduction of open-systems hardware, networking platforms, interoperable standards, and a fertile environment for software all point to a greater number of new products and services delivered in shorter amounts of time.

For IT professionals charged with installation, operation, and maintenance of storage networking infrastructure, the variety of choices will only increase. Understandably, that can be a blessing in disguise. Most IT surveys cite storage professionals' plans to work with a smaller number of vendors in deploying solutions. At the same time, only through the widespread choices will those managers be able to dramatically improve their environments. The selection of vendors with products that have been certified to comply with industry standards will enable users to broaden and enhance their storage environments while assuring interoperability. In the long run, adoption of and adherence to standards will contribute to simplified management and operations while preserving choice and flexibility.

As we enter a post-Internet boom economy and mindset, with a back-to-reality assessment of true needs and objectives, the overwhelming consensus around storage deployment is simplicity. Distracted by what *can* be accomplished compared to what *should* be accomplished, the industry may well have let the innovation cycle get the upper hand. Taming and managing that cycle, both for IT users and producers, requires incrementing to simplicity. Designing effective policies for enterprise storage helps IT professionals get there.

11.2 Clearing the Decks: Core Versus Context

The first step of incrementing to simplicity requires separating core and context functions. In a keynote presentation at Storage Networking World, the industry's premier conference event, Geoffrey Moore outlined his approach to clearing the decks as a means to create competitive advantage. Moore argued that by managing non-core business functions defined as context, companies free time to focus on business functions that build and sustain value. This section covers the key points of that presentation.

11.2.1 Success via Differentiation and Identification of the Core

Ultimately, companies succeed or fail based on their ability to create value for customers above and beyond what can be delivered by competitors. Competitive differentiation can be created in areas such as operational excellence, particularly in commoditized markets, or product leadership, where performance measures dwarf other offerings. In each case, companies succeed by identifying differentiation points and intensely focusing on their delivery.

Business functions and processes that directly impact differentiation create sustainable advantages and are classified as *core*. All other functions that support corporate commitments are classified as *context*. For any young business to succeed, its core must be differentially better than its competition. As such, younger companies spend more time, talent, and money on core functions. As these businesses grow, supporting functions explode and resource allocation shifts towards context instead of core, as shown in Figure 11–1.

As competition gets wind of new core functions, they replicate them to the point where any core function eventually becomes context. Without continually expanding and focusing on core functions, domination by context is inevitable. In the data storage industry, new capabilities may start out on the top of the food chain as core functions, but slowly migrate downward to where they become context. Since the context functions still require management and resource attention, higher core functions may become missed opportunities due to lack of focus, as shown in Figure 11–2.

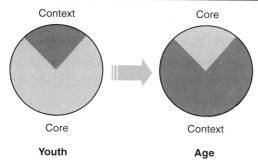

Figure 11–1 Context buildup. *(Source: The Chasm Group)*

11.2.2 Storage Infrastructure as Competitive Differentiator

For many companies, limited external visibility of the data storage infra-structure makes it hard to put storage on a list of core functions. More often than not, storage is a supporting function within the organization and better classified as context. However, since a preoccupation with context detracts from an intense focus on core, the connection may be closer than realized. Therefore, limiting the managerial attention and resources for routine data storage functions can positively increase the organization's ability to develop core functions.

Classifying data storage application across core and context initiates a planning process for managing human and capital resources, and ultimately setting organizational policies for storage. As shown in Figure 11–3, each

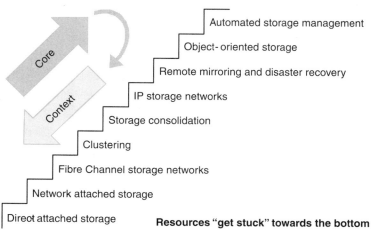

Figure 11–2 Core functions eventually end up as context. *(Source: The Chasm Group)*

	Core Be Effective	**Context** Be Efficient
Mission Critical Be Safe	*Whatever It Takes* Applications Military, Space, Physics, SSPs, Surveillance	*No Surprises* Applications EPR, CRM, SCM, PDM
Supporting Be Frugal	*More Productivity* Applications Seismic, Medical, CAD, Genomic, Audio/Video	*Cost Savings* Applications Internal Web, Compliance, Email

Abbreviations: **SSP**–Storage Service Provider, **ERP**– Enterprise Resource Planning, **CRM** – Customer Relationship Management, **SCM** – Supply Chain Management, **PDM** – Product Data Management, **CAD** – Computer Automated Design

Figure 11–3 Storage classification including operating goals (italics) and applications. *(Source: The Chasm Group)*

quadrant of applications has varying operating philosophies and goals. For mission-critical core applications, such as those in the military, the operating philosophy is, "Be safe and effective," and the operating goal is to do "whatever it takes." At the other end of the spectrum, for applications such as internal Web sites and email, the operating philosophy is, "Be frugal and efficient," and the operating goal is cost savings.

As shown in Figure 11–3, the most common storage investments exist in context-related applications such as enterprise resource planning, customer relationship management, email, and internal Web systems. The buildup in context results in management allocation towards those functions and, ultimately, a risk-averse strategy with little innovation.

Recapturing the time and attention to devote to forward-thinking core functions requires taming context. This is exactly the message resonating through the storage community about complexity of the storage infrastructure. Too many IT administrators are spending more time on storage as it grows as opposed to less as they get better able to manage it. The difficulty in achieving simplicity holds everyone back.

11.3 Defining Simplicity

Today, most IT managers find themselves continuously adding more storage infrastructure, both hardware and software, and simultaneously increasing the complexity of their environment. While the cost of storage infrastructure continues to decline, the myriad cost-effective choices continues to increase in management costs. To address these concerns, some IT organizations purposely restrict vendor selection to only one or two players. This helps mitigate the troubleshooting and management complexity. Other organizations and vendors are working hard to implement sophisticated automation of routine storage management practices to drive down management costs in line with infrastructure costs, as shown in Figure 11–4.

Many of the management burdens escalating in current environments are routine tasks falling into the context category. Functions such as volume allocation, backups, and restores consume inordinate amounts of IT professionals' attention. So, the ideal path is to move from that of *context overload* in current environments to that of *managed context* required for survival.

Achieving storage simplicity requires driving both infrastructure and management costs to decline in parallel while increasing functionality and value.

Simpler storage infrastructure. Throughout the book, we have seen how integrating storage platforms into a common IP and Ethernet technology infrastructure delivers a flexible, adaptive storage architecture. The open-systems ecosystem driven by lower cost and more commoditized hardware and software sets the stage for simpler storage infrastructure.

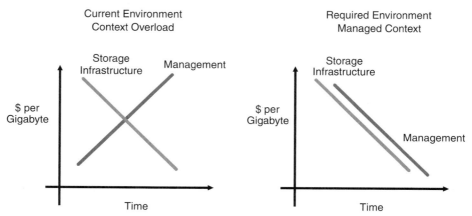

Figure 11–4 Moving to a managed context environment.

Simpler management. Simpler management requires that routine processes and practices be automated in software. But no software package exists to automate undefined processes. Therefore, achieving simpler management of the storage domain begins with a plan of attack outlined in the following section.

Ultimately, the combination of simpler storage infrastructure and management leads to the following:

- Scalable, adaptive, flexible infrastructures

- Shorter return on investments through cost-effective implementation

- Reduced administration costs by automating labor-intensive processes

- Secure, reliable storage platforms

11.4 Managing Storage: A Plan of Attack

Storage professionals need to harness and shape their IT departments with a coordinated plan of attack. The Data Mobility Group, led by John Webster and Perry Harris, has created just such a plan. This section presents their research.

The race to recapture time and storage resources, such as unused capacity, led to the creation of dozens of storage management products. Primarily software-driven, these products range from point solutions for specific tasks such as volume allocation to broader management oversight of large enterprise storage deployments.

For a storage professional looking to deploy a storage management solution, the product landscape can be overwhelming. Organizationally, the scope of functions that fall under the storage management domain can span several individuals. The first steps to achieving management simplicity require a framework to address broader issues of managing storage domain.

What should a storage management group within the larger enterprise IT department look like? What skill sets should be represented within this group? How should the group be structured? What disciplines should be practiced? These are just a few of the questions that need to be answered.

While it would be a gross oversimplification to say that storage was once a simple matter of plugging an array into a SCSI port, compared to the array of alternatives available today, the past was clearly a lot simpler. The days of one-size-fits-all SCSI are long gone.

Storage as an enterprise core competency is becoming exceedingly complex as this brief, but by no means exhaustive, list of technologies involved with the new world of networked storage illustrates:

■ Fibre Channel fabric architectures

■ Ethernet and IP networking

■ Server clustering

■ Data backup and restoration

■ Wide- and metropolitan-area networking protocols

■ Bridging, routing, and switching

■ Host bus adapters and drivers

■ Object modeling

■ Data traffic management

■ Diagnostic and recovery technologies

■ Enterprise management applications

■ Database and file system architectures

■ Security

Given this complexity, it is becoming increasingly common to find storage management groups within enterprise IT departments. Once a decision is made to form such a group, the next challenge is how to break management into manageable pieces and determine which disciplines each group member should represent.

11.4.1 Practice Disciplines

Think of enterprise storage management as a practice composed of a number of definable discipline areas. Each area can be further broken down into specific disciplines or tasks. Both management tasks and software-based management applications can be grouped under each discipline area.

For the purposes of this outline, we consider three discipline areas: managing the storage environment as a business entity, managing data from the standpoint of the storage environment, and using the storage environment to manage and mitigate corporate risk.

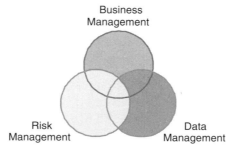

Figure 11–5 Practice disciplines for managing the storage domain. *(Source: The Data Mobility Group)*

There are no hard boundaries between discipline areas. In fact, management practices and products that fall under one area could also overlap with the other two. For example, copy functions that have been placed under the data management heading are also a critical component of business continuance (under risk management) and are becoming critical enablers of content distribution services (under business management). The discipline areas and overlap are shown in Figure 11–5.

Dividing storage management first into discipline areas provides a method for identifying and assigning specific disciplines to each group member. Depending on the specifics of the organization, it may also be useful to add or further subdivide practice areas.

11.4.2 Business Management

The *business management* discipline area includes management of the storage domain as a business entity, complete with customer service levels (both internal and external) and a method for tracking usage and applying chargeback. The basic functions of this grouping are outlined in Figure 11–6.

Business Management Objective
• Management of storage domain as business entity

Implementation examples
• Service Level Agreements (SLAs)
• Tracking and usage charge-back
• Quality of Service (QoS)
• Hardware and software decision making

Figure 11–6 Business management practice objectives and implementation examples.

A quick look back in storage history to storage service providers (SSPs) helps clarify this discipline. In spite of their hyperbolic track records, SSPs were successful in understanding at least one key component of storage—that storage provisioning is a business. By implementing sophisticated systems to administer and track usage across multiple customers, the SSP model evolved into a storage utility, analogous to an electric or other utility-based service. Today, many IT managers are looking to reproduce such storage utility models within their own enterprises.

In the case of an enterprise-based storage utility, customers are users represented by departments or applications and can be managed the same way that SSPs managed their outsourcing customers—via service level agreements (SLAs).

Many of the provisions covered in SLAs fall under this discipline area, including on-demand capacity provisioning, quality of service (QoS), continuous availability, and performance monitoring and management. Since the storage utility is run as a business, amortizing the cost across the entire user base provides a lower cost to each user than does operating independent environments. A comprehensive overview of storage service provider models was covered in Chapter 7, "Options for Operational Agility."

The business management practice also includes hardware and software selection. Balancing the double-edged sword of choice, this group must decide between fewer vendors favoring a simplified support model with less price flexibility and a multivendor solution favoring a potentially more complex support model but with greater price flexibility. Since the business management practice understands the ultimate needs of the customers (departments, specific applications, service levels), this group should lead product selection. However, for practical implementation reasons, all discipline areas should be involved in choosing new products.

11.4.3 Risk Management

Risk management includes the use of the storage domain to mitigate corporate risk through the use of well-established backup and recovery procedures, business continuance, disaster recovery, and most recently, security functions. The storage domain is also a good place to focus attention when implementing compliance with regulatory requirements. Examples in the United States include the Securities and Exchange Commission (SEC) for public companies and the Health Insurance Privacy and Accountability Act (HIPAA) for health-care organizations.

A tightly integrated combination of storage hardware, software, and networking services can be used to secure and protect data from unforeseen catastrophic events, human error, or malicious intent. Consequently, storage platforms can now be thought of as places to manage and mitigate enterprise risk. With the increasing dependence on corporate data, concentrating risk management into a discipline area ensures proper oversight and organizational management of this function. The primary areas of risk management are outlined in Figure 11–7.

Four major IT disciplines relating to risk management can be applied to the storage environment:

Disaster recovery and business continuity. Storage can be used to replicate data inside and outside the data center, effectively mitigating the risk of data loss from a variety of systems outage. Good business continuance and disaster recovery plans use technologies like mirroring and remote copy to protect data against these types of outages. As such, this discipline is codependent with the data management discipline area.

Backup and restore. Backup and restoration technologies mitigate enterprise risk by enabling users to restore backed-up data to its last uncorrupted state. Simply copying data to secondary storage devices, however, does not ensure complete data protection, since copy functions can propagate corrupted data along with good data. Close, knowledgeable, managerial attention must be brought to bear when restoring corrupted data to ensure that data has been recovered successfully.

Security. There is a growing realization that masking and zoning techniques do not go far enough in protecting networked storage-based data. Networked storage security will become more robust

Risk Management Objective
• Use of the storage domain to mitigate
  corporate risk

Implementation Examples
• Disaster recovery and business continuity
• Backup and restore
• Security

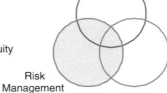

Risk
Management

Figure 11–7 Risk management practice objectives and implementation examples. *(Source: The Data Mobility Group)*

over time, but an understanding of storage-based security techniques is essential even now.

Regulatory compliance. Every major industry segment has some set of regulatory requirements—be they imposed by governmental agencies such as the SEC or industry-specific organizations such as JHACO—that require ongoing compliance. Failure to comply with these requirements can often expose the enterprise to significant risk. Compliance often involves the long-term storage (seven years or more) of digitized records and images, and presents IT managers with significant challenges relating to extreme scalability of the supporting storage infrastructure and migration of data through time and across media, application, and operating system changes.

11.4.4 Data Management

The data management practice includes the effective presentation of data contained within the storage domain through storage-based file systems and copy functions. It also includes effective storage infrastructure design for maximum performance. The primary objective and implementation examples are shown in Figure 11–8.

This discipline area serves as a foundation for business management and risk management with basic functions acting as building blocks for other areas. Data management will become more important over time as more file management capabilities move into the storage domain. Storage-based file management systems can protect shared data—accessed by multiple applications, servers, or users—from loss or corruption while maintaining a high degree of data availability for all authorized applications or users.

Copy functions fall into the data management practice. These functions are essential to the storage domain's risk management capabilities for func-

Data Management Objective
• Effective presentation of data within the storage domain using storage-based file systems and copy functions

Implementation examples
• Storage-based file systems (e.g., NAS)
• Copy functions for content distribution, performance optimization
• Network storage design and architecture

Data Management

Figure 11–8 Data management practice objectives and implementation examples. *(Source: The Data Mobility Group)*

tions such as backup and replication. Copy functions also enable new Web-facing applications by presenting data in multiple forms for specific use. Additionally, copy functions can enhance performance by distributing content to multiple locations, simplifying access across geographic areas.

A subset of policy-based automation also falls under the data management practice. As mentioned earlier in this chapter, few, if any, industries are immune to regulatory oversight, and many require long-term retention of digitized records. The automation of corporate policies covering records retention can be programmed such that user productivity is enhanced and storage management is greatly simplified. An example would be an email management application that sorts through an email user's in-box and offloads certain documents to a centralized records retention facility, relieving users of this burden and freeing up disk space on email servers.

11.4.5 Shaping Storage Domain Management

The storage management plan outlined through the business, risk, and data management practices can be implemented within an existing enterprise IT department with minimal disruption. This plan can also be used to structure the operational and organizational management of a new team formed to absorb the larger responsibilities of a growing IT storage domain.

IT skills related to backup and recovery, performance, security, and networking have existed for years in the data center. Implementing this organizational plan gives these traditional skills a networked storage focus. It further leaves room to incorporate additional skills to align an enterprise storage management group with present and future business needs.

Implementation of the plan mandates attention to specific management policies for the storage domain. The following section presents a sampling of such policies. It is by no means an all-inclusive list, but rather intended to assist in the creation of company- and department-specific storage domain management.

11.5 Creating Effective Policy Systems

While it would be nice to envision a single, comprehensive approach to administering storage policies, no such method exists. Organizing a storage domain management system, from IT manager and administrator duties to individual policies such as disk quotas, is inherently a company-specific task. Therefore, storage management policies must be aligned with policies that govern the enterprise as a whole.

As networked storage environments grow larger and more complex over time through the implementation of new vendor technologies and architectures, it becomes more difficult and time consuming to manage them. Also, the job of the storage administrator becomes more critical as more users come to depend on the 24/7 functioning of the storage network. Implementing software applications that streamline the process of storage management should be considered whenever and wherever possible. If storage management and administration remains largely a manual process, it becomes more susceptible to downtime, errors, and data loss, consequently exposing the enterprise to greater risk. Software automation is key to solving these problems. Storage management software allows for the automation of policies that can assure consistent, efficient, reliable operation and scaling of the storage environment without disruption. Policy automation also frees invaluable administrative time and talent that can now be focused on more strategic core processes that can bring enhanced business value and reduced business risk to the organization.

The previous section covered a plan of attack that began with a breakdown of functions across business, risk, and data management tasks. This section covers examples of more specific storage policies within each practice area that can be implemented through the use of software applications or manually in cases where no software to automate policy-based management exists.

11.5.1 Business Management Policies

Integrating the storage domain with corporate accounting requires a set of business-specific policies.

- **Reliable service (SLAs).** Agreed upon SLAs, outlined in more detail in Chapter 7, allow IT managers to set multiple levels of service ranging from mission-critical to "temporary-outage acceptable" storage. Specific QoS settings facilitate priority of one SLA over another. Figure 11–9 shows an example of implementing transport-based QoS in a storage network. In this case Online Transaction Processing (OLTP) traffic (A) is given priority over other types of traffic that are likely to be less critical, such as the corporate file server.

- **Monitoring and reporting.** Monitoring and reporting software tools facilitate tracking policies to charge for departmental usage.

- **Vendor selection.** Vendor selection policies drive product choice and ultimately storage domain deliverables. Comparison checklists, such as

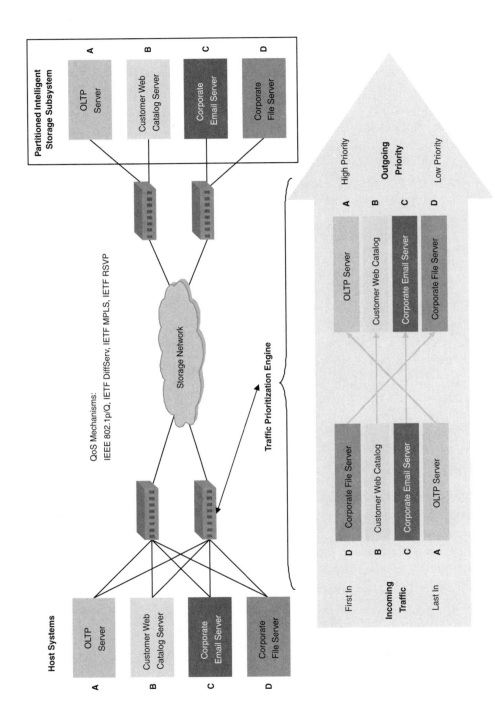

Figure 11–9 Implementing quality of service policies.

		SAN / DAS			NAS	
		Vendor A	*Vendor B*	*Vendor C*	*Vendor A*	*Vendor A*
Discover	Topology					
	Logical relationships					
Monitor/ Report	Array, SAN, NAS, and host health					
	Array performance					
	SAN performance					
	Host performance					
	Database performance					
	Configuration/utilization					
Provision	Filesystems and volume managers					
	Zoning					
	LUN masking					
	Storage devices					
Automate	Alert resolution					
	Provisioning					
	Replication					

Figure 11–10 Storage networking open management checklist. *(Source: EMC Corporation)*

the sample in Figure 11–10, assure that IT managers choose products that will provide open-systems management flexibility.

11.5.2 Risk Management Policies

Today's backup and restore software does a very good job of managing data protection. Additionally, remote replication packages facilitate recovery from unanticipated disasters. Other policies that require consideration under the risk management practice include the following:

■ **Site/physical environment.** As storage environments become more complex architecturally and heterogeneous from a multiple-vendor solution perspective, the complexity and cost of managing remote disaster recovery locations increases substantially. Who, therefore, is responsible for the computing environment, facilities recovery, transportation logistics, and cost in case movement to a second site is required?

■ **Personnel and management.** What is the management and operational staffing structure, and who are the backup personnel available in case primary managers and subordinate staff are unavailable? What is the management chain of responsibility?

- **Security.** What is the security framework for determining data access? Who will maintain access codes and authorization in the event of system failures? Is data security aligned with corporate security policies?

- **Disaster recovery scenarios.** Who is responsible for outlining and testing disaster recovery scenarios? Who declares a disaster and under what circumstances? Who is responsible for the restoration of production systems and data at the recovery site? Who is responsible for linking the recovered systems to business units needing access to these systems? Who is responsible for assuring system performance, availability, and security? Who is responsible for backing up the recovery site and restoring it to a new production location when it becomes available?

- **Governmental and industry-related regulatory agencies.** Who interfaces with those individuals within the enterprise responsible for maintaining ongoing compliance with outside regulating authorities? Is there a periodic compliance review process? If so, who manages this process? Can individuals or organizations outside the enterprise be used to validate the process by which compliance is ultimately achieved?

11.5.3 Data Management Policies

Careful formulation of data management policies will facilitate administration of the entire storage domain. For example, establishing an email-retention policy will allow administrators to offload and save in a centralized location those message and attachments deemed important to the enterprise while discarding the rest. This process can serve risk management by ensuring compliance with records retention requirements while, at the same time, freeing up capacity on production systems that can be used by business-related applications.

Data management policies cannot and should not be formulated by IT staff in a vacuum. Data management policies should be established via consensus with business-line managers and corporate officers. Included are policies relating to

- **Copy functions.** Who is responsible for copying what types of data: operating systems, application programs, control files, application data, fixed content, and so on? Who determines to where and when it is copied?

- **File systems.** Who determines the best locations for differing kinds of data: database files, fixed content, streaming data, shared data, program files, and so on? Who determines when data needs to be migrated to devices with differing operational and economic characteristics?

- **Storage growth and allocation.** Who tracks storage utilization and determines saturation levels? Who determines when additional space, such as LUNs and physical volumes, need to be allocated?

- **Data retention.** Who determines what data must be retained and for what period of time, and what data can be ultimately discarded? Who is responsible for ongoing data-retention policy review?

- **Content distribution guidelines.** Who determines what data needs to be distributed and to whom? Who controls access to the distributed data and assures data security? Who determines when distributed data can be deleted?

- **Availability and performance requirements.** Who tracks data traffic and delivery performance? Who establishes limits as to performance acceptability? Who has responsibility to reconfigure the environment to restore performance and availability requirements?

- **Data migration.** When certain types of data must be retained for extended periods of time (medical records or audit data, for example), who is responsible for migrating stored data to updated storage formats, updated versions of operating systems, and updated versions of applications?

11.6 Outsourcing for Management Simplicity

With a storage domain management framework in place and the appropriate set of policies implemented to maintain ongoing administration, IT managers can decide whether outsourcing makes sense for their organization. Outsourcing has long been used in the business community, both as a means to achieve lower costs for services and, more importantly, as a means to leave management attention free to focus on competitive differentiation.

Referring back to our discussion of core and context, IT professionals would be well served to consider the questions outlined in Figure 11–11. The answers to these questions will help determine if outsourcing portions of the

- Will outsourcing free up key talent?
  - If you and your team were freed from what you are doing now, what could you do to create additional shareholder value?
    - Could your team be used on core work?
- Is talent currently context-burdened?
  - What do you and your team do today that you would be willing to surrender, provided you were assured the work would be handled correctly?
    - Is context holding you back?

Figure 11–11 Considerations for outsourcing. *(Source: The Chasm Group)*

storage domain, such as backup and recovery functions, will provide the IT team with time to focus on core-enhancing functions.

If the answer to both of these questions is yes, then outsourcing will likely make sense. However, there is a distinct possibility that a series of questions such as these could lead to outsourcing as well as elimination of resources within the IT department. Travel this road of exploration appropriately.

Justifying the outsourcing decision requires a careful look at labor, capital, utilization, and opportunity. A simple calculation will typically weigh the cost of labor and capital. The guiding principle is that an outsourcing firm will be able to provide services across a wide customer base at a lower cost than any single customer could do individually. Therefore, weighing labor and capital into the equation typically justify the effort. However, the opportunity component, specifically the time, talent, and management attention that can be refocused on core-enhancing opportunities, is where the real returns lie, as shown in Figure 11–12.

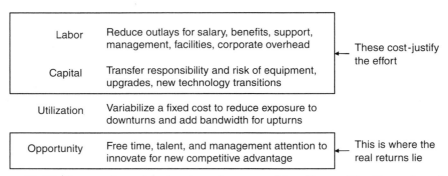

Figure 11–12 Outsourcing-related costs and opportunities. *(Source: The Chasm Group)*

11.7 Chapter Summary

Managing the Storage Domain

- Storage management costs continue to increase as a portion of resources spent on storage infrastructure.

- Companies must identify means to tame escalating management costs to maintain base level efficiencies.

11.1 Incrementing to Simplicity

- The high-technology industry is driven by an appetite for simpler, easier, faster solutions fed by a continuous rollout of new inventions.

- Storage networking is in the middle of a tumultuous cycle of new product introductions, architectures, standards, and business models.

- Choice presents a double-edged sword—most IT managers cite plans to work with fewer vendors to minimize maintenance complications.

- At the same time, fewer choices restrict the openness of total solutions.

- Taming the escalation of management costs requires a path towards simplification—both product *and* management oversight.

- Designing effective policies for the storage domain helps IT professionals get there.

11.2 Clearing the Decks: Core Versus Context

- Business success depends upon the ability to focus on clear competitive differentiation.

- Functions that contribute to competitive differentiation are defined as core.

- All other supporting functions are defined as context.

- Businesses naturally evolve from more core to more context—over time, more resources are required to support core functions, resulting in added context.

- Most core functions eventually end up as context as competitors replicate successful business practices.

- The single largest problem companies face in dealing with context is the lack of management attention that can be spent on core.

- For most companies, the lack of external visibility to the storage infrastructure makes the storage domain context.

- However, a preoccupation with context detracts from attention to core.

- Capping managerial attention on context functions can positively impact the organization's ability to refocus on competitive differentiation.

- Storage applications can be segmented across core and context, as well as mission-critical and supporting functions.

- Each quadrant of applications has a different operating strategy and goal.

- Segmenting applications allows IT professionals to assess if resources are allocated appropriately.

11.3 Defining Simplicity

- Most IT departments that continue to add new storage infrastructure see an increase in management costs.

- While the cost of the storage infrastructure (hardware, software) declines, management costs have not followed a similar path.

- The buildup in management costs, particularly routine functions, can lead to context overload.

- To move to managed context, IT professionals must simplify both acquisition and management costs.

- The combination of simplified environments results in

  - Scalable, adaptive, flexible infrastructures.

  - Shorter return on investments through cost-effective implementation.

  - Reduced administration costs by automating labor-intensive processes.

  - Secure, reliable storage platforms.

11.4 Managing Storage: A Plan of Attack

- The race to recapture time and storage resources led to dozens of storage management product introductions, the scope of which can be overwhelming.

- Before identifying and selecting storage management products, storage managers must first set organizational structures for managing the storage domain.

- Practice disciplines exist within the larger storage environment and can be used to segment and structure organizational management responsibility.

- These areas include business management, risk management, and data management.

- **Business Management Objective**

  - Management of storage domain as business entity.

  - Implementation examples include service level agreements (SLAs), tracking and usage charge-back, quality of service (QoS), and hardware and software decision making.

- **Risk Management Objective**

  - Use of the storage domain to mitigate corporate risk.

  - Implementation examples include disaster recovery and business continuity, backup and restore, and security.

- **Data Management Objective**

  - Effective presentation of data within the storage domain using storage-based file systems and copy functions.

  - Implementation examples include storage-based file systems (e.g., NAS), copy functions for content distribution and performance optimization, and network storage design architecture.

11.5 Creating Effective Policy Systems

- Storage specific and enterprise-wide policies need to be aligned.

- Policies can be automated through software or administered manually.

- Business management policies such as SLAs, omnitoring, and vendor selection drive consistency of operation.

- Risk management policies such as site/physical environment, personnel, security, and disaster recovery drive preparedness for unseen events.

- Data management policies such as file systems, storage allocation, and data retention facilitate administration of the entire storage domain.

11.6 Outsourcing for Management Simplicity

- Outsourcing can serve as an effective means to remove context-heavy functions from the daily routine and focus attention on core-enhancing functions.

- IT managers must consider the following questions:

  - Will outsourcing free up key talent? (If you and your team were freed from what you are doing now, what could you do to create additional shareholder value? Could your team be used on core work?)

  - Is talent currently context-burdened? (What do you and your team do today that you would be willing to surrender, provided you were assured the work would be handled correctly? Is context holding you back?)

- If the answer to both questions is yes, then outsourcing will likely make sense.

- However, possibilities exist that exploring questions such as these could lead to outsourcing and elimination of resources within the IT department.

- Returns from outsourcing activity come from reduced labor and capital costs, but more importantly from freeing management time and attention to focus on core-enhancing activities.

12 Perfecting the Storage Engine

The preceding chapters supplied tactical and strategic advice applicable to storage infrastructure build-out. Approaching the completion of our optimized storage deployment roadmap, Chapter 12 drafts an outline of current and future trends in enterprise storage. This knowledge can help IT professionals chart a custom course for their respective companies.

Improvements on the technology roller-coaster ride never end. Already, emerging patterns appear towards the next waves of innovation—across infrastructure, intelligence, and management. Taking a peek into the future, we examine these patterns more closely.

Perhaps the most important lesson to gain from witnessing the dramatic change in the planning, deployment, and management of storage is the need to continually evolve. The broad strategic goals of the book and this chapter will survive technology shifts. IT professionals should craft their own strategic missions to provide guidance across seemingly ambiguous landscapes. A clear, centered approach with agreed-upon objectives across the organization helps clarify complexity.

The tactical recommendations will also outlast short-term changes in underlying technology improvements. Think of the tactical objectives as the first level of strategic implementation. Storage teams' goals should encompass the following examples, but should also be complemented by company-specific tactical initiatives.

Emerging technology patterns are just that—visible glimpses of the future that will likely morph into concrete implementations. While we are not yet able to pinpoint the ultimate particulars, certain discernable patterns merit consideration today as part of our broader enterprise storage planning processes.

12.1 Strategic Objectives

12.1.1 Create Offensive as Well as Defensive Strategies

The preservation of data assets will remain a critical function for IT departments and storage professionals. However, the increasing growth and availability requirements for storage are likely to overburden storage administrators without additional help. As outlined in Chapter 11, "Managing the Storage Domain," clearing the decks of repetitive, labor-intensive functions defined as context provides the time and attention required to invest in new core functions. New functions might include changing the storage architecture, platforms, and management systems for more flexible, adaptive approaches.

Of course, the introduction of offensive approaches to storage networking must be in concert with defensive approaches. Due to continuous short-term requirements, the shift typically requires a medium- to long-term planning process, as shown in Figure 12–1. Fortunately, the planning, development, and implementation of defensive storage networking deployments often fit hand in hand with offensive approaches. Well-designed storage networks, particularly those that incorporate existing and new technologies such as IP networking, deliver the resiliency to serve both objectives.

12.1.2 Segment Strategies with Portfolio Management

Portfolio management enables IT managers and senior executives to segment, prioritize, and track IT projects. In a research survey conducted by Mainstay Partners in 2002, fewer than 21 percent of the companies had a process for prioritizing digitization efforts. Ultimately, this often leads to cancelled or poorly executed projects, difficulty in measuring project returns, and missed opportunities to tie technology projects to business strategy.

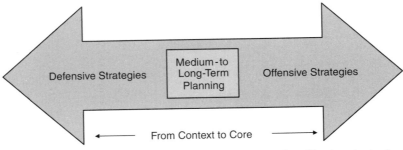

Figure 12–1   Use a medium- to long-term planning process for offensive strategies.

Today's high-growth storage environment can involve dozens of projects at a time, ranging from capacity expansion, to storage allocation, to backup and recovery procedures, to automated management.

A portfolio framework, such as that outlined in Figure 12–2, is a starting point for storage professionals charting a project management course. The first tier of projects fall under *optimization* and represent incremental improvement in existing processes for productivity improvements. These optimization projects need not necessarily involve new technology additions, but rather may simply be a reorganization of current infrastructure and management tools. Nontechnical processes, such as redefined administrative steps, may also contribute to optimization.

The *reconstruction* tier goes one step further and typically involves new technology deployments. As opposed to linear improvement growth, reconstruction generates dramatic "step-function" improvements. The *invention* tier represents the greatest level of complexity, and accordingly the highest returns. New project deployments are the only way to achieve such returns, and IT managers and senior executives should recognize their inherent risk.

The development and management of a technology project portfolio requires well-defined and clearly communicated goals across multiple departments within the organization. Figure 12–3 highlights several key steps through this process.

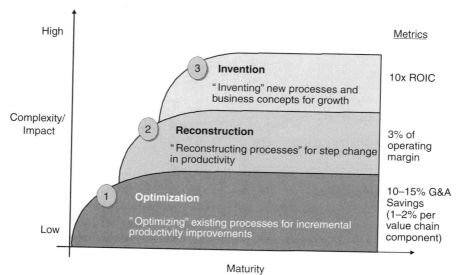

Figure 12–2 Sample portfolio segmentation: optimizing, reconstructing, inventing. (*Source: Mainstay Partners*)

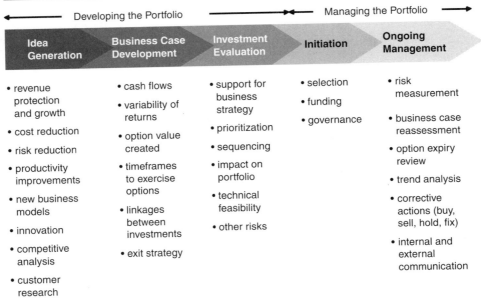

Figure 12–3 Creating and managing the IT portfolio. *(Source: Mainstay Partners)*

Ultimately, according to Mainstay Partners, successful portfolio management provides the following benefits:

■ Single set of metrics for evaluating investments.

■ Consistent method for communicating internally and externally.

■ Less waste due to dead ends or missed opportunities.

■ Ability to stratify cost of capital according to risk/return profile.

■ Consensus across the business around initiative priorities.

■ Allows everyone to provide insight into the opportunities that exist in the firm.

The scope of storage administration within any medium to large organization now encompasses a diverse project portfolio, and the user scope extends far beyond a limited data center focus to one with global reach. Implementing a portfolio management process tailored to storage requirements helps structure and monitor organizational effectiveness.

12.2 Tactical Goals

Historical computing evolution and storage sector innovation influence new deployments. The first wave of storage networking adoption, starting in the late 1990s through 2003, helped shape the basic understanding of networked storage benefits and implementation practices. Coupling that understanding with historical computing patterns and sector innovation leads to identifiable trends useful in all types of storage planning.

12.2.1 Adapt to Infrastructure Fluidity

As we have seen throughout the book, implementing even the most basic storage network initiates a functional separation between servers and storage that in turn presents more choice and flexibility to storage architects. Once the primary server-to-storage connection traverses a network, the functional breakdown can continue by adding custom-tailored storage components. The increased performance of commodity servers coupled with specialized software means that many of these storage components can be produced and deployed rapidly and at a relatively low cost.

The introduction of function-specific storage nodes—ranging from NAS heads to protocol converters to virtualization engines—delivers infrastructure fluidity. For the storage domain, this flexibility will continue through the use of more specialized storage nodes across a wider functional spectrum.

IT project planners need to recognize this trend and plan accordingly. Including both custom storage hardware and more commodity-oriented platforms in new deployments guarantees a hedge on future hardware and software directions.

12.2.2 Use Distributed Resources and Intelligence

Tightly coupled with the emergence of infrastructure fluidity is the use of distributed resources and intelligence. Fluidity implies the ability to easily move within set boundaries, and with IP networks in the storage equation, those boundaries reach further than ever before. Much like water will follow the path of least resistance directly into the gravitational pull, storage processing will ultimately find a home in the nodes that can deliver the most functionality and reliability at the lowest cost. As more storage nodes become networked together, storage administrators will have the option to transfer tasks accordingly. Similarly, it will become easier to remove storage bottlenecks by adding scalable storage-processing power.

Nearly every large server and storage vendor now touts the promise of harnessing distributed resources and allocated IT services on demand. All of this functionality rides upon a coherent infrastructure, which in the case of storage comes from well-architected Fibre Channel and IP storage networks.

12.2.3 Prepare for Geographic Integration and Consolidation

Large corporations' dispersed offices have for years been linked together with IP networks servicing enterprise applications. Further, many corporations have linked upstream to suppliers or downstream to customers through electronic data interchange (EDI). That time-tested connectivity has removed many geographic barriers to everyday business.

Storage now enters that playing field through the emergence of IP storage. For internal and external applications, the ability for storage data to freely travel across secure IP networks radically changes the traditional notion of the storage footprint. Whereas it previously covered the confines of a data center, it now covers the globe.

Following the natural inclination of business solutions towards lower cost solutions, imagine factoring power consumption into the storage location decision. Assuming adequate bandwidth, it may make sense to locate large storage arrays requiring intense power and cooling close to power-generating faculties. While this example may seem farfetched to some, it highlights the unrestricted storage movement that is likely to influence future storage decisions.

12.2.4 Continually Monitor Organizational Structure and Utility

The earnings-driven corporate mantra of "do more with less" isn't likely to go away any time soon. As such, recurring high-cost components of technology infrastructure—specifically labor—will continue to be targeted for cost savings. Previously, storage administration has been a relatively labor-intensive process compared to other areas of IT deployment. Advances in hardware and software management are starting to change that, and now fewer individuals are needed to oversee larger storage domain operations.

Centralizing responsibility to a smaller storage professional team means more decision-making authority. For example, even though more functions may be automated, that small group will still determine storage rules and permissions for the same customer base. Theoretically, this seems like an ideal opportunity to streamline and concentrate responsibility within a highly skilled storage administration team.

However, rules are easily managed; exceptions are not. The possibility exists that exception management—modifications to rules, one-time changes, and extraordinary circumstances—can overwhelm reduced administration teams. Continually monitoring the structure and utility of the department ensures the storage administration team has the appropriate level of resources and the ability to accommodate unanticipated exception handling. A feedback process incorporating storage customers provides one manner to measure effectiveness. Rather than viewing this as a "complaint" structure, storage professionals should view it as a method to anticipate future requirements and should set the technical direction accordingly.

12.3 Storage Advances to Watch

The maturity of storage networking solutions, from the basic hardware infrastructure to the overall management, sets the stage for incremental advancements. Striving to extract additional performance and functionality at reduced costs, future storage networking products have to dig deeper or smarter into the functionality layers. In this section, we explore a few of those options.

12.3.1 Application-Specific Storage

Application-specific storage is one method to enhance the performance and functionality characteristics. By designing storage systems that tie directly into defined application requirements, users get the benefit of a custom-fit solution. The most common examples of application-specific storage include those focused on Microsoft Exchange and Oracle databases.

In the case of these particular applications, unique requirements directly reliant upon the storage system make "application awareness" a useful feature. For example, a storage system aware of the allocated capacity assigned to a Microsoft Exchange server could automatically provision more storage once that capacity was nearing full utilization. This helps administrators avoid the trouble of manually adding capacity and, more importantly, frees them from the requirement to continually monitor the system.

Similarly, table space for an Oracle database—or any other database, for that matter—could be automatically increased based on communication between the database application and the storage subsystem. In doing so, the increment must be large enough to prevent fragmentation and allow adequate performance.

The interaction between applications and storage subsystems can take place via a variety of mechanisms, such as Simple Network Management Protocol (SNMP) traps or the increasingly more sophisticated XML-based exchanges, such as those using the Common Interface Model (CIM) specification developed by the Storage Networking Industry Association.

Storage professionals looking to improve overall system functionality will benefit from assessing application-specific requirements and working to match those with more intelligent storage systems.

12.3.2 Automation

As discussed throughout the book, the management component is usually the largest ongoing expense of storage systems. The plethora of hardware and software products tailored to solve specific problems can lead to an inordinate time commitment for simple administrative tasks. For example, setting up and configuring a remote replication system for offsite storage can take anywhere from weeks to months. Creating a duplicate database for testing and experimentation can take hours or days. These functions and hundreds of others often require so much manual involvement that they are viewed as too troublesome to implement.

Storage management systems continue to offload more administrative tasks from storage professionals through a variety of intelligence mechanisms. At the most basic level, management systems use pattern identification to trigger alerts or traps that can be sent to administrators. This frees IT professionals from day-to-day oversight functions, but still requires them to act on the information. An example of pattern recognition might be a database table reaching allocated capacity on a volume.

The next step in the intelligence spectrum is independent decision making. In this stage not only can the system detect patterns, but it can also act on a predefined set of rules. Taking our previous example one step further, when a database table approaches maximum capacity of a volume, the management software could expand that volume by assigning more storage from a *free-space* pool. In this case, a pattern was identified and a solution applied without manual intervention.

The previous examples represent relatively closed sets of functionality with defined parameters. In the case of the decision process, an administrator still had to define a free-space pool in order for the system to automatically allocate storage. Only part of the process has been offloaded.

Peering further in to the future, the only practical way for administrators to cope with the data set growth and reliability requirement increases is through centralized automation. Through these systems, agents will act on an array of input criteria to determine an action set. Let's take the previous example one step further. The database described happens to represent mission-critical e-commerce data. In expanding the volume, the system must ensure that additional storage will have the same performance characteristics as the original storage. It also needs to confirm that access to the expanded volume can support mission-critical applications. The agents will do this by exploring the storage network access paths between the database server and additional storage. Further, since this database requires synchronous replication, the system will need to confirm that the remote site has the expansion capability as well and that the data set increase and resulting replication traffic can be sustained on the allocated bandwidth of the remote link. Finally, all of this must take place without any data loss or system interruption. A graphic outline of intelligence systems is shown in Figure 12–4.

As evidenced by the numerous system requirements, automated storage systems will require complete knowledge of the entire infrastructure and the ability to act upon that knowledge. This implementation style is often classified as true utility computing where proper storage can be delivered anytime and anywhere. Most large system and storage vendors have automated management programs underway, and this area will continue to be a driving sector for storage area networking improvements in the future.

12.3.3 New Platforms

The increasing digitization of corporate assets now drives enterprise storage growth across a number of categories. While previously storage growth may have been limited to databases residing on mainframe computers—a fairly localized and contained infrastructure—distributed systems, desktop PCs, and the use of Internet-oriented applications precipitate a wider

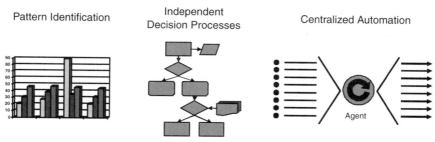

Figure 12–4 Types of intelligence systems.

spectrum of storage categories. Key storage category metrics include the following:

- Where is the data stored?

- How frequently is the data accessed?

- How frequently is the data changed?

- Who needs to access the data?

- What are the longevity requirements?

- What is the underlying data structure?

- What are the security requirements for the data and infrastructure?

Since answers to these questions vary, each category of data emerges with its own requirements. Block-accessed SANs and file-accessed NAS have served multiple storage categories respectively. More recently, the emergence of object-oriented storage systems, such as content-addressed storage, has helped satisfy requirements for the fixed-content storage category largely represented by digitized corporate assets that are created once, do not change, must be accessed by numerous users, and have extensive longevity and data protection requirements.

But even within these primary categories of block, file, and object-oriented approaches, distinct variations exists. Consider the difference between managing millions of short, text-based emails and managing hundreds of thousands of large, image-based medical x-rays, cat scans, or MRIs.

As subcategories expand, we are likely to see a drill-down to more specific storage platform subsets or entirely new approaches. Storage administrators can benefit from storage platform customization by tracking storage categories, growth, and usage patterns.

12.3.4 Declassifying Storage Networking

During the first few decades of computing, storage was an integrated part of the overall solution. The shift from DAS to NAS mandated a separate technology classification and launched an entire industry specifically focused on the storage component. Soon enough, many organizations realized that the storage piece often outweighed the server piece in terms of dollars spent on acquisition and maintenance. More vendors entered the market, more products were introduced, and the multibillion-dollar storage industry took on a life of its own.

Jump to today's environment—a collection of disparate storage resources that serve different purposes within the organization, require an inordinate amount of manual administration, and cannot be easily integrated with one another. To some degree, the *classification* of storage as a separate system component has caused considerable headaches.

IP storage networking is not the panacea to solve this problem. Integration of storage into mainstream computer communications systems is. It just happens that the means to accomplish that task is through the use of a communications protocol more widely used than any other the technology industry knows—the Internet Protocol.

Sometimes the storage industry (and many other industries, for that matter) get swept up in the debates over lower-level technologies and user-level insights. The very introduction of IP storage networking as a term initially incited a riotous uproar from the Fibre Channel community, and an ensuing debate continued to ricochet for years in the media. The proponents of IP storage networking, your author included, would have been better served by calling the technical advancements integrated storage networking.

Providing a means for storage components to interact seamlessly with other computing components is the first step towards *declassifying* storage networking. This does not imply declassification from the security sense of the word, but rather the elimination of a separate category and a more complete integration with the overall computing system.

Open, interoperable communications serves as the first step. IP storage, in its many permutations, will pilot distinct and diverse storage resources towards a cohesive communications model. This is not to say that other communications methods will disappear. Fibre Channel and yet-to-come technologies will prosper and serve respective purposes. But the glue from a global to local perspective will be the ubiquitous IP network.

Abstraction layers between storage consumers and storage repositories can then facilitate a more accurate matchmaking scheme. Underlying virtualization layers will serve storage management applications in providing the right storage to the right user at the right time. These matchmaking skills are still in their infancy, yet promise to radically improve gaps that exist today.

Finally, the incremental addition of intelligent services and the use of automated systems will hone matchmaking and maintenance skills to a level of specificity likely unattainable through manual administration. Whether through pattern recognition, decision process, or self-directed intelligent agents, incorporation of artificial intelligence to storage management will drive complete system and storage integration, and ultimately the declassification of storage networking.

12.4 Chapter Summary

Perfecting the Storage Engine

- Technology improvements operate in a continuous cycle.

- Strategic and tactical goals can outlast innovation cycles.

- Technology patterns, even not fully defined, assist in the planning and deployment process.

12.1 Strategic Objectives

- Create defensive and offensive strategies.

- Investments in storage networking equipment appropriately selected and deployed can serve both objectives.

- Segment strategies with portfolio management.

- The dramatic size and scope of storage requirements mandate an evaluation and prioritization process.

12.2 Tactical Goals

- Adapt to infrastructure fluidity.

- More commoditized products based on server platforms means a greater variety of functionality across the end-to-end storage chain.

- Use distributed resources and intelligence.

- Network flexibility and infrastructure fluidity will push solutions to solve bottlenecks throughout the system.

- With storage as part of the IP landscape, the geographic reach for integration and consolidation will extend globally.

- Continually monitor organization structure and utility.

- The trend towards more automated storage administration will put policy administration in the hands of fewer individuals.

- Feedback processes incorporating storage customers provides one manner to measure effectiveness.

12.3 Storage Advances to Watch

- Tightly coupled interaction between applications and storage requirements (application-specific storage) enhances performance and functionality.

- Growth in data storage and reliability requirements mandate centralized storage automation.

- Manual administration will be augmented with pattern identification, independent decision processes, centralized automation, and new platforms.

- Current and future platforms will emerge based on data-usage patterns.

- The classification of storage as a separate component led to separation from an integrated system.

- Integrating storage networking with other system components will take place through improved communications, abstraction, and added intelligence.

- Ultimately, storage networking will merge back into mainstream computing functions.

IT Service Recovery Strategy: Best Opportunity for Success

Executive Overview

Predefined methods for business recovery provide templates for IT service recovery planning. They typically leave out three key issues in need of a strategy:

- How to deal with distributed systems

- How to avoid data destruction in a disaster

- How much to invest in recovery facilities

How Do You Deal with Distributed Systems?

- The *distributed architecture* paradigm drastically increases the complexity of business continuity planning.

- To succeed, business continuity planning has to focus on an IT service recovery model.

> RECOMMENDATION: Designate the "custodian" of an IT resource as responsible for the recovery of the IT services after a disaster.
>
> RECOMMENDATION: Focus on improving the IT documentation necessary for business continuity.
>
> RECOMMENDATION: Organize IT documentation by "service," with individuals responsible for recovery assigned the responsibility for maintaining the documentation.

How Do You Avoid Data Destruction in a Disaster?

■ You can purchase new hardware, build new buildings, even hire new employees, but you *must* have an intact "copy" of your data for successful recovery.

■ Storing the copy in a remote location decreases your risk of losing both the original and the copy in a disaster.

■ The potential exists in a disaster to lose all data changes that have occurred since the delivery of the last copy of the data to the remote location.

■ Options exist to speed up the movement of the copy to the remote location.

RECOMMENDATION: Implement a second-generation storage network with remote disk mirroring. (This will have to be approached on an incremental basis to avoid a large one-time infrastructure investment.)

RECOMMENDATION: Replace the current tape-based disaster backup strategy inherited from the mainframe with remote disk mirroring.

RECOMMENDATION: Locate the remote disk mirror in a remote location. Potential vendors exist in most metropolitan areas.

RECOMMENDATION: Store the IT documentation electronically in the SAN to take advantage of the remote disk mirroring.

How Much Do You Invest in Recovery Facilities?

■ Your recovery facility strategy determines how soon services will be available again following a disaster.

- The tasks required to build a recovery facility are about the same amount of work before or after the disaster.

- The only way to decrease the time it takes to get the recovery facility in service is to put some or all of the recovery facility in place before the disaster. The more you put in place before the disaster, the sooner you will have IT services after a disaster.

- The more you put in place before the disaster, the higher your overhead costs to maintain the recovery facilities until the disaster.

- A disaster is not a certainty. The money spent before the disaster amounts to insurance against lost IT services.

- Lacking a risk assessment on paper, an organization's budget tends to make more decisions concerning the recovery facility than concerning the threat of a disaster.

RECOMMENDATION: Create a formalized risk assessment process. (Security issues contain a parallel requirement for predictable risk assessments.)

RECOMMENDATION: Identify the acceptable downtime for each IT service based on the documented risk assessment.

RECOMMENDATION: Identify key vendors for replacement equipment.

RECOMMENDATION: Establish lead time for replacement equipment in the event of a disaster.

RECOMMENDATION: Establish the need for a recovery site based on lead time rather than acceptable downtime.

RECOMMENDATION: Document and maintain all of this information in an SLA for IT customers to consider in gap analysis.

Evolution to a SAN Environment

Incremental Steps to a Second-Generation SAN

The creation of a SAN envisioned in the recommendation can be approached on an incremental basis:

1. *Select backup/remote disk mirroring software.* The current backup software should be reviewed to ensure it addresses the near real-time disk performance required for the remote disk mirroring. Since software tends to evolve version to version, the evaluation point is likely to be whether the software has the feature when you need it.

2. *Upgrade the distribution switch to support SAN throughput speeds.* Minimum speed will be Gigabit Ethernet. Some vendors will enter at the 10 Gigabit Ethernet speed. This throughput requirement may force the replacement of the existing distribution switch within your infrastructure.

3. *Install a standalone iSCSI disk system and HBA.* Second-generation iSCSI disk systems and HBAs were introduced in 2002. This step allows the iSCSI interface to be proven without any other components in the mix. Implementation on a non–mission-critical server should provide the experience needed for further evolution.

4. *Convert standalone iSCSI disk system/HBA to the distribution switch.* This step allows the iSCSI interface to prove itself through the distribution switch. Use of the non–mission-critical server from Step #3 should provide the experience needed to assure confidence.

5. *Implement a second host on the distribution switch to create a SAN.* This step creates a SAN in the central office. Again, adding a second non–mission-critical server is recommended. Once proven, the inclusion of mission-critical servers can be considered.

6. *Implement remote storage with communications.* Additional outlays will have to occur to implement the remote disk space with communications links. The most likely link will be Gigabit Ethernet.

7. *Implement remote Disk Mirroring over the communications link.* This step may force you to revisit the software question considered in Step #1.

These steps would provide easily managed steps with little or no risk of failure on a large expenditure. With the potential exception of Step #6, the other steps would fit into the current replacement process typically employed within Information Technology.

Strategic Decisions

Issues IT Business Recovery Planning Has to Address

In planning for recovery of IT services, most organizations follow variants of these basic steps.

- Provide top-management guidelines.

- Identify serious risks. (See Chapter 5 concerning risk assessment.)

- Prioritize the services to be maintained, and standardize their maintenance.

- Assign the disaster team.

- Take a complete inventory.

- Document the plan.

- Train employees.

- Test the plan.

- Review with all employees.

For the most part, business continuity planning for IT services involves following the outlined actions and completing templates. The three notable exceptions are the strategy employed to deal with distributed systems, the strategy for backups, and the recovery facility.

Distributed Systems Strategy

A majority of the publications concerning IT service recovery focus on the recovery of the central IT facility. This historical focus derives from the mainframe architecture typical of customers interested in business continuity.

The *distributed architecture* paradigm shift has drastically increased the complexity of IT service recovery for an organization.

Increased Documentation Volume

Any IT service recovery process depends on the quality of the documentation. Replacing equipment destroyed in a disaster requires up-to-date inventories of the hardware and software, configuration settings, etc. needed to rebuild the environment. The distributed architecture's replacement of the mainframe with smaller computers means more documentation to create and maintain.

The New IT Service Recovery Model

Other than for central operations, the reasons for a central facility have all but disappeared. A majority of the equipment works just fine on someone's desk. Most communications equipment ends up distributed through the wiring closet. Physical security requirements mandate "secure" facilities, not "central" facilities.

The organization has become the "IT facility." Business continuity planning has adapted to this shift by focusing on an *IT service recovery* model. The model works, but it increases the number of technical decisions documented in the business continuity planning process. The increased technical content increases the number of trained personnel who have to be involved in the planning process. At a certain point, no one individual has the ability to review the validity of the plan's contents.

Blurring Roles

Lower equipment prices place more services and applications within reach of a business unit's operating budget. Today's business environment involves more IT purchases within the business units than within the central IT department.

Most organizations that have experienced a disaster uncover mission-critical business units dependent on self-acquired IT services lost in the disaster. There are methods to combat this issue, but all of them increase the complexity of the business recovery planning process within the organization.

Backup Strategy

You can purchase new hardware, build new buildings, even hire new employees, but the data that was stored on the old equipment cannot be bought at any price. You must have a copy not affected by the disaster, preferably one easily restored to the new equipment. The following sections explore a number of options available to help ensure that such a copy of your data survives a disaster at the primary facility.

Offsite Tape Backup Storage

This option calls for the transportation of backup tapes made at the primary computer facility to an offsite location. Choice of the location is important. You want to ensure survivability of the backups in a disaster, but you also need quick availability of the backups.

This option has some drawbacks. First, it takes time to move the backup tapes offsite. A disaster striking at the wrong moment may result in the loss of all data changes that have occurred from the time of the last offsite backup. There is also the time, expense, and energy of having to transport the tapes. In addition, physical damage or loses can occur when transporting tapes. Finally, there is a risk that all of this ongoing effort may be worthless in a disaster.

The complete recovery of a system from a tape backup has always been an intricate, time-consuming process rarely undertaken by organizations unless necessary. The increased difficulty caused by multiple systems has alarmed industry experts. Citing 60 to 80 percent failure rates as justification, industry experts have always advocated testing the recovery process when the backup process changes. Few organizations have the resources for one full-scale test, let alone a test every time the backup changes. As a result, most recovery processes go untested until a disaster strikes.

Some organizations contract with disaster recovery companies to store their backup tapes in hardened storage facilities. These can be in old salt mines or deep within a mountain cavern. While this certainly provides for more secure data storage, regular transportation of the data to the storage facility can become quite costly. Quick access to the data can also be an issue if the storage facility is a long distance away from your recovery facility.

Automated Offsite Backup

This option calls for a backup system located at a site away from the primary computer facility with a communications link coupling the backup system to the primary computer facility. The remote backup system copies operating system data, application programs, and databases at designated times from the primary facility's servers or SAN.

A majority of the installed backup systems use tape libraries containing some degree of robotic tape handling. Optical and magnetic disk-based systems used to be the high-priced option for those desiring higher speeds or a permanent backup. Waning prices have allowed more consideration for business needs in media selection.

A majority of the time, the communications link is the primary bottleneck in remote backup implementations. The fastest options use peripheral, channel-based communication, such as SCSI, SSA, ESCON/FICON, and Fibre Channel over fiber-optic cable. Communications service providers typically have dark fiber, but they make their money selling widely used provisioned services. Channel-based services usually require your own private network infrastructure. You will pay for the installation of the fiber either up front or in a long-term lease. These costs tend to limit you to campus backbone networks.

Channel-based networking costs make front-end network-based (Ethernet, TCP/IP, etc.) backup solutions the volume leader in the market. Concessions on speed allow you to leverage your existing network infrastructure and expertise. Done outside peak hours to avoid degrading performance, the backup uses capacity that sits idle in most private networks.

Remote backup does not provide up-to-the-second updates available from the next two options. It does provide a means for conveniently taking backups and storing backups offsite any time of the day or night. Another huge advantage is that backups can be made from mainframes, file servers, distributed (UNIX-based) systems, and personal computers. Although such a system is expensive, it is not prohibitively so.

A Windows-only solution can be moderately priced depending on the exact features, and typically includes a general backup strategy that scales well as you install additional servers. Incremental costs include occasional upgrades to larger tape drives and faster communications.

Split-Site Server Array

Based on OLTP specifications, a server array maintains the integrity of the client's business transaction during a server failure within the array. For example, an Internet shopping application may allow you to place several items into your shopping cart before buying them. A server failure in a server array will go unnoticed. In a failover server cluster, the contents of the shopping cart will disappear unless additional client-side software exists within the application to conceal the server failure. This is shown in Figure A-1.

Splitting the server array by location further reduces the risk to service and data loss. The two halves use fiber-optic cabling (the campus backbone network would be suitable) for communication within the array, while an additional network connection provides client access. The server array appears to the client as one server. Behind the scenes, the server array uses all of the purchased resources to provide transaction throughput exceeding the throughput of a single server, all the while updating both copies of the data—

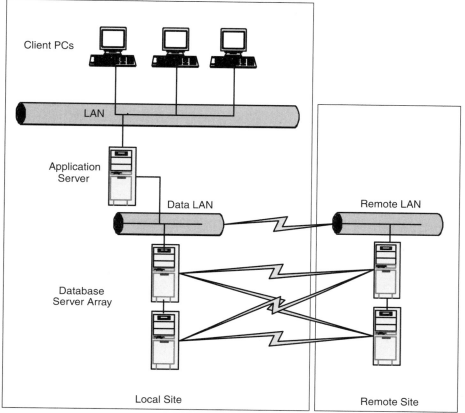

Figure A-1 Split-server site configuration.

one in the primary facility and the other located in the remote site in real time. Distance limitations and the price of dark fiber make this solution a good fit in a campus setting between buildings.

Remote Disk Mirroring

Remote disk mirroring extends RAID Level 1 to provide 100 percent duplication of data at two different sites. A disk subsystem located at a site away from the primary facility communicates with the local disk subsystem. The two disk subsystems each record a copy of the data for fault-tolerant operation. In a primary facility disaster, you have an almost up-to-the-second copy of the data at the remote site. Remote disk mirroring deals with the bandwidth bottleneck between the two locations by buffering peak demand within the remote disk mirroring process. The buffered data could be lost in a disaster unless saved in the original server during the outage. A basic remote disk mirroring configuration is shown in Figure A-2.

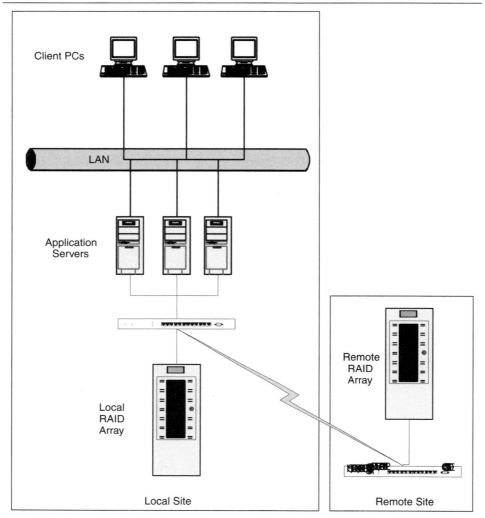

Figure A-2 Remote disk mirroring configuration.

You can simplify the recovery process by locating the remote disk subsystem at your recovery site. It does not require an entire computer system at the remote site, just the disk subsystem. This option originated in the mainframe disk market, but distributed SANs are making it available to those using distributed architectures.

Industry experts acknowledge that the remote disk mirror significantly reduces the risk of data loss in a disaster. Unlike tape-based backups, the remote disk mirror is almost a duplicate of the original. Instead of recovering data, the recovery effort focuses on restoring the primary site's half of the

SAN and the computer systems lost in the disaster. The complete recovery of each computer system remains an intricate, time-consuming process, but employing contract personnel can assist in these efforts. Industry experts advocate periodically testing the accessibility of the remote disk mirror after disconnection from the primary site. Most organizations have a couple of hours to devote to these tests to ensure the safety of their data.

Final Observations

Market trends indicate network-based storage is replacing server-imbedded storage. The network storage market offers both SANs and NAS. NAS devices connect to the front-end network (Ethernet, TCP/IP, etc.) as a replacement for a file server. Typically, a NAS uses a slim microkernel specialized for handling file-sharing I/O requests such as NFS (UNIX), SMB/CIFS (DOS/Windows), and NCP (NetWare).

SANs can be broken into two components:

- The storage plumbing that provides the network connectivity between end storage devices.

- The software to provide management capabilities for the network. There are many issues to consider when evaluating a software solution for your backup needs, from hot database backup, backup software performance, cross-platform issues, network performance, reliability, ease of use, disaster recovery, and administrative issues to your choice of tape hardware and automation issues.

Today, a SAN can cost two to three times the price of a NAS device for the same amount of disk space. This price reflects the number of additional components involved:

- Fibre Channel Arbitrated Loop (FC-AL) Switch

- Fibre Channel-based Disk Space

- Fibre Channel Host Bus Adapters (FC-AL HBA)

- Storage Network Management Software

- (Optionally) SCSI-to-Fibre Channel Converters

For the added cost, you receive higher transfer rates per second in device-level block-mode transfers typical of disk devices. These speeds easily sustain the throughput necessary for an active relational database management system such as Oracle or SQLServer.

There are other deficiencies in current storage network implementations. There are a limited number of Fibre Channel component vendors. Even so, interoperability between different vendors' hardware components is not a sure thing. Fibre Channel network experience comes at a premium. Those with experience will typically attest to higher administrative requirements compared to Ethernet. Extending Fibre Channel beyond the "dark fiber" campus requires bridging to IP. Fibre Channel over IP protocols extends the Fibre Channel-based SAN to metropolitan networks. It also adds infrastructure costs.

The evolution of Ethernet into the Gigabit and 10 Gigabit range created a great deal of strategic thinking in the SAN market. Why not eliminate Fibre Channel (FC-AL) in favor of a Gigabit Ethernet infrastructure? Most places looking at a SAN already have an existing investment in Ethernet technology with an existing knowledge base of their workings. An Ethernet-based storage network would use the same Ethernet switches as your front-end network, taking advantage of VLAN technology to ensure quality of service. The jump to a metropolitan network uses the same technologies as your existing Internet access. A new open standard, Internet SCSI (iSCSI), aims at dumping Fibre Channel in favor of Gigabit Ethernet.

Technically, iSCSI has been relatively easy to implement. A number of vendors offer components and management software. For example, you can buy a Gigabit Ethernet SAN infrastructure that allows you to convert your existing external SCSI or Fibre Channel storage into a SAN. The solution has demonstrated the viability of iSCSI-based SANs using first-generation prototype iSCSI host adapters and various types of storage.

As second-generation iSCSI host adapters and storage become a common option, anyone with a Gigabit Ethernet switch will be able to create a SAN with the right storage management software. Extend the Gigabit Ethernet infrastructure to a remote location, and you have the desired remote disk mirroring.

Recovery Facility Strategy

Destruction of the centralized IT facility in a disaster may take an extended period to repair or rebuild. In the interim, it may be necessary to restore computer and network services at an alternate site. There are a number of strategies for this recovery facility; each has its own tradeoffs. More than any other decision, the recovery facility strategy determines how soon services will be available again following a disaster.

Some generalizations are worth considering:

1. The tasks required to build a recovery facility are about the same whether they are done before or after the disaster.

2. The only way to decrease the time it takes to get the recovery facility in service is to put some or all of the recovery facility in place before the disaster. The more you put in place before the disaster, the sooner you have IT services after a disaster.

3. The more you put in place before the disaster, the higher your overhead costs to maintain the recovery facilities until the disaster.

4. A disaster is not a certainty. The money spent before the disaster amounts to insurance against lost IT services.

The various recovery facility strategies have developed to address an organization's willingness to gamble with the uncertainty of a disaster.

No Recovery Site

All organizations start out at this point. It allows the organization to include the extent of the disaster in its planning decisions. A minor disaster, such as a leaking roof, may involve rebuilding part of the existing facility. On the other hand, a major disaster like a landslide wiping out a primary facility might call for the creation of a completely new replacement facility at another site.

Temporary recovery facilities may be required to provide critical IT services, such as phones. A minor disaster may mean temporarily relocating equipment in the existing facility, while a major disaster may require a whole new site for the recovery facilities while the replacement primary facilities are being rebuilt.

Two main factors largely determine the time that it takes to reestablish IT services:

- The extent of the disaster

- The quality of the documentation not destroyed by the disaster

Still, maintaining no recovery site is appropriate where IT services are small or restoration of IT services is not critical.

Recovery Partnerships

Some organizations team up with others in a partnership with reciprocal agreements to aid each other in the event of a disaster. These agreements can cover simple manpower-sharing all the way up to full use of a computer facility. Often, however, since the assisting partner has to continue its day-to-day operations on its systems, the agreements are limited to providing access for a few key, critical applications that the disabled partner must run to stay afloat while its facilities are restored. The primary drawback to these kinds of partnerships is that it takes continual vigilance on behalf of both parties to communicate the inevitable changes that occur in computer and network systems so that the critical applications can make the necessary up-front changes to remain operational. Learning that you cannot run a payroll, for instance, at your partner's facility because it no longer uses the same computer hardware or operating system is not acceptable.

One of the most critical issues involved in the recovery process is the availability of qualified staff to oversee and carry out the tasks involved. This is often where disaster partnerships can have their greatest benefit. Through cooperative agreement, if one partner loses key personnel in the disaster, the other partner can provide skilled workers to carry out recovery and restoration tasks until the disabled partner can hire replacements for its staff. Of course, to be completely fair to all parties involved, the disabled partner should fully compensate the assisting partners for use of its workers unless there has been prior agreement not to do so.

The use of reciprocal recovery agreements of this nature may work well as a low-cost alternative to hiring a disaster recovery company or building a hot recovery site. In addition, reciprocal recovery agreements can be used in conjunction with other arrangements, such as the use of a cold recovery site, described below. The primary drawback to these agreements is that they usually have no provision for providing computer and network access for anything other than predefined critical applications. Therefore, users will be without facilities for a period until systems can be returned to operation.

The same two factors still largely determine the time it takes to reestablish IT services:

■ The extent of the disaster

■ The quality of the documentation not destroyed by the disaster

Cold Recovery Site

A cold recovery site is an area physically separate from the primary facility where space has been identified for use as the temporary home for the computer and network systems while the primary facility is being repaired. There are varying degrees of "coldness," ranging from an unfinished basement to space where the necessary raised flooring, electrical hookups, and cooling capacity have already been installed, just waiting for the computers to arrive.

The following factors determine the time it takes to reestablish IT services:

■ The degree of "coldness" in the cold recovery site

■ The quality of the documentation not destroyed by the disaster

Contracted Disaster Recovery Company

A number of companies provide disaster recovery services on a subscription basis. For an annual fee (usually quite steep), you have the right to a variety of computer and other recovery services on extremely short notice in the event of a disaster. These services may reside at a centralized hot site or sites that the company operates, but it is necessary for you to pack up your backup tapes and physically relocate personnel to restore operations at the company's site. Some companies have mobile services, which move the equipment to your site in specially prepared vans. These vans usually contain the entire necessary computer and networking gear already installed, with motor generators for power, ready to go into service almost immediately after arrival at your site. (Note: Most disaster recovery companies that provide these types of subscription services contractually obligate themselves to their customers to not provide the services to any organization who has not subscribed, so looking to one of these companies for assistance after a disaster strikes will likely be a waste of time.)

The following factors determine the time it takes to reestablish IT services:

- The extent of the disaster

- The clarity of the contractual obligation

- The ability of the contracted vendor to deliver as obligated when a disaster occurs

- The quality of the documentation not destroyed by the disaster

Hot Site

This is probably the most expensive option for being prepared for a disaster and is typically most appropriate for very large organizations. A separate computer facility, possibly even located in a different city, can be built, complete with computers and other facilities ready to cut in on a moment's notice in the event that the primary facility goes offline. High-speed communications lines must join the two facilities so that users at the primary site can continue to access the computers from their offices. Hot sites, however, do not have to be interlinked with the primary facility. A secondary live facility, with computer equipment of similar size, operating system, and so on can be considered a hot site in that the only requirement to become operational is data and application restoration.

The following factors determine the time it takes to reestablish IT services:

- The extent of the disaster

- The degree of "heat" in the hot site

- The quality of the documentation not destroyed by the disaster.

IT Service Recovery Documentation

What Information Do You Need?

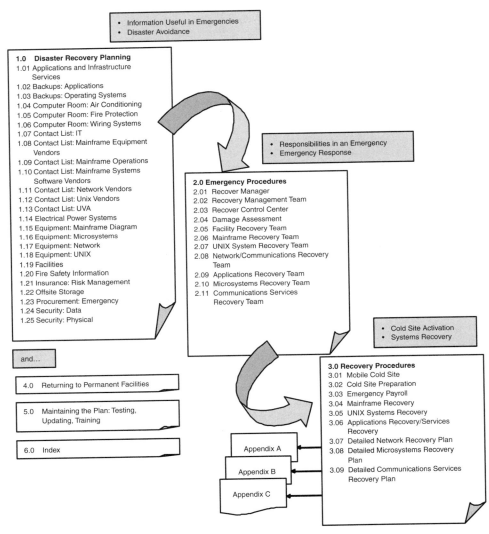

- Information Useful in Emergencies
- Disaster Avoidance

1.0   Disaster Recovery Planning
1.01 Applications and Infrastructure Services
1.02 Backups: Applications
1.03 Backups: Operating Systems
1.04 Computer Room: Air Conditioning
1.05 Computer Room: Fire Protection
1.06 Computer Room: Wiring Systems
1.07 Contact List: IT
1.08 Contact List: Mainframe Equipment Vendors
1.09 Contact List: Mainframe Operations
1.10 Contact List: Mainframe Systems Software Vendors
1.11 Contact List: Network Vendors
1.12 Contact List: Unix Vendors
1.13 Contact List: UVA
1.14 Electrical Power Systems
1.15 Equipment: Mainframe Diagram
1.16 Equipment: Microsystems
1.17 Equipment: Network
1.18 Equipment: UNIX
1.19 Facilities
1.20 Fire Safety Information
1.21 Insurance: Risk Management
1.22 Offsite Storage
1.23 Procurement: Emergency
1.24 Security: Data
1.25 Security: Physical

- Responsibilities in an Emergency
- Emergency Response

2.0 Emergency Procedures
2.01 Recover Manager
2.02 Recovery Management Team
2.03 Recover Control Center
2.04 Damage Assessment
2.05 Facility Recovery Team
2.06 Mainframe Recovery Team
2.07 UNIX System Recovery Team
2.08 Network/Communications Recovery Team
2.09 Applications Recovery Team
2.10 Microsystems Recovery Team
2.11 Communications Services Recovery Team

- Cold Site Activation
- Systems Recovery

and...

4.0   Returning to Permanent Facilities

5.0   Maintaining the Plan: Testing, Updating, Training

6.0   Index

Appendix A

Appendix B

Appendix C

3.0 Recovery Procedures
3.01 Mobile Cold Site
3.02 Cold Site Preparation
3.03 Emergency Payroll
3.04 Mainframe Recovery
3.05 UNIX Systems Recovery
3.06 Applications Recovery/Services Recovery
3.07 Detailed Network Recovery Plan
3.08 Detailed Microsystems Recovery Plan
3.09 Detailed Communications Services Recovery Plan

Figure A-3 Sample IT service recovery outline.

Roadblocks to Quality IT Service Recovery Documentation

Successful IT service recovery depends on the quality of the documentation not destroyed by the disaster. So, what keeps organizations from maintaining quality documentation for IT service recovery?

1. *Lack of experience.* Most people have not experienced a major business disaster that destroys their entire work environment. Further, few of us are interested in experiencing something like the Oklahoma City bombing to further our education in IT service recovery. The absence of experience forces organizations to depend on classroom training, designated experts, and simulated disasters to educate employees on what information they need to recover IT services after a disaster. Still, these forms of education do not convey the real impact of a disaster.

2. *Lack of interest.* While organizationally essential, IT service recovery typically does not garner an employee's personal concern unless management demonstrates an interest. Management leads by example when it consigns recovery planning to a lower priority than day-to-day operations. Moreover, while maybe not intended, recovery planning inadvertently scrutinizes what it attempts to recover. It should come as no surprise that the effort frequently uncovers chronic organizational shortcomings in need of improvement. Unless management has a formalized quality management program in place, these inefficiencies tend to fall to the pressures of day-to-day activity. Employees are quick studies. It will not take long before they do not even bother to report these issues to management. Employees quickly learn that there is no glory in recovery planning.

3. *Dynamic environment.* As little as 10 years ago, a purchase influencing IT services had the potential of being a huge occurrence. Today, the rate of IT service–related purchases have increased to a daily flow. Configuration changes now occur on a daily basis. The software "bug" detected yesterday may be enough to develop a test patch you can download today. Browse a site on the Internet, and it will update the software on your computer to make sure your browser can handle the site's special features. After the data, IT recovery depends heavily on the hardware and software inventory. Today's business environment is so dynamic, this changes every day. There are software tools available that will generate viable configuration documentation.

4. *Increased information volume needed for recovery.* The configuration parameters in today's desktop operating systems exceed tenfold the parameters found in yesterday's mainframe. The standardized configuration frequently used to ease administrative workload in the mainframe environment has given way to unique configurations on every computer. The real kicker is that some of these parameters, especially security-linked parameters, overtly alter your ability to use your recovery data. The absence of these parameters can stall your recovery process. In time, experimentation may grant access to the data, but the shear volume of parameter combinations makes this a very time-consuming route. Worst case, you may learn the right combination eludes discovery.

5. *Lack of testing.* There are essentially two methods for verifying the validity of IT service recovery plans. You can have a disaster that forces you to use the plan, or you can simulate a disaster much the same way you would a fire drill. Not surprisingly, those organizations that test their plan have proven to be more successful in a real disaster. Unlike a fire drill, the time required for full testing of a disaster recovery plan often takes days. Organizations that implement disaster simulations for testing purposes frequently limit their tests to a fixed period. The test involves walking through the recovery process and documenting each problem encountered until you have to stop or the allotted time runs out. Early tests frequently stop before the time expires, as someone discovers the simulated disaster destroyed some information key to recovery. Comparing the documentation from one test to another provides a good gauge on the improvements made in the recovery plan.

6. *Lack of controls.* In this context, "control" refers to the policies, procedures, practices, and organizational structures designed to provide reasonable assurance that business objectives will be achieved and that undesired events will be prevented or detected and corrected. Organizations that fall short in addressing internal controls normally find it very difficult to maintain useful IT service recovery documentation. The preliminary assignment to develop a business recovery plan may produce the finest documentation money can buy, but following formation, the quality of the plan will hinge on the organization's controls.

IT Service Recovery Risk Assessment

IT service recovery decisions attempt to balance a relatively complex cost model:

1. Predisaster Costs: Insurance

   a. Recovery planning

   b. Prepurchased recovery resources

   c. Ongoing maintenance of recovery documentation and resources

2. Postdisaster Costs: Damage Recovery

   a. Recovery activity outlined in the recovery plan

   b. Postpurchase of recovery resources

   c. Intangible costs of the disaster

The executive discussion on the correct balance between predisaster and postdisaster costs can be resolved through a risk assessment focused on the impact of a disaster. This may be better termed a business impact analysis, as the focus of this risk assessment is to

1. Identify assets

2. Identify associated risks

3. Prioritize the assets' importance to the business

4. Outline safeguards needed to mitigate these risks

Identifying Assets

Start the process by creating a list of assets deemed important to the business. In some cases, combining general assets into one category makes sense. Specific assets such as mail servers and individual software packages should be identified separately. It's useful to record a person who is responsible for each asset. Today's information-centric businesses should focus on identifying critical information within business transactions, as this information is often irreplaceable in catastrophic disasters.

Identify Risks

A recent poll listed CIOs' top five concerns in the following order:

1. External hackers

2. Internal hackers

3. Terrorism

4. Natural disasters

5. Economy

This type of information can be very subjective. Opinions change based on circumstances and events. This forecast information deserves ongoing examination and backing by upper management.

Larger organizations frequently have specialists responsible to provide this component in the form of a list of threats. Even in the absence of such specialists, it is in an organization's best interest to focus on event assessment independent of impact assessment. Forecasting the chances of a fire, flood, server failure, or other disaster involves a completely different set of skills than establishing the impact of these events.

Asset Importance to the Business

Risk can be broken into two parts: the chance an incident will arise and the impact of the incident on the organization when it occurs. Successful organizations focus on these two elements separately, even though both elements must be considered.

Prioritizing an asset's importance to the business can best be accomplished by considering how the asset impacts the services being provided to the customers. This value, as opposed to the purchase price, is the critical dimension. You may notice assets that are comparatively cheap to replace whose absence stops a critical service.

In the case of IT services, this involves a service-by-service outline, the elements of which can turn out to be very extensive. Possible issues worth including are

- Lost revenue

- Threats to life and limb

- Excess expense

- Lost productivity

- Damage to assets

- Customer dissatisfaction

- Violations of law

- Career damage

By considering this information, management will find it a lot easier to make informed decisions on the amount of "insurance" to invest.

Mitigating Risks

This entire document provides strategies for mitigating disaster risks to IT services and data loss, so there is no need to repeat them here. The strategies outlined are by no means the complete list, but a broad spectrum of options to get the process started.

Resources will often become the deciding factor in what safeguards are deployed to mitigate risks. While behavioral safeguards may be implemented with policy, the remainder will involve some degree of resource commitment. This is where a good business-impact analysis report will come in handy.

By providing decision makers with the information that went into the selection of safeguards, you allow everyone to discuss the issues on equal footing. In the absence of detailed information on why you want to spend money, the decision will invariably turn to how much the safeguard costs the organization.

The business impact assessment helps the discussion stay focused on the real issues—the risks to assets and how these risks can be reduced. Once developed, you can keep this information on file and periodically review and update it.

An ongoing demonstration of management interest through periodic review is an essential component of disaster recovery. A formalized risk assessment process will make the renewal of these reports an objective for all managers within the organization.

Good risk management is good organizational management. It entails not only programmatic and technical expertise but also good communications among all the members of the team. The risk assessment process enables risk identification, assessment, prioritization, action planning, and communication among team members. No one person on a program knows all the risks. Risk identification and management is everyone's responsibility. The important points are to keep it simple, tailor the process to meet the program needs, and follow up on a regular basis.

The Need for Speed!

A Technical Briefing for Those Interested in Bits and Bytes

During the course of developing this information, I came across a number of subtle but noteworthy differences between system peripherals and networks that can easily mislead individuals comparing disk I/O specifications with network I/O specifications.

While theoretical throughput specifications suggest speed, they mislead in the same way horsepower specifications oversimplify the speed of an automobile. Throughput specifications suggest a potential limit on the maximum speed.

A majority of today's communications protocols use layering concepts outlined in the OSI model. Each layer decreases the "user" data throughput below the maximum by taking a percentage of the bandwidth for layer-to-layer information. In contrast, peripheral devices and system bus communications use electrical signals at board level. Maximum throughput is much more theoretical with the potential for bottlenecks created by a specific card design. In the end, these "cards" have to communicate over wire, fiber, or wireless. As technology pushes processor speeds, all of these communication methods tend to converge.

The figures in Table A–1 may aid individuals interested in a comparison.

TABLE A–1 COMMUNICATION MECHANISMS, PROTOCOLS, SPEEDS, AND DISTANCES

Type	Name	Maximum Throughput	Distance
Connection Service	Dial-Up Modem	9.6, 14.4, 28.8, 33.6, 56 Kbps	
Network Service	Packet Switched (X.25)	56 Kbps	
Network Service	Switched 56/64	56 Kbps, 64 Kbps	
Connection Service	Fractional T1	$N \times 64$ kbps	
PC Connection	Serial Port	115 Kbps	
Network Service	ISDN BRI	BRI 64–128 Kbps	
Connection Service	ISDN DSL (IDSL)	144 Kbps	
Printer Connection	Standard PC Parallel Port	115 KB/s (920 kbps)	
Network Service	ISDN PRI	PRI 1.544 Kbps	
Connection Service	Consumer DSL (CDSL)	128 Kbps Upstream 1 Mbps Downstream	
Connection Service	G.Lite ADSL	520 Kbps Upstream 1.5 Mbps Downstream	
Connection Service	Rate Adaptive DSL (RADSL)	1 Mbps Upstream 7 Mbps Downstream	

Type	Name	Maximum Throughput	Distance
Connection Service	Asymmetric DSL (ADSL)	1 Mbps Upstream 8 Mbps Downstream	
Connection Service	T1	24 × 64 Kbps = 1.5 Mbps	
Connection Service	Symmetric DSL (SDSL)	160 Kbps 208 Kbps 784 Kbps 1.5 Mbps	
Connection Service	High Bit Rate DSL (HDSL/HDSL-2)	768 Kbps 44 Mbps (HDSL-2) 1.544 Mbps 2.048 Mbps	
Connection Service	Very High Bit Rate DSL (VDSL)	1.6–6.4 Mbps Upstream 13–52 Mbps Downstream	
Local Network	Ethernet	10 Mbps (shared)	100 m
Local Network	Wireless Ethernet	11 Mbps (shared) & 54 Mbps	
Local Network	Switched Ethernet	10 Mbps (node to node)	100 m
Local Network	Token Ring	4, 16 Mbps	125 m
Device Interface	USB Version 1.0	12 Mbps	
Personal Network	Wireless Personal Area Network – "Bluetooth"	20 Mbps (shared)	10 m
Card Interface	PCMCIA Bus (16-Bit)	20 Mbps	
Printer Interface	ECP/EPP parallel port	3 MB/s (24 Mbps)	
Card Interface	PCMCIA Bus (32-bit) CardBus	40 Mbps	
Device Interface	SCSI-1	5 MB/s (40 Mbps)	6m
Connection Service	T3	672 × 64 kbps = 44.7 Mbps	
Network Service	Frame Relay	56 Kbps–45 Mbps	
Network Service	Sonet OC-1	51.84 Mbps	
System Bus	ISA – Original PC	8 MB/s (64 Mbps)	

(continued)

Type	Name	Maximum Throughput	Distance
Device Interface	SCSI-2		
	Fast SCSI,		
	Fast-10	10 MB/s (80 Mbps)	3m
Local Network	Fast Ethernet	100 Mbps	100 m
Local Network	FDDI/CDDI	100 Mbps	10 km
Local Network	Fast Token Ring	100–128 Mbps	125 m
Device Interface	ESCON	17 MB/s	3 km
		(136 Mbps)	
Device Interface	IDE	3.3–16.7 MB/s	
		(26.4–133.6 Mbps)	
Network	Sonet OC-3	155.52 Mbps	
Device Interface	Ultra SCSI,		
	Fast-20	20 MB/s	1.5 m
		(160 Mbps)	
Device Interface	SCSI-2,	20 MB/s	1.5 m
	Fast Wide SCSI,	(160 Mbps)	
	Fast-10		
Device Interface	UltraIDE	33 MB/s	
		(264 Mbps)	
Device Interface	Ultra Wide SCSI,		
	Fast-20	40 MB/s	1.5 m
		(320 Mbps)	
Device Interface	Ultra2 SCSI	40 MB/s	12 m
		(320 Mbps)	
System Bus	Micro Channel –	40 MB/s	
	Original	(320 Mbps)	
Device Interface	IEEE-1394 Firewire	100–400 Mbps	4.5 m
Device Interface	USB Version 2.0	480 Mbps	
Network Device	Sonet OC-12	622.08 Mbps	
Device Interface	SCSI-3,		
	Ultra2 Wide (U2W)		
	SCSI,	80 MB/s	12 m
	Ultra2 LVD SCSI,	(640 Mbps)	
	Fast-40		
Device Interface	FICON,	100 MB/s	10 km
Storage Network	Fibre Channel (FC-AL)	(800 Mbps)	
Local Network	Gigabit Ethernet	1000 Mbps	550 m

Type	Name	Maximum Throughput	Distance
Device Interface			
Storage Network	iSCSI	1000 Mbps	
System Bus	PCI (32-bit/33 MHz)	132 MB/s (1,056 Mbps)	
System Bus	VESA VL-Bus (Limited to 486 CPU)	132MB/s (1,056 Mbps)	
System Bus	Micro Channel – RS6000	160 MB/s (1,280 Mbps)	
Device Interface	Ultra3 SCSI, Ultra160/m	160 MB/s (1,280 Mbps)	12 m
Device Interface	SSA	160 MB/s (1,280 Mbps)	2.4 km
System Bus	PCI (64-bit/33 MHz) PCI (32-bit/66 MHz)	264 MB/s (2,112 Mbps)	
System Bus	PCI-X (32-bit/66 MHz)	264 MB/s (2,112 Mbps)	
Network	Sonet OC-48	2,488.32 Mbps	
Device Interface	Fiber Channel (FC-AL)	100–400 MB/s (800–3,200 Mbps)	
System Bus	PCI (64-bit/66 MHz) (Limit 1 per System)	528 MB/s (4,224 Mbps)	
System Bus	PCI-X (64-bit/66 MHz) PCI-X (32-bit/133 MHz)	528 MB/s (4,224 Mbps)	
System Bus	PCI-X (64-bit/133 MHz) (limit 1 per system)	1,060 MB/s (8,480 Mbps)	
Connection Service			
Network Service	ATM	1.5, 25, 100, 155, 622, 2,488, and 9,953 Mbps	
Network	Sonet OC-192	9,953.28 Mbps	
Network	Sonet OC-768	38,813.12 Mbps	

Please do not consider this a trustworthy source for data in critical situations. The data, collected from numerous Web sites, may contain errors or outdated information. Occasionally, different sites contained different data. In attempting to provide the theoretical maximum throughput, the table lists the highest throughput found. This list is not anywhere near conclusive.

B

The Broadview Storage Perspective

Storage Perspective

January 2003

NEW YORK

SILICON VALLEY

BOSTON

LONDON

BROADVIEW INTERNATIONAL LLC
MEMBER NASD
MEMBER SIPC

Agenda

Storage market drivers and valuation considerations

Segment focus

- Storage management software
- Storage systems
- Storage components and semiconductors
- Emerging technologies
    - Storage virtualization

Broadview overview

Storage Market Drivers And Valuation Considerations

BROADVIEW

336

Storage Capacity Demands And Budgetary Constraints Drive Innovation

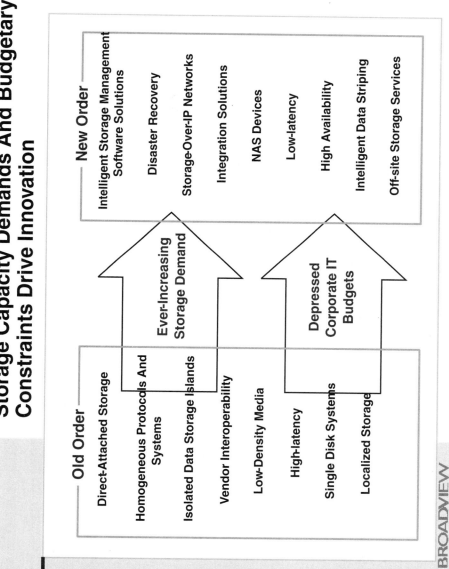

Old Order

- Direct-Attached Storage
- Homogeneous Protocols And Systems
- Isolated Data Storage Islands
- Vendor Interoperability
- Low-Density Media
- High-latency
- Single Disk Systems
- Localized Storage

Ever-Increasing Storage Demand

Depressed Corporate IT Budgets

New Order

- Intelligent Storage Management Software Solutions
- Disaster Recovery
- Storage-Over-IP Networks
- Integration Solutions
- NAS Devices
- Low-latency
- High Availability
- Intelligent Data Striping
- Off-site Storage Services

Innovation Is Taking Place Within Each Segment Of The Storage Market

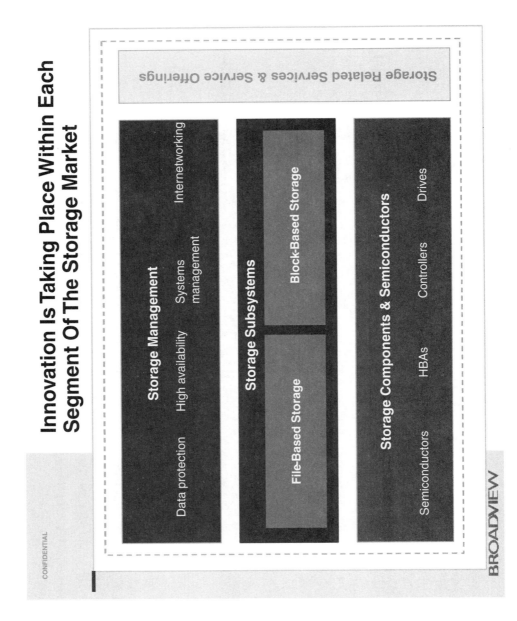

Storage Related Services & Service Offerings

Storage Management

Data protection High availability Systems management Internetworking

Storage Subsystems

File-Based Storage Block-Based Storage

Storage Components & Semiconductors

Semiconductors HBAs Controllers Drives

BROADVIEW

338

Battles Are Being Waged Within Five Key Areas

The Issue	Challenges	Battlegrounds	Predicted Outcomes

Heterogeneous Protocols and Interconnects	Trimmed IT staffing/expenditure budgets
	Lack of wide-area transport, security, QoS
	Lack of adopted standards
		IP Storage
		  – iSCSI
		  – FCIP
		  – iFCP
		InfiniBand
			Fibre Channel-based standards will be the short-term winners
			IP storage will find shared implementation with Fibre Channel throughout the corporate network environment

Virtualization	Complexity and interoperability issues Manageability issues across heterogeneous systems	Different vendors are addressing virtualization from different perspectives Hardware vs. software based Standards vs. proprietary In-band vs. out-of-band	Vendors that address both scalability and compatibility across heterogeneous systems will win
Complete End-to-End Solution	One-stop-shop for end-to-end storage needs Vendors without an adequate portfolio to meet customer's needs	Systems integrators without product offerings and equipment vendors without design services vs. full-service vendors	Equipment vendors that address end to end system needs (equipment, software and design and integration services) will ultimately dominate the market
Disaster Recovery	Increasing risk of data loss due to faulty hardware, virus, and security threats High availability	Tape backup vs. RAID backup Server architecture (standalone, rack mount, or portable) Offsite vs. onsite	Heterogeneous solutions will win as DR is widely adopted Technology minimizing time -to-recovery at a valuable cost will win customer support
Storage Services	Increased storage system complexity and executive level scrutiny Increased number of choices with respect to architecture, technology, vendor, etc.	Equipment and software vendors offer increased services and encroach on core system integrator markets SSP's are moving towards a software oriented model	CTO's will place greater reliance on system design, integration and monitoring services Equipment vendors able to provide front-end design and integration services will win

Increased Demand For End-To-End Vendor Solutions Drives M&A And Partnerships

Partnerships and M&A Are the Most Popular Means for Systems Vendors to Provide an End-to-End Solution

Components	Networking Equipment	Storage Subsystems	Software/ Applications	Services
Semiconductor	Director	Disk Subsystem	Data Protection	Systems Integration
HBA	Switch/Hub	Tape Subsystem	High Availability	Storage Service Provider
Controller	Routers/ Extenders	Network-Attached Storage	System Management	General Service Provider
M&A will help legitimize evolving IP based interconnect standards, but until winning standards are more clearly defined, incumbents will choose partnership over acquisition	Convergence of the SAN, LAN, and WAN will continue driving investment in the storage networking equipment sector, further hastening development of competing IP based interconnect standards	Pricing pressure and rapid product innovation cycles will lead to increased market consolidation with exit opportunities for only a select few	Vendors will look to software to differentiate core offerings and build credibility and viability in the marketplace Firmware (hardware vendor specific software) will need to overcome perceived customer lock-in bias	Vendors are looking to services to grow revenue by generating increased customer account control and by harnessing a heterogeneous product knowledge - base

BROADVIEW

Market Fundamentals Remain Strong & Poised To Support A Broader Market Recovery

Private Equity

Remains an active market for financial investors ($1.6B invested) in 2001 despite retrenchment by strategic investors

Valuations across all areas of storage networking-related technologies experience downward pressure

Partnerships

Emerging players seek relationships with storage incumbents to promote their solutions

Storage networking offerings are considered critical complements to other related technologies (networking, web acceleration)

Mergers and Acquisitions

Many buyers view storage networking technology as a long term growth opportunity

Established players are building broader solutions through acquisition, especially in software and services

Players in adjacent markets (e.g., data networking) use M&A to gain a foothold in the storage market

Public Markets

A limited number of pure play public storage vendors creates de facto gorillas (Veritas, EMC, Brocade)

Storage companies have experienced greater stock price volatility in the current market

Strong private companies will gain early access to the public markets when the IPO window reopens

Storage Market Dynamics

341

Segment Focus:
Storage Management

BROADVIEW

Storage Management Market Segmentation

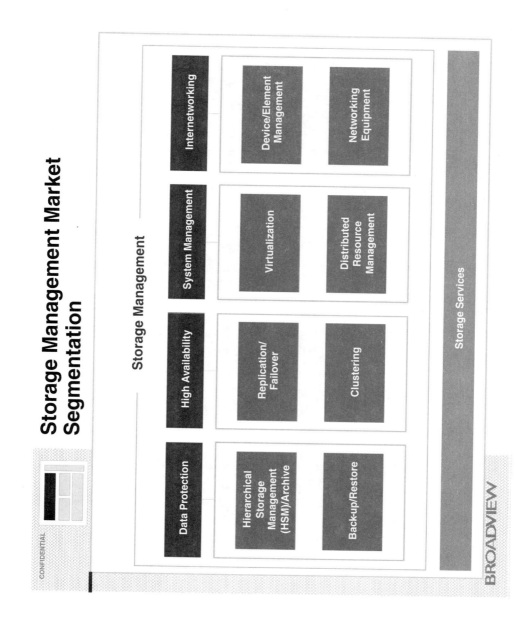

Characteristic Market Dynamics

Data Protection

HSM/Archive

Mature market; most vendors provide some offering

Content management and search/archive functionality represent areas of differentiation

Back-up/Restore

Mature segment characterized by numerous point solutions and functionalities

Server-less backup promises to be a growth opportunity

WAN-enabled back-up/restore driven by increased bandwidth and demand for disaster recovery

High Availability

Replication/Failover

Growing interest in disaster recovery and 24x7 networked storage drives demand for WAN-enabled replication

Becoming a standard feature of most enterprise SAN and NAS offerings

Clustering

Increased adoption of VI (virtual interface) and NAS drives demand for clustering

Infiniband promises low latency and high performance

Cluster management software still considered nascent

System Management

Virtualization

Actively funded area; likely to see considerable M&A and partnership activity in the near future

Competing technology approaches stalling market adoption

Distributed Resource Management

Distributed storage management is a key storage system end-user requirement

Software and equipment vendors must focus on interoperability and overcome vendor lock-in concerns

BROADVIEW

344

Storage Management Market Map: Software And Systems Vendors

Data Protection		High Availability		System Management		Internetworking		Managed Storage Service Providers
HSM/Archive	Backup/Restore	Replication/Failover	Clustering	Virtualization	Distributed Resource Mgmt.	Device/Element Management	Networking Equipment	

Managed Storage Service Providers: Accellion, Amerivault, Arsenal Digital Solutions, CNT (BI-Tech), Datalink, Glasshouse, Livevault, Managed Storage Intl, NaviSite, Scale 8, StorageAccess, StorNet, StorageProvider

Networking Equipment / Device/Element Management: EMC, IBM, McDATA, Vixel, BakBone, Softek (Fujitsu), TantiaTechnologies, XIOtech, 3PARdata, SANgiaSystems

Distributed Resource Mgmt.: IBM, Computer Associates, BMC, ADIC, Hitachi Data Systems, Softek (Fujitsu), QLogic, StorageNetworks, TrueSAN Networks, PowerQuest, Software Partners, StorageNetworking Technologies

Vi/sion Software, AppIQ, Accellion, ArkivioSoftware, CreekPath, Intermine, InterSAN, InvioSoftware, Lane15, NorthernParklifi/OuterBay Tech, Radiant Software, Storability, StorLogic, Tek-Tools, TeraCloud, Vsto

Virtualization: Hewlett-Packard, Sun Microsystems, FalconStor, StorageTek, KOM Networks, DataCore Software, DantaDevelopment, 3PARdata, StoreAgeNetworking Technologies, VicomSystems

Agile Storage, Alacritus, Cloverleaf, Incipient, LeftHandNetworks, LSI Logic, Monosphere, Pirus, Sanrad, StorageQuest, StoreAge, Zambeel

Clustering: Hewlett-Packard, Dell, Polyserve, SanIndic, SistineSoftware

Replication/Failover: Veritas, Network Appliance, CNT, Legato, Softek (Fujitsu), FalconStor, Crossroads, OLogic, TrueSAN, DataCore Software, XIOtech, NSI Software, Troika Networks, MangoSoft, Zerowait

Backup/Restore: IBM, EMC, Computer Associates, BMC, ADIC, Dell, Brocade, Hitachi Data Systems, BakBone, Softek (Fujitsu), FalconStor, StorageTek, StorageNetworks, TantiaTechnologies, Innovation Data Processing, PrincetonSoftech, KOM Networks, PowerQuest, Software Partners, DantaDevelopment, VicomSystems, BlueArc, XIOsoft

Atempo, Avamar, CommVaultSystems, Connected, iVault, LandS, Permabit, Kashya, Knox Software, MiraLink, Microlite, Neartek, NovaStor, St. Bernard, Storactive, Syncsort, Unitrends, V.Comm

HSM/Archive: IBM, EMC

FileTek, QstarTechnologies, Zantaz

BROADVIEW

345

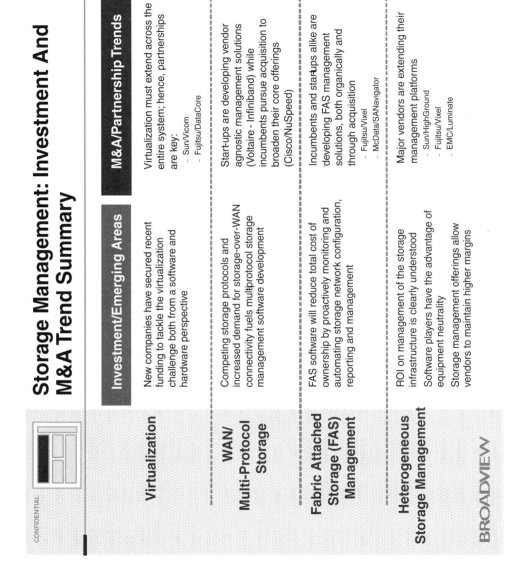

Storage Management: Investment And M&A Trend Summary

	Investment/Emerging Areas	M&A/Partnership Trends
Virtualization	New companies have secured recent funding to tackle the virtualization challenge both from a software and hardware perspective	Virtualization must extend across the entire system; hence, partnerships are key: – Sun/Vicom – Fujitsu/DataCore
WAN/ Multi-Protocol Storage	Competing storage protocols and increased demand for storage-over-WAN connectivity fuels multiprotocol storage management software development	Start-ups are developing vendor agnostic management solutions (Voltaire - Infiniband) while incumbents pursue acquisition to broaden their core offerings (Cisco/NuSpeed)
Fabric Attached Storage (FAS) Management	FAS software will reduce total cost of ownership by proactively monitoring and automating storage network configuration, reporting and management	Incumbents and start-ups alike are developing FAS management solutions, both organically and through acquisition – Fujitsu/Vixel – McData/SANavigator
Heterogeneous Storage Management	ROI on management of the storage infrastructure is clearly understood Software players have the advantage of equipment neutrality Storage management offerings allow vendors to maintain higher margins	Major vendors are extending their management platforms – Sun/HighGround – Fujitsu/Vixel – EMC/Luminate

BROADVIEW

Segment FocusStorage Systems

BROADVIEW

Ongoing Battles Will Determine Where Network Intelligence Is To Reside

Intelligence is becoming increasingly distributed and expanding into the network and numerous battles are being waged:

– Software (e.g., virtualization, intelligent management)

– Appliances (e.g., virtualization, security appliances)

– HBA/controllers (e.g., intelligent RAID controllers, virtualization on the HBA, applications moving to the line card)

– Directors/Routers (e.g., virtualization, security, QoS at each port via specialized storage semiconductors)

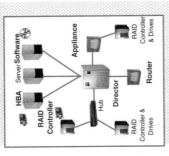

HBA Server **Software**

RAID Controller

Appliance

Hub

Director

Router

RAID Controller & Drives

RAID Controller & Drives

Bold indicates where intelligence resides on the network

> **Ultimately, intelligence will be distributed to several parts of the network**

BROADVIEW

348

NAS Incumbents Face Challenges From A Slew Of New Entrants

Hardware

Number of new entrants with low manufacturing cost structures entering the NAS market

Using off-the-shelf software toolkits to create low-cost solutions targeting the small- to medium-sized enterprise

New offerings able to operate in heterogeneous storage environments

Software

Software is rapidly becoming the differentiating factor for NAS vendors

Microsoft and Veritas offer two popular software toolkits for NAS vendors

- Microsoft's Server Appliance Kit already has 15% of the NAS market, with Compaq, Dell, HP and IBM all using it in their NAS devices

Startups beginning to emerge with more powerful software offerings

NAS-SAN Convergence

A whole new class of players is redefining how NAS systems are implemented

- NAS is increasingly being used as a front-end for the SAN

- New offerings mix block and file-based technologies

- Networking becoming an increasingly important component of next-generation NAS appliances

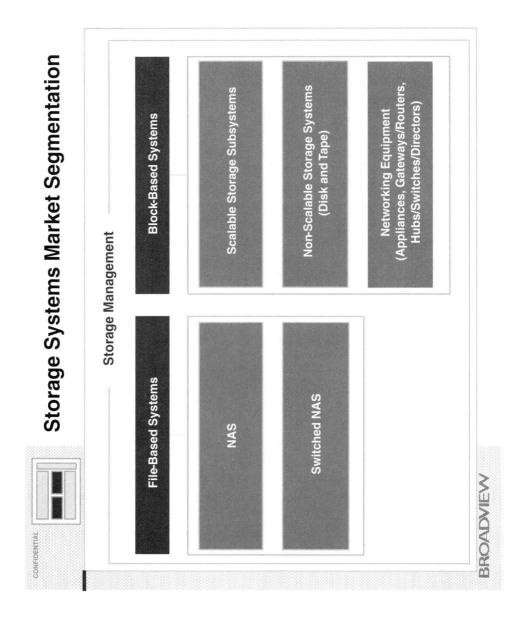

Storage Systems Market Segmentation

350

Characteristic Market Dynamics

File-Based

NAS

NAS becoming the preferred architecture for small and medium enterprises

Traditional hardware vendors entering the fray using low-cost hardware and software toolkits

Switched NAS

Next-generation NAS boxes incorporate SAN-level switching capabilities

Increasingly used as front-ends for SANs

Block-Based

Scalable Subsystems

Incumbents being challenged by upstarts designing "SAN-in-a-Box" systems

Very large venture financings in this space will lead to a shakeout among next-generation startups

Non-Scalable Subsystems

Disk and tape arrays are becoming commodities

Disk market continues to show robust growth due to decreasing cost of acquisition

Tape subsystems showing some resurgence with recent trend toward disaster recovery

Networking Equipment

Actively funded area; likely to see considerable M&A in the near future, especially in next-generation switches

Fibre Channel will remain dominant within the SAN for the foreseeable future, as companies work to add intelligence to FC switches before moving to IP storage Fabric switches and directors will continue to dominate

Battles regarding where intelligence will reside will keep market in flux

SAN island connectivity is a desired feature, especially for disaster recovery

Migration to native-IP routers continues to get pushed out

351

Storage Systems Market Map

Private Company
Public Company

File-Based		Block-Based					
		Scalable Subsystems	Non-Scalable Subsystems			Networking Equipment	
NAS	Switched NAS		Disk	Tape	Appliances	Gateways/Routers	Hubs/Switches/Directors
HP					HP		
IBM			IBM			IBM	IBM
StorageTek			StorageTek			StorageTek	StorageTek
Sun			Sun				Sun (Pirus)
Dell			Dell			Dell	Dell
			Hitachi			Hitachi	Hitachi
SanOne			SanOne			SanOne	
			Cambex			Cambex	
MTI			MTI			Cisco/Andiamo	Cisco/Andiamo
RARE				RARE			
Network Appliance			Network Appliance		Troika		Troika
Raidtec			Raidtec		Raidtec		
Syred			Syred		Syred		
Adaptec (Tricord)			Adaptec	ADIC		ADIC	
			Cybernetics				ATTO
EMC			Dot Hill		EMC	Brocade (Rhapsody)	
						McDATA	
LSI Logic			LSI Logic			Nishan	
			Qlogic	nStor	Spinnaker		Qlogic
Spinnaker			Nexsan		Nexsan		
			Chaparral				Chaparral
					Candera (Confluence)		Candera

Private Companies

NAS	Switched NAS	Scalable Subsystems	Disk	Tape	Appliances	Gateways/Routers	Hubs/Switches/Directors
Agile Storage	BlueArc	3ParData	Baydel	Ampex	FalconStor	Akara	Emulex
Auspex	EqualLogic	YottaYotta	DataDirect	DynaTek	Neoscale	Apcon	High Velocity Systems
BigStorage	Ibrix		Disc	Exabyte	Netezza	CNT	INRANGE
Exavigor	Intransa		Dot-Hill	Maxoptix	Onaro	Crossroads	Intransa
Islon Systems	Lefthand Networks		Eurologic	Overland	SANgate	Digital Interfaces	KTI Networks
Maximum Throughput	Panasas		Imperial Technology	Periso	StorageQuest	Gennoco	Maranti
Microtest	Z-Force		Integrix	Plasmon	Storigen	SANCastle	MaXXan
Network Storage Solutions			Maxtor	Qualstar	Surgient	SAN Valley	Nautiicus Networks
Procom Technology			Platypus	Quantum	Vicom	Stonefly	Sanera
Quartet Network Storage			RAID	Sony	Vividon	Networks	SanRad
Snap Appliance			Seagate	SpectraLogic	Vormetric	TD Systems	Systran
Zambeel			Solid Data Systems	Straightline		Voltaire	Vixel
			Xyratex	Tape Labs			
			Zzyzx				

352

Storage Systems: Investment And M&A Trend Summary

	Investment/Emerging Areas	M&A/Partnership Trends
NextGeneration Protocols	Tremendous investment is going into a number of new transport protocols designed to displace Fibre Channel - IP Storage — InfiniBand	Most of the activity has been in partnerships, with limited M&A activity - Adaptec/Platys - Qlogic/Little Mountain Group
NAS/SAN Convergence	Many companies emerging to provide NAS products with SAN functionality iSCSI integration into NAS enables single server to storage connection for blocks and files	Market still nascent, but several software acquisitions - LeftHandNetworksNorthFork
Disk Arrays Increasingly Commoditized	As SAN becomes increasingly heterogeneous, disk arrays from third-party vendors sufficient for data storage	Increased use of EMS and CMS companies to manufacture drive arrays
Intelligence Within the Network	Increasing intelligence in the fabric drives TCO down "Next-generation" switching advancing beyond protocol conversion to include additional intelligence within the fabric	Hardware and software to facilitate management within the fabric - McData/SANavigator - Sun/Pirus - Brocade/Rhapsody Networks - Cisco/Andiamo

BROADVIEW

353

Segment Focus:Storage Components And Semiconductors

BROADVIEW

Fibre Channel Will Continue To Dominate While IP Storage And InfiniBand Develop

	Key Considerations	Target Market	Role in Storage
Fibre Channel/ Fibre Channel Over IP (Tunneling)	Leverages Fibre Channel's strength and existing penetration in storage	Large enterprise customers	Fibre Channel remains dominant within the SAN Additional intelligence and management on FC hardware will keep FC in the driver's seat
iSCSI (Native IP)	TCP-offload and emergence of iSNS standards are crucial Lower cost and technology familiarity will drive adoption 10GbE will also help to drive IP storage	Small- and medium sized enterprise customers Complementary alternative for departments or workgroups in larger corporations	Initially, iSCSI will gain traction in small to medium enterprises, beginning in 2004 Complementary technologies (e.g., TCP-offload) will accelerate adoption, but suppliers are struggling to stay alive
InfiniBand	Faltering industry support Higher speed (10x) products will drive limited adoption	Lower-end server market, especially until 10x products ship	Will likely be used primarily as a server interconnect, but overall future remains dubious

BROADVIEW

355

Leaders in the Networked Storage Market Will Be Companies Who Can Effectively Move and Control Data

The increase in "fixed content" data (*i.e.* x-rays/medical imaging, business docs, financial services docs) is dramatically changing the way that data is handled

An increasing amount of data is only being moved, not processed

Files no longer need to be cycled through application server's processors after their original write to the storage pool, and can be read directly to clients, thus conserving mission critical server processor cycles

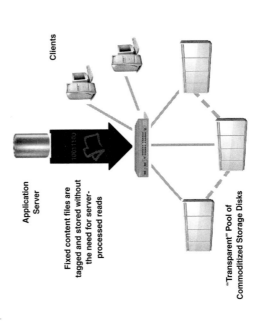

Clients

Application Server

Fixed content files are tagged and stored without the need for server-processed reads

"Transparent" Pool of Commoditized Storage Disks

Storage Components Market Segmentation

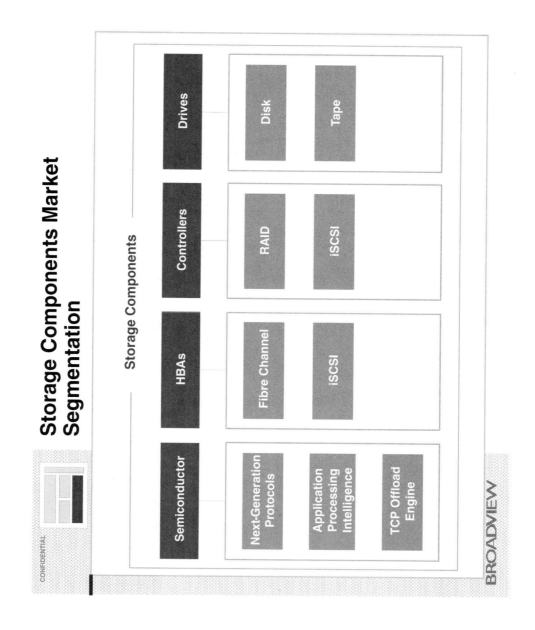

Storage Components

Semiconductor	HBAs	Controllers	Drives
Next-Generation Protocols	Fibre Channel	RAID	Disk
Application Processing Intelligence	iSCSI	iSCSI	Tape
TCP Offload Engine			

Characteristic Market Dynamics

Semiconductor

Next-Generation Protocols

IP storage very slow to develop, with iSCSI in the lead

Infiniband future uncertain, with initial traction several years away

Application Processing Intelligence

Virtualization, security, and QoS are all moving from software onto silicon

TCP Offload Engines

Will act as a catalyst for IP storage

Products already shipping

HBA/Controller

HBA

Top vendors control market, with over 80% market share

Incumbents using M&A as a means to gaining next-generation protocol expertise

Controller

Mature market, with controller vendors moving up market into more value-added products

Drives

Tape

Mature industry, with few players remaining in the market

Long tail, especially to due to recent disaster recovery trend

Disk

Mature industry, with major consolidation having already occurred

Serial ATA and other interface technologies emerging as new battleground

Drive manufacturers moving upstream into NAS boxes and other higher-value added product lines

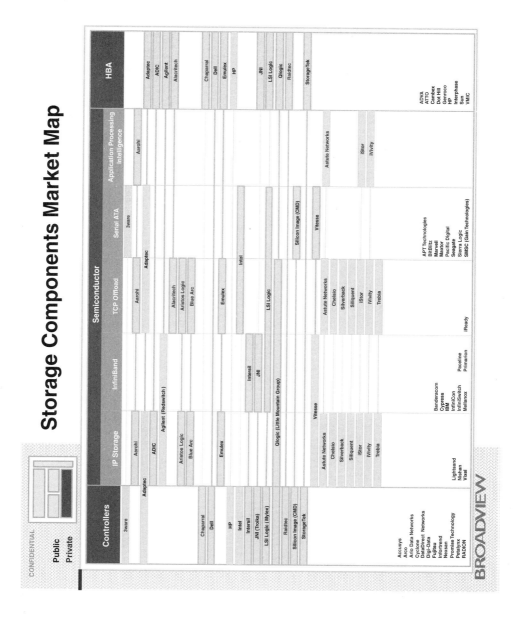

Storage Components Market Map

Index

informIT

YOUR GUIDE TO IT REFERENCE

Articles

Keep your edge with thousands of free articles, in-depth features, interviews, and IT reference recommendations – all written by experts you know and trust.

Online Books

Answers in an instant from **InformIT Online Book's** 600+ fully searchable on line books. For a limited time, you can get your first 14 days **free**.

Catalog

Review online sample chapters, author biographies and customer rankings and choose exactly the right book from a selection of over 5,000 titles.

Register
Your Book

at www.awprofessional.com/register

You may be eligible to receive:

- Advance notice of forthcoming editions of the book
- Related book recommendations
- Chapter excerpts and supplements of forthcoming titles
- Information about special contests and promotions throughout the year
- Notices and reminders about author appearances, tradeshows, and online chats with special guests

Contact us

If you are interested in writing a book or reviewing manuscripts prior to publication, please write to us at:

Editorial Department
Addison-Wesley Professional
75 Arlington Street, Suite 300
Boston, MA 02116 USA
Email: AWPro@aw.com

Visit us on the Web: http://www.awprofessional.com